THE DOOMSDAY BOOK

Can the World Survive?

Gordon Rattray Taylor

A FAWCETT CREST BOOK

Fawcett Publications, Inc., Greenwich, Conn.

THE DOOMSDAY BOOK

THIS BOOK CONTAINS THE COMPLETE TEXT
OF THE ORIGINAL HARDCOVER EDITION.

A Fawcett Crest Book reprinted by arrangement with
The World Publishing Company

Library of Congress Catalog Card Number: 75-124280

Printed in the United States of America
September 1971

for Rodney and Betty

Population Crash

And I saw another angel ascending from the east, having the seal of the living God: and he cried with a loud voice to the four angels, to whom it was given to hurt the earth and the sea, saying, Hurt not the earth, neither the sea, nor the trees. . . . The first angel sounded, and there followed hail and fire, mingled with blood, and they were cast upon the earth: and the third part of trees was burnt up, and all green grass was burnt up. And the second angel sounded . . . and the third part of the creatures which were in the sea, and had life, died. . . . And the third angel sounded . . . and the third part of the waters became wormwood; and many men died of the waters, because they were made bitter. And the fourth angel sounded . . . and the day shone not for a third part of it, and the night likewise. And the fifth angel sounded . . . and there arose a smoke out of the pit, as the smoke of a great furnace; and the sun and the air were darkened by reason of the smoke of the pit. And there came out of the smoke locusts upon the earth. . . . And in those days shall men seek death, and shall not find it; and shall desire to die, and death shall flee from them. By these three was the third part of men killed, by the fire, and by the smoke, and by the brimstone. . . . And the rest of the men which were not killed by these plagues yet repented not of the works of their hands, that they should not worship devils, and idols of gold, and silver, and brass, and stone, and of wood.

THE REVELATION OF ST JOHN THE DIVINE,
Chapters 7, 8, and 9

Acknowledgements

I AM particularly grateful to the Conservation Foundation in Washington, who allowed me to use their library and gave me other help; and to Dr. Göran Löfroth of Stockholm University, who supplied me with numerous uniquely valuable reports prepared for the Committee for Natural Resources of the Swedish Natural Science Research Council and other documents; and to Dr. C. R. Manders, Scientific Officer, British Embassy, Tokyo, who supplied copious material about Japan.

I am also most grateful to the following who gave up valuable time to discuss specific problems: Prof. R. A. Bryson (University of Wisconsin), Prof. C. LaMont Cole (Cornell University), Dr. F. Fraser Darling and Dr. Ray Dasmann (Conservation Foundation), Prof. Kingsley Davis (International Population and Urban Research, University of California, Berkeley), Prof. Paul Ehrlich (Stanford University), Dr. F. R. Fosberg (Smithsonian Institution), Lyle Saunders (The Ford Foundation), Dr. Glenn Seaborg (US Atomic Energy Commission), S. Fred Singer (US Department of the Interior), Dr. Harold A. Thomas (Center for Population Studies, Harvard University), Dr. T. Tucker (Bristol and Avon River Authority), Stewart L. Udall (Overview), Dr. H. van der Schalie (University of Michigan), R. M. Westebbe (International Bank for Reconstruction and Redevelopment), and Dr. Gale Young and colleagues (Oak Ridge National Laboratory).

I also owe warm thanks for help and information to: Dr. Lewis S. Anderson (Population Council, Turkey), Dr. J. M. Barnes (MRC Toxicology R.U.), Dr. W. G. Belter (US Atomic Energy Commission), Dr. J. Bettelheim (Power Research Institute, Prague), Dr. J. O. Blomeke (Oak Ridge National Laboratory), Dr. S. Boyden (Australian National University), Prof. Dr. K. Bullrich (Institut für Meteorologie, Mainz), John Clark (American Littoral Society), Prof. Barry Commoner (Washington University), Dr. A. H. Conney (Burroughs and Wellcome, N.Y.), Dr. A. J. Coutu (N. Carolina State University), H. J. Frith (CSIRO, Canberra), Dr. J. W. Gofman (Lawrence Radiation Laboratory), Dr. E. D.

Goldberg (Scripps Institution of Oceanography), Dr. Harriet L. Hardy (Occupational Medical Service, MIT), Dr. Matthew Huxley (National Institutes of Health), Prof. Dr. O. Jaag (Anstalt für Wasserversorgung, Switzerland), Niels Johannsen (Copenhagen), Dr. F. S. Johnson (Southwest Center for Advanced Studies), Prof. C. Junge (Max-Planck Institut für Chemie), G. Kazantzis (Middlesex Hospital), Prof. V. A. Kovda (University of Moscow), Prof. P. J. Kramer (Duke University), H. H. Lamb (Meteorological Office), Leif Larsen (*Politiken*), Dr. P. J. Lawther (St. Bartholomew's Hospital Medical School), Howard Lewis (National Academy of Sciences), Dr. P. Leyhausen (Max-Planck Institut für Verhaltensphysiologie), Dr. J. E. Lovelock, Thomas F. Malone (Travelers' Insurance Co.), Dr. H. G. Masterson (Central Electricity Research Laboratories), Mme M. de Meuron-Landolt (*Atomes*), Dr. J. A. Mihursky (University of Maryland), N. T. Mitchell (Ministry of Agriculture, Fisheries and Food), W. E. Moran (Population Reference Bureau), Dr. R. J. Murgatroyd (Meteorological Office), Dr. K. Myers (CSIRO, Australia), Dr. A. Nelson Smith (University of Swansea), Dr. Hans Palmstierna (Government Environmental Committee, Sweden), Dr. F. Pasquill (Meteorological Office), Dr. C. C. Patterson (California Institute of Technology), H. W. Patterson (Acres, Ltd.), W. H. Pawley (Food and Agriculture Organization), Dr. P. Pockley (Australian Broadcasting Commission), Fred Poland (*Montreal Star*), Dr. H. F. Robinson (University System of Georgia), Dr. A. J. W. Scheffey (Williams College), Prof. H. W. Schlipkoter (Med. Inst. für Lufthygiene und Silikoseforschung, Düsseldorf), E. Sochor (UNESCO), Dr. P. V. Sukhatme (Food and Agriculture Organization), O. J. Du Temple (American Nuclear Society), Dr. V. Timbrell (MRC Pneumoconiosis R.U.), Dr. F. E. Volz (HQ Air Force Cambridge Research Laboratories), C. C. Warnick (University of Idaho), Kjell Wase (National Nature Conservancy Office, Stockholm), and Dr. Charles F. Wurster (State University of New York).

Contents

THE
DOOMSDAY
BOOK

1 Man the Microbe

PUT BACTERIA in a test-tube, with food and oxygen, and they will grow explosively, doubling in number every twenty minutes or so, until they form a solid, visible mass. But finally multiplication will cease as they become poisoned by their own waste products. In the centre of the mass will be a core of dead and dying bacteria, cut off from the food and oxygen of their environment by the solid barrier of their neighbours. The number of living bacteria will fall almost to zero, unless the waste products are washed away.

Mankind today is in a similar position. The population is growing explosively, but the waste products of technology are beginning to take their toll. The pollutants which poison our air and water are not just an unfortunate by-product of technology; they pose a threat to life precisely because man's growth has been so abnormally rapid. They are part of the feedback mechanism by which nature seeks to limit excessive growth.

The eventual population crash, when the complexities of large scale become overwhelming, has yet to come. If the experience of other species can be taken as a guide, the population will fall to something like one-third the peak figure. All animal populations exhibit population explosions from time to time. All such explosions end in crashes. Will man prove the only exception? Or will his technological skill enable him to postpone the apocalypse, so that he flies higher only to fall further?

Man is only one of three million species in the world. But today he consumes more food than all other land animals put together. Roughly, the numbers of any species are inversely proportional to their size. For obvious reasons there are far more mosquitoes than elephants in the world. For his size, man was once a rare species. The population of the Stone Age has been estimated at a million or so. Neanderthal man, it has been estimated, lived at a density of one person to 2–5 square miles. His numbers were conditioned by the density and distribution of game and edible plants, as well as by the risks of being eaten by a leopard or dying of fever. On balance, he just about replaced himself, and if a run of good luck caused the population to rise, he would cut it back by abortion, infanticide, or prolonging lactation. In the inter-glacial period, however, a dramatic change took place: thanks to a series of technological advances, man's numbers began to increase steadily.

Even so, it took until 1850 for the world's population to reach a billion. But it took only until 1930 to add a second billion, a mere 80 years. By 1960, a third billion had been added—after only 30 years. The fourth billion will have been reached by 1975, a bare 15 years more. But the pace gets ever faster: a fifth billion by 1985–6, a sixth by about 1993–6, a seventh by the year 2000 or soon after. This is not a population *explosion*, for in an explosion the particles lose speed as they move outwards. Here the speed is increasing all the time. Clearly the expansion cannot continue at this rate indefinitely—but so far there is no sign at all of slowing down. At the moment, as you read these lines, the earth's population is growing at the rate of almost a hundred people a minute.

So, if we have problems of crowding, pollution and a disturbed balance of nature now, what shall we have in thirty years or so? It is plain as a pikestaff that unless something very drastic is done, the situation will be literally intolerable. The impact of so many people will go far beyond a simple dirtying-up of our surroundings. It could drastically change the climate. It could disturb the balance of nature so radical-ly as to make life impossible for man in anything like his present numbers: for man's continued existence depends upon the existence of many other species of plants and animals, upon which he feeds, and these in turn depend on others. But food is not the only thing on which life depends. The life cycle depends on the bacteria which destroy dead organisms, and on those organisms which restore to the air the oxygen that man and animals consume, to name but two. It is this complete network of relationships which is at risk.

If this is the case, why have scientists not warned us long ago? The answer is: they have, but only now are the warnings being relayed by the mass media. They are warnings not just of difficulties but of a major disaster.

WORDS OF WARNING

As long ago as 1959, Dr David Price of the US Public Health Service said: 'We all live under the haunting fear that something may corrupt the environment to the point where man joins the dinosaurs as an obsolete form of life.' And he added ominously: 'And what makes these thoughts all the more disturbing is the knowledge that our fate could perhaps be sealed twenty or more years before the development of symptoms.'

Even earlier than this, in 1957, Professor F. R. Fosberg made a slightly different point: 'It is entirely possible that man will not survive the changed environment that he is creating,' he said, 'either because of failure of resources, war over their dwindling supply, or failure of his nervous system to evolve as rapidly as the change in environment will require.'

The world remained notably unmoved, and in 1968 Dr Fraser Darling, Scottish-born research director of the Conservation Foundation in Washington, told the representatives of 70 nations in Paris, assembled to discuss just this problem, 'The fear is now whether we can rehabilitate, or are causes and consequences setting up their own repercussive oscillations to an extent we cannot control?' The calling of this meeting at least was a sign of progress, and the delegates adopted, with an unanimity rare in international gatherings, a whole set of recommendations for tackling the problem.

But these are men professionally concerned with health and conservation. What about hard-headed administrators? The President of the Rockefeller Foundation, in a report issued about the same time as the meeting in Paris, wrote: 'We are on the threshold of a new ecological crisis, because of our failure to establish a balance between resources, their utilization and our requirements.' The inventor of the term 'ecosphere', Professor LaMont Cole, was prepared to put it more strongly. In an article starkly entitled 'Can the World be Saved?' he lamented 'man's apparent intention to damage beyond repair the ecosystems which sustain him'. Not only Americans are concerned. For instance, Göran Löfroth, a Swedish scientist, asserts: 'There is at least the possibility of a human tragedy of global proportions occurring if our present practices continue unrestrained. Must we demand the evidence of catastrophe before we act?'

Though I could extend the list easily enough, I shall cite just one more, Professor Barry Commoner, director of Washington University's Center for the Biology of Natural Systems. In his book *Science and Survival* he declares: 'I believe that the cumulative effect of these pollutants, and their interactions and amplification, can be fatal to the complex fabric of the biosphere. And because man is, after all, a dependent part of this system, I believe that continued pollution of the earth, if unchecked, will eventually destroy the fitness of this planet as a place for human life.' You cannot put it plainer than that.

These are fantastically strong assertions, yet they have caused relatively little impact. By and large, men do not conduct their affairs as if the planet were on the verge of becoming uninhabitable. The threat is too serious to take seriously. Are these scientists grossly overstating their case to gain attention? If so, they have defeated their own ends. Or are they in earnest, and are we too complacent or unimaginative to listen?

Part of the difficulty, I suspect, is that they have not spelled out their predictions in sufficient detail. Words like 'the complex fabric of the biosphere' are too general and abstract to mean much to anyone who is not a biologist, most of whom have never heard a word like 'biosphere' before. My object in writing this book is therefore to make the predicted breakdown as explicit as is possible in the present state of our knowledge. It is a book about the next thirty years—a survey of the problems which are looming, not a summary of those we already know about. It has little to say about smog and industrial effluent, much about climate and the great cycles on which all life depends.

SPACESHIP EARTH

For millions of years we have known a world whose resources seemed illimitable. However fast we cut down trees, nature unaided would replace them. However many fish we took from the sea, nature would restock it. However much sewage we dumped into the river, nature would purify it, just as she would purify the air, however much smoke and fumes we put into it. Today we have reached the stage of realizing that rivers can be polluted past praying for, that seas can be overfished and that forests must be managed and fostered if they are not to vanish.

But we still retain our primitive optimism about air and water. There will always be enough rain falling from the skies to meet our needs. The air can absorb all the filth we care to put in it. Still less do we worry whether we could ever run short of oxygen. Surely there is air enough to breathe? Who ever asks where oxygen comes from, to begin with? They should—for we now consume about 10 per cent of all the atmospheric oxygen every year, thanks to the many forms of combustion which destroy it: every car, aircraft and power station destroys oxygen in quantities far greater than men consume by breathing.

The fact is, we are just beginning to press up against the limits of the earth's capacity. We begin to have to watch what we are doing to things like water and oxygen, just as we have to watch whether we are over-fishing or over-felling. The realization has dawned that earth is a spaceship with strictly limited resources. These resources must, in the long run, be recycled, either by nature or by man. Just as the astronaut's urine is purified to provide drinking water and just as his expired air is regenerated to be breathed anew, so all the earth's resources must be recycled, sooner or later. Up to now, the slow pace of nature's own recycling has served, coupled with the fact that the 'working capital' of already recycled material was large. But the margins are getting smaller and if men, in ever larger numbers, are going to require ever larger quantities, the pace of recycling will have to be artificially quickened.

All we have is a narrow band of usable atmosphere, no more than seven miles high, a thin crust of land, only one-eighth of the surface of which is really suitable for people to live on, and a limited supply of drinkable water, which we continually reuse. And in the earth, a capital of fossil fuels and ores which we steadily run down, billions of times faster than nature restores it. These resources are tied together in a complex set of transactions. The air helps purify the water, the water irrigates the plants, the plants help to renew the air.

We heedlessly intervene in these transactions. For instance, we cut down the forests which transpire water and oxygen, we build dams and pipelines which limit the movement of animals, we pave the earth and build reservoirs, altering the water cycle. So far, nature has brushed off these injuries as pinpricks. But now we are becoming so strong, so clever and so numerous, that they are beginning to hurt.

The area in which our arrogance has become most obvious is that of pollution. It is beginning to dawn on us that we are affecting our health and the viability of animals. It is a newer idea that it also poisons plants. In the US, damage to nursery gardens and vegetable growers is already put at $500m. (£200m.) a year, not counting possible indirect losses resulting from changing the climate by pollution. In one county of Florida alone, farmers have had to abandon 150,000 acres of pasture. Most orchid growers have left New Jersey because ethylene from cars damages the flowers. In California, 10,-000 acres of pines have been damaged. Near Niagara Falls farming is 'almost finished'. These are facts which only came to light after the Clean Air legislation of 1967.

POLLUTION AND SUPER-POLLUTION

Pollution—the simple, visible kind of pollution—is now worldwide. When Apollo 8 took photographs of the earth's surface, where did they reveal the most serious smog and polluted air? Not over Los Angeles, which has somehow got the reputation of having the biggest and nastiest smogs, but over Osaka and Tokio in Japan. Along this strip 34 tons of dirt a month fall on every square kilometre, compared with a mere 17 tons in New York. Coastal vessels collide regularly or run aground, because they cannot see each other's navigation lights in daylight, or because light-buoys are invisible. Traffic policemen go back to the police-station after four hours on duty and breathe pure oxygen from cylinders, to re-oxygenate their carbon-monoxide-loaded blood. In cafés and arcades coin-in-the-slot machines dispense oxygen to shoppers who feel themselves about to collapse. In school, the children wear face-masks while they do their lessons on smog-warning days.

Smogs are now found near most large cities and it is not true that a temperature inversion is needed for their formation: sunlight alone is the precondition. The Po Valley is just right for smog. So is Durban in Africa, Rio de Janeiro, Sydney ... of course London and New York have smogs. Anyone who has flown across the Atlantic from Europe is likely to have noticed the sharp onset of industrial haze as the coast is reached, and if he continues to Chicago, say, he will, on most days, see the pall darken over the cities, such as Buffalo, Detroit, and Chicago itself. In researching this book, I flew down to the Oak Ridge National Laboratory, 20 miles from Knoxville, Tennessee. Out at Oak Ridge, the air was crystal-clear. As I approached Knoxville, it grew hazier and from the plane, after take-off, I could see the wide pall lying down-wind from the city. But, compared with Los Angeles, Knoxville is quite small, and Tennessee is a remote and mostly rural state.

Again, everyone knows that Lake Erie is badly polluted. But few people realize that most of the important lakes of Europe are dead or dying. The Lake of Zurich has been devoid of life ever since the introduction of piped sanitation at the close of the last century. The Tegernsee, claimed by many as the most beautiful lake in Germany, has been rendered abiotic by the sewage from the surrounding hotels. The North Italian lakes are, with the exception of Lake Garda, polluted either by industrial effluent or by sewage, or both. Lake Orta, with its island and ancient basilica, has been completely dead since the twenties. The list runs on, from the Schliersee in Austria, through many Swedish lakes, to Lake Balaton in Hungary.

Even the Russians have pollution problems, and currently a movement is developing to protect Lake Baikal, the deepest freshwater lake in the world, from the effluent of a growing pulp and paper industry. One-third larger than Lake Erie, Baikal is a place of almost mystic importance to Russians, the scene of many an ancient legend. Russia has river pollution problems too. Moreover, each country affects others.

The Dutch, at the mouth of the Rhine, receive the effluent of Germany higher up. The Swedes complain that their rivers are made acid by the sulphur oxides which are washed down in the rain, and originate in the Ruhr, the centre of German steel making, and in Britain.

It was Professor Larry Slobodkin of the Department of Biology at Stony Brook (State University of New York) who told me why Scottish fish-farming experiments came to grief. By closing off the end of a loch, seeding it with fish fry and dumping nutrients into the water, the Scots found they were able to grow large numbers of easily-caught fish. The food on which the fish thrived were the larvae of a brine-shrimp from San Francisco Bay. These stand up to being transported in a dormant condition and are equivalent to live food. But as the Bay was filled in and polluted the supply dried up, and an alternative had to be found. The Great Salt Lake also provides such larvae, but when these were placed in the loch, all the fish died. It turned out that the Utah farmers use heavy loads of pesticide, which drain into the lake and get into the brine-shrimps. The quantity is not enough to kill them, but when the Scottish trout have eaten a few hundred of them and concentrated the pesticide from all of them in their own tissues, the load has become a lethal one. Thus the desire of the Utah farmers to grow more cereal affects Scottish attempts to produce more protein. That's the kind of world it now is.

The existence of environmental pollution has recently gained recognition as a major problem—but pollution is only part of the story. It is not simply that we load the environment with gases, acids, metals and assorted poisons which comprise a damage to health. It is rather that we alter the environment in every possible way. We dump heat into it, and dust particles; we fell forests and pave over fields; we decimate one species of animal, and cultivate another; we make noises and dump trash. There is a limit to how much of this treatment it can take.

If we dump sewage into a stream, on a small scale, the stream dissolves it and purifies it. Ten miles downstream the water is pure again. But if we dump large quantities of sewage, we end by killing the purifying bacteria, and then the stream has lost its power to purify. It can no longer deal even with the small quantity of sewage which it once accepted without difficulty. The system has broken down. For this overwhelming kind of pollution we need a new term: I call it *super-pollution*. The same thing is true of man's impact on the environment in general. It can take so much heat, so much dust; it can stand the felling of so many acres of forest and the paving of so many acres of soil; but the point is finally reached at which the whole natural system collapses. This we call an ecological catastrophe, and we do not know whether such catastrophes can ever be put right. They may be irreversible, or to reverse them may take so long that for all practical purposes the damage is permanent.

The kind of breakdown which most alarms biologists at present is not a simple physical alteration in the air or water, but a breakdown of these biological chains of cause and effect. The kind of process they have in mind is vividly instanced by Konrad Lorenz in his book *King Solomon's Ring*. Describing an aquarium, he notes what happens when 'children and adults alike are unable to resist the temptation of slipping just one more fish into the container, the capacity of whose green plants is already overburdened with animals. And just this one more fish may be the final straw which breaks the camel's back. With too many animals in the aquarium, a lack of oxygen ensues. Sooner or later some organism will succumb to this and its death may easily pass unnoticed. The decomposing corpse causes an enormous multiplication of bacteria in the aquarium, the water becomes turbid, the oxygen content decreases rapidly, then further animals die and, through this vicious circle, the whole of our carefully tended little world is doomed.'

Any closed world of organisms in which life is maintained is called an ecosystem, from the Greek word for household, *oikos*. Aquaria and spacecraft are simple examples, containing few species, and the relationships between them and their environment (the study of which is known as ecology) are easily understood. Spaceship Earth is a vast ecosystem, sometimes called the ecosphere, in which the relationships are still far from being understood. Ecologists therefore slice it into convenient fragments, such as a deciduous forest, which they examine, disregarding its surroundings and taking the soil and climate as given.

The disaster which scientists apprehend is an ecological disaster, and it is because few people understand about the fragility and complexity of ecosystems that their warnings have met so little response.

Super-pollution is now world-wide in an even fuller sense than is pollution. The carbon dioxide and the dust particles which are beginning to affect the climate are spread throughout the atmosphere: over India the dust is found at a height of over 20,000 feet above the ground. There is DDT at this level too, and in the bodies of Indians DDT is present in almost twice the quantities present in the bodies of Americans, which in turn is twice the British level. It is also widely spread through the animal world, even including penguins. Lead is present in the Pacific Ocean and in the air above it, in amounts many times the pre-industrial level, as it is also in the Arctic snows. Cadmium is found in the kidneys of Japanese in even greater amounts than are found in the kidneys of Americans. And it is impossible to take a 50-gallon sample of water from the sea anywhere in the world without finding measurable amounts of man-made radio-activity.

Does this matter? Man has abused the environment before. Most of the great deserts are the results of misuse of soil and water. The Rajputana desert in India, all 250,000 square miles of it, was once heavily populated. The hard-tramped soil, denuded of vegetation, blew away, while the dust it became altered the weather, reducing the rainfall. In Roman days, the granary of the empire was in North Africa, where today the anchors of ships and ruined villas testify to a long-lost prosperity. Even now, the process has not ceased—the Sahara eats up another 30,000 acres every year.

Man's situation differs from that of the bacteria in the test-tube in two important respects. First, he is not alone in the test-tube, but is one of three million species, each one of which is dependent on many others for its existence. The annihilation of species on which man depends can harm man as much as if the damage were done to him in the first place. Secondly, he does not live between inert glass walls, but in a complex environment of air and water, soil and energy. Damage to that environment can damage man directly or damage him indirectly by handicapping species on which he depends.

THE PEOPLE PROBLEM

The heart of the problem is the prevalence of people. If the world's population were 10 or 15 million, we could pollute as much as we liked. The sea would cheerfully absorb the lead, mercury and assorted filth we poured into it. Unless we all gathered into half a dozen great cities, for some unlikely reason, we could not create a serious smog. The heat and the dusts we should create would have no measurable effect on the climate, and even the radiation problem would be a minor one. The whole population of Elizabethan England could have been sustained by a single nuclear power station. While all radiation does some harm, when it encounters living things, the chances of individuals intercepting any would be much reduced.

Conversely, at a world population of 7 billion or more, even primitive technologies would create some impact. The sewage produced by these 7 billion people would be none the smaller and the rivers could not easily absorb it. (But of course, we could never actually support so many with a primitive technology. We should certainly need transport systems to shift the food from where it was grown to where it was to be eaten, to say nothing of fertilizer factories and motorized ploughs.)

In short, the more people the world carries, the more careful we have to be about what we do with technology and its by-products, the narrower the safety margins.

According to current forecasts, the world's population, which is doubling every 35 years, will be at or near 7 billion by the year 2000. This is unlikely to be an over-estimate for all previous forecasts have proved too low—demographers seem to find it hard to believe their own figures, and hope for a decline in the speed of advance. So far there is no sign of it. And of course it is not going to stop when it reaches 7 billion. It may double again by 2030—if the world has found out how to feed 14 billion people.

This doubled population will, we must assume, be very much more industrialized than today. Advanced countries are expected to increase output by a factor of at least five times. Developing countries will at least have established extractive industries, backed by roads, airports and power-stations, and will be trying to export in order to be able to pay for imported food and skills. Technology itself will have become more sophisticated and various. Doubtless new materials, even harder to dispose of than glass and plastic, will have been invented. New drugs, reagents and pesticides with unsuspected side-effects will have been invented. New means of transport will abound: hovercraft will skim over lakes and commons to invade the once quiet areas beyond, as snowmobiles now invade the silence of winter. A flurry of rocket-belted enthusiasts will leap about like grasshoppers, while overhead the skip-liners, circumnavigating the globe in five or six hours, will emit their sonic booms.

More people with more technology spells more pollution, more environmental distortion and less privacy. Much of the damage will come from the attempts which will necessarily be made to feed the ever-increasing number of mouths, and to house their owners. The crash of falling timber, as forests are felled, will be echoed by the thunder of explosives, as canals and harbours are blasted into existence.

It is obvious that this process cannot continue for ever: when will the poison-point come? Some maintain the world could support 15 billion people, one or two have put the figure as high as 30 billion. The earlier figure could come in the lifetime of those now living, so the question is not an academic one. It is my belief that the collapse will come considerably before this level is reached, perhaps quite soon.

PYRRHIC VICTORY

Naturally, as the problem grows more pressing, man will try to meet it. But as he is rather ignorant of the delicate web of relationships which go to make up his environment, his efforts to postpone the crisis may be the very thing which will bring it on. Or perhaps nature will take a hand: famine, plague and war are the classic controls on population. Any one or a combination of all three could cut the population back before environmental collapse occurs and thus, perhaps, give mankind a new lease of life and an opportunity to repeat his folly. And now we know that nature has yet another card up her sleeve: the undermining of potency and fertility at many points when crowding begins to create stresses, and eventual death from stress diseases. This is perhaps the most likely outcome, and there are signs that it is already beginning to happen.

For my part, I think man will surmount most of the dangers described in this book, but at tremendous cost and by a very narrow margin. In doing so, I fear, he could create a way of life which would scarcely be worth living. By a tremendous technological effort, he may succeed in detoxifying the soil; he may clean the air enough to breathe, and purify at least some of the water. He may avert starvation by giving up beefsteaks in favour of algae and converted petroleum, and sacrificing such unnecessary luxuries as sugar and alcohol. He may have to do without the private car and forgo the luxury of a full-length bath. He may have to live in domes and tunnels in the Arctic, or on islands in the sea, giving up the pleasures of owning a garden or the smell of grass after rain.

If, by drugs or conditioning processes, people are led to accept such a life without too much regret, what kind of a victory will that be? Science-fiction writers of the more serious sort, from George Orwell onward, have warned us of a nightmare world in which man continues to exist, but desperately, frustrated and unfulfilled.

How much satisfaction would there be in a world where all the rivers, though not actually useless, were too foul to swim in; a world where no one could pick an apple from the tree without risking poisoning; a world without privacy or quiet, without green fields or blue skies . . . a world in which people lived like battery hens? It is this kind of solution which seems to me most probable.

What kind of solution will this be? A world in which everyone has to work many hours a week to re-establish an approximation to the conditions which, at a more reasonable level of population, nature would provide free of charge would make a mockery of technology. This would be a technological treadmill, on which man has to pedal furiously just to remain in the same place. And even this solution only continues to be possible if population growth is eventually brought under control and the level stabilized.

What, then, should we be doing? The first step, incredibly enough, is still to gain more visibility for the problem. Although pollution, in the narrow sense, is at last becoming a public issue, with the polluters fighting every inch of the way, there is still little or no recognition of the wider issue of environmental integrity, and the risks attached to wrecking it. That is what this book is about. That, and what we should do about it.

Time is the enemy. The question is not 'how can we cope?' but 'can we cope in the time available to us?' Or is it even too late already?

2 The Planetary Engineers

A NEW TERM has begun to creep into the jargon: global engineering or, as some prefer it, planetary engineering. It reflects the realization that man can now carry out engineering works which, together and sometimes even singly, can affect everybody on earth. At present, most of them do so by virtue of the fact that—intentionally or otherwise—they affect the climate or some aspect of the climate. But others shift the crust of the earth, causing earthquakes in the process. Plans are in hand to reverse the flow of rivers, create inland seas, change the course of ocean currents, melt the polar ice-caps, join and separate continents, create and eliminate islands, regulate the weather, change the composition of the atmosphere and raise the temperature of the earth. All these plans, if executed, will of course have drastic ecological consequences besides.

Further in the future, so vaulting has man's ambition become, lie projects for altering the atmosphere of Mars and the climate of Venus to make them habitable, the capture and towing back to earth of asteroids or their use to construct a new planet, and the complete taking apart and rebuilding of Jupiter, this last a brain-child of Professor Freeman Dyson of Cornell.

In March 1968, so large did these prospects loom that a symposium was organized under the joint auspices of the US Department of the Interior and the National Research Council, the chair being taken by the Deputy-Assistant Secretary for Scientific Programs of the Department of the Interior, Mr S. Fred Singer. 'We are moving into the age of planetary engineering,' he said in his opening address, 'and now is the time to discuss proposals for modifications and their consequences, before the need for such modifications becomes urgent.' Stewart L. Udall, Secretary of the Interior at that time, delivering the keynote address, warned listeners that various engineering modifications of the earth's surface might have undesirable ecological consequences.

Let us have a look at some of the projects in question. Many of them concern the hydrology of the planet—that is, the cycle through which water passes. Evaporated from the sea, some of it falls on the land and is absorbed, while another part runs back to the sea by way of rivers. Some accumulates in underground strata, or aquifers. Some gets into plants or animals and is transpired. Man now interferes with every one of these stages.

The limitation of run-off by building dams is old stuff. The recharging of aquifers has become a commonplace more recently. Attempts to increase precipitation (rainfall or snow) are still somewhat experimental. Recently, in Swiss, Austrian, Italian and Scottish resorts, snow generation has been employed, using sprinklers in conjunction with freezers, while in the western United States and in Hawaii sprays running on wheels are moved electrically across the crops so as to simulate an actual rain-storm. In Chile, Dr C. Marangunič has successfully turned snow to water, by using four aircraft to dust a mixture of lamp-black on the Coton glacier in the Andes. The operation released two million gallons of water daily, and the cost was recovered after the flow had continued for 81 days.

But hydrologists dream of much more ambitious efforts than these. Thus Drs R. J. Chorley and R. J. More believe it should be possible to put more water into the atmosphere for the rainmakers to work on by increasing the rate of evaporation. This might be done 'by chemical methods, heating the surface water, increasing wind speeds, etc.'. The reason it has not been tried, they say, is lack of data on ocean temperatures and how they are linked with rates of evaporation, 'but satellite sensing may remedy this deficiency in the near future and make experimental work possible.'

In other parts of the world, you might prefer to reduce evaporation, and this could conceivably be achieved 'by putting huge quantities of dust or metallic needles into stationary orbit'. This would reduce the temperature of the sea beneath and so reduce evaporation.

More godlike still, you might alter the course of storms, while 'more ambitious projects make it likely that hurricanes can be suppressed or damped down by the seeding of the rising air in the cumulus eye-wall, widening the ring of condensation and updraught.' This would decrease the rotation rate of the hurricane and hence lower wind speed. In addition, the sea ahead of the storm might be spread with oily materials in order to stop surface evaporation and so cut off the hurricane's energy supply. When it is remembered that 30 per cent of the rainfall in Texas in August, and of Louisiana and Connecticut in September, are derived from hurricanes, while the Atlantic City–New Jersey area gets as much as 40 per cent of its September rainfall from this source, the economic significance becomes obvious. But these writers admit that 'even such apparently beneficial attempts may represent potentially dangerous tampering with the natural global moisture economy.'

Man's first attempt to damp down a hurricane was made in August 1969, when Hurricane Debbie was seeded with silver iodide crystals: five hours later, the wind-force had diminished by 31 per cent. Next day, with no seeding, they intensified, and a second seeding was made. The wind again dropped by 15 per cent. The director of Project STORMFURY, Dr R. Cecil Gentry, after four months' analysis of the data, reported: 'The data suggests we did modify the hurricane.'

Soviet weathermen have substantially reduced hail damage by firing shells containing silver iodide into hail-producing clouds. Attempts to suppress lightning have already met with a degree of success. The clearing of fog from airports is becoming routine and eventually it should be possible to clear hundreds of square miles in this way. Thomas F. Malone, Director of Research for Travelers Insurance Co., which has an extensive environmental research programme, considers, 'There is a high probability that the last third of the twentieth century will witness gradual perfection in the technology of meaningful, local weather control.' But he thinks the chances of being able to control hurricanes more dubious.

The US government has a $13m. project, named SKY-WATER, for regulating rainfall, and the Russians are reported to be in the same business on an even larger scale. Another approach, proposed by physicists, is to coat deserts with tar or to dust them with black particles, which would increase their absorption of solar heat.

This heat would warm the air, which would rise, creating a 'thermal mountain' and causing clouds to form. Rainfall would then increase downwind. Here again Messrs More and Chorley warn us that we should go cautiously. 'The unknown dangers attendant upon such large-scale tampering with the delicately-balanced world hydrological cycle must postpone such schemes until theoretical mathematical models simulating the behaviour of the earth-atmosphere system have been developed, so that all possible effects can be predicted in advance.'

The use of computers is opening new vistas. Malone says: 'Quite clearly, within the next decade or so, it will become possible to explore, through simulation techniques, an almost unlimited array of deliberate interventions in natural atmospheric processes and to assess possibilities and limitations.'

My own modest prediction is that we shall never be able to predict 'all possible effects' with complete confidence, and that, sooner or later, global disasters will occur, if we get so far. However, I do not expect to see large-scale control of weather attempted before the end of the century. In this chapter I want to describe a number of projects which are a good deal nearer: some, at least, may be launched in the next decade. Prominent among them are various fantastic schemes of dam-building, designed to create vast inland seas. Since engineers are now rather good at dam-building and the financing problems are well understood, it is a foregone conclusion that some of these plans will go ahead.

WATERWORKS

'Damn the river and blast the mountain!' roared the general, when told that his army could not advance because of natural obstacles. So they did. The same forceful spirit of progress seems to have infected both Russian and American planners.

The Russians have for some time been considering a number of alternative plans for irrigating Central Asia and making hydro-electric power at the same time. In its latest form, which has been approved by the Science and Technology Council of the USSR's Ministry of Electric Power, a vast dam, 78 metres high and not less than 60 kilometres long, will be built at the confluence of two great rivers, the Irtysh and the Ob, which flow towards the Arctic. This dam will cause the water to back up the Irtysh and its tributary, the Tobol, until, with a little aid from a canal 575 miles long, it overflows the watershed and runs down towards the Aral Sea. This will rise many metres, until in turn it opens up an ancient river bed and feeds the Caspian. At the same time this will create an inland sea with a surface as large as Great Britain—90 per cent of the flooded area being at present impassable marshland.

Unfortunately this will take all the water from the lower 640 miles of the Ob, which carries ships of considerable size. So another dam on the Yenisei, one of the world's largest rivers, will create a vast reservoir 200 miles long, which will feed, via another canal, into the headwaters of the Ob. A further deepwater canal will link this whole system to Lake Baikal more than 500 miles to the east, thus creating a deep-water shipping route 5,000 miles long from the Caspian to Baikal. It will also provide 12,900 megawatts of electric power.

One reason for the USSR's rather fervent interest in this project is the fact that the Caspian Sea is vanishing—a piece of unplanned global engineering of a spectacular order, since the Caspian, at 150,000 square miles or so, is the largest lake in the world. In the past 20 years the water-level has fallen 6 feet, as a result of the industrialization of the lower Volga Valley and the construction of numerous hydro-electric schemes. Hundreds of fishing villages, active in 1939, now lie tens or even hundreds of miles from the lake shore. Soviet hydrologists predict that the fall will continue: it will have dropped another 6 feet by 1980.

The scheme, which will take 20 years to execute, is expected to moderate the climate of western Siberia, permitting agriculture to spread north. But some Soviet scientists are apprehensive about this plan. They think the cooling of air masses above the lake may have an undesirable effect on the fertile steppes to the south. Others think the underlying strata may not be able to support the weight of millions of tons of additional water. The Ob reservoir may raise the whole water table, creating marshes even greater than those which are to be flooded. The diminished salinity of the Aral, and to some extent the Caspian, may affect the fishing, while the ice which in winter locks the mouths of the Yenisei and the Ob may melt later in the early summer. Studies of these problems are continuing.

The originator of this super-project, in its present form, is a Soviet engineer, M. M. Davidov, who has developed projects for diverting the Ob made more than half a century ago, in Czarist times, by a Russian named Demchenko.

Even this grandiose scheme pales in relation to the plan, prepared by America's Hudson Institute, to dam the Amazon, creating an inland sea one-third the size of France. The Amazon is the world's greatest river: it carries one-fifth of all the water carried by all the rivers of the world, and the silt it transports colours the water 200 miles out to sea. At least ten of its tributaries are each larger than the Mississippi. But its rate of fall is very slight, and the inland sea will only be 100 feet above sea level. There is a natural site for the dam near Obidos, about 1,000 miles from the coast, where the river flows between two lines of hills 40 miles apart. The dam would thus be long, but not high. Depending on the level to which the water is raised, the area flooded would be from 46,000 to 70,000 square miles (120,000 to 180,000 sq. km.), according to the Hudson Institute. My estimate is that it would be at least twice that.

In addition to the main sea, it is proposed to create subsidiary lakes on the tributaries by means of inexpensive earth dams; some of these would be as much as 200 miles long and 10 miles wide. This is, of course, far larger than any artificial lake yet made and there could be from 25 to 40 of them. The cost of the main dam is put at $800m. and of the subsidiary dams at $250m. To equip the dam with electric generating equipment would cost between $5 billion and $6.5 billion. Of course, the forest tribes of the Amazon are not consumers of electricity, so transmission lines to major cities like Rio de Janeiro, Montevideo, São Paulo and Buenos Aires will be required. More practically, some of it could be used to extract aluminum from bauxite, a process which depends on cheap electricity. At present about a quarter of the world's bauxite is extracted in Surinam and Guyana and shipped to areas where cheap current is available, such as Kitimat and Lake Volta.

There are certain drawbacks to this scheme, to be sure.

The population of the Amazon basin is unknown, but a good guess would be somewhere between half a million and a million people, almost all living near the rivers, which provide the main lines of communication. If the scheme went ahead, a great part of these would have to leave their villages and fields, or hunting areas, and would starve to death in the surrounding towns. If it were proposed to flood 100,000 square miles or so of Canada or the mid-West, no doubt some of the inhabitants would write to their Congressmen. Fortunately, the Amazon tribes have no Congressmen. Of less importance than their misery, but still not negligible, is the fact that they provide one of the last largely unexplored fields of anthropological study, from which we might learn vital facts about human behavior.

The proponents of the plan concede that 'significant disruption of the ecological balance of the area' is possible and that in a country so large 'some surprises are probable'. Furthermore, they agree, the formation of this vast inland sea may affect the climate, while the holding-back of the rich silts could affect the fishing off Florida. (It could affect it even more off Brazil, but this they ignore.) What would happen to the billions of forest trees, many of which would stick out of the 100-foot-deep water or remain out of sight to wreck boats? The Hudson Institute hopes they could be dredged out. Decaying, they would eutrophicate* the water. No fish could survive there until long after they vanish. But they do not expect these prospects to prevent construction of the dam, on the grounds that they have never made any difference in the past. As a final underlining of their cynical lack of human feeling they add that it would be far too costly to make good maps of the area, which is largely unmapped, but these are not essential—i.e. if the flooding drowns a few tribes who were not evacuated because they were supposed to be on higher ground, or wipes out a few forest species, who cares? In a later chapter I shall describe in more detail the ecological consequences of this type of operation.

Even more ambitious was the project advanced by H. Sergal to form *two* inland seas in Africa: the Chad Sea and the Congo Sea. Between them, they would have put nearly

---

*A lake which is biologically *too* good, i.e. has too much nutrient in it, so that algae grow profusely and fish die, is said to be eutrophicated.

10 per cent of the African land mass under water. No one regards this as likely to happen, but there are lesser projects for flooding the Sahara which are by no means out of the question. The classic suggestion is to lead the Mediterranean into the Qattara depression, the idea being that, though the lake itself will be salt, the evaporated moisture will fall nearby and render parts of the desert fertile. Recently, a rather more detailed scheme was prepared by Professor Torki to reclaim the area west of Gabès. In Greek times there was a lake here, known as the Lake of Pallas, the remains of an inland sea which covered some 1,500 square miles in the Quaternary period. By AD 43, when Pomponius Melas wrote about it, it was no more than a memory. He described the fishbones, shells, polished stones and old anchors which were to be found far from the banks of the river, thus proving that there had once been a sea there. Also he noted that the trunks of enormous trees were found, showing that the land had once sustained a rich vegetation.

Professor Torki, investigating the possibilities of mining uranium in the area in 1964, came across a ruined Roman villa in a region which is now marshy and uncultivated. Well-preserved mosaics show scenes of hunting and agriculture, and display a slogan which reads 'O Land of Happiness!'

But the steady expansion of the Sahara continues at the rate of 30,000 acres a year. Rainfall declines—it is down 30 per cent since 1910—and temperatures rise. By flooding the area, Professor Torki reckons that the advance of the desert would be stopped, 65,000 tons of fish might be caught, and the area could become a tourist centre. Eventually nuclear complexes could be built, the lake could be desalinated, and fresh water could be led by canals into the Sahara. The area of the sea would be 62 million acres: it would become the Baltic of Africa. Against this, it is objected that rapid evaporation might depress the water table and raise the salt content of the soil.

Australia has long toyed with similar notions. As far back as 1902 Professor J. W. Gregory, of Melbourne University, proposed cutting a channel from Spencer's Gulf to Lake Eyre. Lake Eyre is a vast depression in S. Australia, below sea-level. Evaporation in this torrid region would, it is hoped, increase the rainfall in surrounding areas. Thirty years later,

Dr J. C. C. Bradfield, an Australian engineer, proposed the diversion of various rivers flowing to the east and south, so as to irrigate the interior, and change the climate, but the committee appointed to consider the plan was unconvinced. Recently Professor Gregory's plan has been revived by Ian B. Kiddle, on the basis of fuller understanding of the meteorological problems involved. He argues that the moisture-saturated air mass which has passed the lake will deposit its load only when it passes over higher ground and is thereby forced to expand. It is also an essential feature that the air should not be fully laden with moisture when it arrives. These considerations explain why some other areas, such as the Red Sea, fail to cause rainfall in surrounding deserts.

Once again, Australian experts are sceptical about the benefits of Kiddle's proposals, which would cost, he says, £50m., a sum which he claims would be amortized by the sale of irrigation water. Here again, it is only uncertainty as to the meteorological results which inhibits enthusiasm.

Canada too has a plan to raise the level of Southern Indian Lake, about 500 miles north of Winnipeg in Manitoba, creating a flooded area one-quarter the size of Lake Ontario.

THE EARTHQUAKE MAKERS

The prospect now looms of man being able to cause earthquakes at will, or, what is more probable, of doing so by mistake. The kind of forces he can now release are quite large enough to upset the frequently tenuous balance of forces in the crustal rocks. For example, the 18,000-foot-high Elburz mountains fall steeply away into the 1,000-foot-deep Caspian Sea, creating a situation which is out of balance. In view of this it has been suggested that the disastrous earthquakes which hit Iran and Turkey in 1957 and 1966 were caused by the changes in the level of the Caspian to which I have already referred.

This is pretty much of a guess based on a knowledge of the geology, but there are similar cases where the connection is beyond doubt. A recent and serious example was a severe earthquake which occurred on 10 December 1967, which caused damage throughout India and killed some 200 people in the town of Koynanagar, 150 kilometres SE. of Bombay. This was caused, it is now agreed, by the filling of the reservoir created by the Koyna Dam. The dam is 103 metres high and can retain 2,780 million cubic metres of water. By 1964 this dam had been filled with 2,000 million cubic metres of water, weighing 2 billion tons. As the new lake filled, the first tremor occurred in 1962 when it was holding only 850 million cubic metres. In 1965 there was a stronger shock. In 1967 an earthquake expert read a paper at a Congress on Large Dams, saying that this series of shocks could be attributed to crustal readjustments, but it was expected that they would gradually decrease over a period of some years and finally stop completely. This hope was vain. The December quake had a magnitude of 6.4 on the Richter scale. (The Alaska earthquake was 8.6.) Before the Koyna Dam was built the whole Bombay-Koyna—Poona area had been free from tremors.

The story is much the same at the Kariba Dam in Rhodesia, the world's largest artificial lake, containing 175,000 million cubic metres of water. Filling started in May 1960: the first tremors were recorded in January and February 1962 and were shown to originate in Kariba. In March there were thirty such shocks in five days. By September 1963 they reached a maximum with a quake rated at 5.7 followed three hours later by a 6.1 shock, and by others at 5.8, 5.5 and 6.0. This was the first time artificial tremors reaching a rating of 6 had been created. The area was quite free of shocks before the dam was built.

Fortunately Kariba is in a sparsely inhabited area. Some dams are not, and much smaller dams can cause significant tremors, especially when they are in areas which are already unstable. For instance the dam at Monteynard in the French Alps holds a modest 275 million cubic metres. A few days after it was filled, a series of tremors culminated in a force 5 shock. There have been many others since. This area, in contrast with those I mentioned previously, was known to be somewhat unstable geologically.

Similarly, the artificial lake of Kremasta in Greece, which holds 4,700 million tons of water, caused many earth-slides and fractures: 480 houses collapsed, 1,200 were seriously damaged, one person was killed and sixty injured. As soon as the lake was full a temblor of force 6.2 occurred, preceded by lesser shocks.

The possibility that man might be disturbing the earth's

crustal forces only dawned on scientists in 1945, when D. S. Carder pointed out what was happening at Boulder Dam in Colorado. There had been no shocks in this area for 15 years before the dam was built. Lake Mead, formed by the dam, began to fill in 1935. The first shock came in September 1936. During 1937 more than 100 shocks were felt. The lake was now 400 feet deep and the weight of impounded water 21 billion tons. In some alarm, the authorities installed seismographs around the lake to find out if it could really be the culprit. When the lake reached its full depth of 475 feet, bringing the weight of water to 25 billion tons, the shocks reached a maximum, with further bursts in several subsequent years when the lake was particularly full. In all, 600 tremors were registered in 10 years, the largest of magnitude 5. The case was overwhelming. Imagination boggles, then, at the probable effect of the great inland seas which I have described, such as the Amazon with its 170 billion tons of water.

However, it seems that it does not take billions of tons of water to produce an earthquake. It can be done with much smaller amounts. This emerged when the US army sought to get rid of what it obscurely called 'toxic wastes' from its chemical and biological warfare establishment at Fort Detrick. The nerve gases were stored in steel tanks, destined to be dumped at sea, as later emerged. Other wastes, no doubt equally lethal and unpleasant, were pumped into a well over 12,000 feet deep, specially drilled near their Rocky Mountain Arsenal outside Denver, Colorado. About 150 million gallons were pumped in at up to 200 gallons a minute, beginning in 1962. Following protests, the practice was suspended in September 1963 until September 1964 and finally abandoned in September 1965. The reason for the protests was the occurrence of 710 earthquakes during the period, eighteen of them of force 3 or higher. In the 80 years preceding this, only three had been recorded in the area.

Scientists were surprised that a mere 750,000 tons of water could produce so large an effect. A geologist at the Colorado School of Mines, David Evans, came up with an explanation. The liquid was being pumped into permeable fractured rocks. When the pressure in these layers built up to match that in the overlying layers, slip would occur. This theory leads on to the thought that whenever two masses of rock are under strain, slip could be induced either by pumping water in or pumping it out, depending on whether the permeable rock contained too little or too much. Thus it might be possible to avoid major earthquakes by initiating a gradual slipping, instead. Naturally there is a risk that you might, unless you knew exactly what you were doing, bring on the big earthquake by mistake. Despite this risk, it seems likely that we shall see attempts at earthquake control being made well before the end of the century.

Meanwhile the use of deep wells for the disposal of difficult wastes is growing rapidly: there are now more than eighty substances being disposed of in this way in 150 deep wells spread over nineteen states, quite apart from the 40,-000–50,000 smaller wells used by the oil industry for brine disposal. They too may trigger some earthquakes.

On top of all this comes the reckless staging of nuclear explosions underground. Scientists did not worry too much when the explosions were caused in stable salt strata. They were worried when the AEC staged an explosion beneath Amchitka Island in the Aleutians, not far from the San Andreas fault-line. No harm was caused, as it turned out, but the day could come when the AEC's experts miscalculate or a fault exists of which they do not know.

Professor Gordon MacDonald of the University of California considers that the threat is more than just a local problem. 'It has become clear in recent years that man by his activities has changed conditions in the near-surface layers of the solid earth,' he says. 'These changes have brought about a release of elastic energy which had been built up by tectonic forces acting over geologic time. The energies released in some events are large enough to cause substantial damage to a highly industrialized region.' In other words, he holds that it is not just a question of the earth settling down a little under the added load: it is a question of adding a straw to the camel's back and releasing huge forces which have been built up over aeons. It is like bringing down an avalanche by firing a shotgun.

The fact that there have not, in man's brief memory, been earthquakes in a particular area, he warns, is no guarantee that the region is not under stress. There seem to be several ways an earthquake can be brought about. If you imagine a mass of rock about to slide sideways across another mass of rock, because it is under a lateral pressure, then it may be restrained by simple friction, in which case an increase of pressure may bring it to the point of sliding. Or there may be a projection of some kind or a mass of hard rock lying across the fault, like a huge nail or steel reinforcing bar. If man does something to weaken such a 'lock-point' this could release the movement. Or again, pumping in liquid might act rather like a lubricant, which may be why the Denver wells produced such an unexpected effect.

Furthermore, when the strain is released by one quake, this sets up other strains, usually much greater ones in larger systems. This is why, in natural earthquakes, the initial shock is seldom the worst. For instance, in the Chilean earthquake of 1960, the initial shock of magnitude 7.5 was followed after 33 hours by one of 8.5 (i.e. ten times as strong).

Finally, declares MacDonald, the large earthquakes significantly affect the strain-field of the whole planet. For instance, the Alaskan earthquake produced permanent strain in the Hawaii area, some 2,500 miles away.

What worries MacDonald is the fact that major earthquakes (magnitude 8.5 or more) seem to consist of a series of smaller events (magnitude 6 to 7). Thus the Alaska earthquake, nominally of 8.5, consisted, according to two geologists, Wyss and Brune, of a rapid succession of earthquakes of magnitude 6.8. Now the man-made disturbances are approaching this critical magnitude 'and there is a not insignificant probability that a man-made event could set off a catastrophic earthquake.' And today the increasing complexity of society, as MacDonald points out, makes us more vulnerable. If San Francisco were again hit by a temblor like that of 1902, ten times as many people could be killed and the damage would be measurable in billions of dollars, rather than millions.

As if this were not enough, he points out that quakes can lower the water-table, depriving man of far more water than can ever collect in the reservoirs which he builds.

He therefore urges increasing the insignificant sums we at present spend trying to understand these processes, and careful study before anyone launches engineering works or atomic explosions of the kind described. But first of all it is essential to get people to recognize the existence of the danger. To this I would add the plea that no nation should unilaterally engage in engineering activities which could affect other nations or even the whole planet, without world agreement. The Amchitka explosion, for one, was in the same category as the Starfish explosion in the stratosphere, which weakened the van Allen belts, or the infamous 'needles' experiment which so alarmed the radio-astronomers.

THE NUCLEAR BULLDOZER

It was Harold Brown, the director of the Livermore Laboratory in Berkeley, California, who first put forward the idea of using nuclear explosives to dig a canal. The year was 1956, and the Israeli-Arab war had closed the Suez Canal. Brown suggested that the world's shipping could be saved its enforced journeys round the Cape of Good Hope by digging a new canal across the Sinai Peninsula, running from the Gulf of Aqaba to the Mediterranean. This could be easily done by using nuclear explosives to blast a furrow through the desert.

Though the idea was politically impractical, the idea of using nuclear explosions as a super bulldozer, capable of moving masses of earth rapidly, took root. Always anxious to find new justification for its existence, the Atomic Energy Commission set up a team under the general heading Project PLOWSHARE. One of the applications dreamed up by this group was to dig a harbour at Cape Thompson. The journal *Environment*, published by the American Committee for Environmental Information, tersely summarized the risks thus: 'There were no compelling economic reasons for the harbour, and Alaskan Eskimos were already getting more radioactivity in their diet than other people. Eskimos eat caribou; caribou eat lichen; lichen concentrates cesium-137 and strontium-90 from fallout.'

The Eskimos and others protested so strongly against the radiation risks that the idea was dropped.

The American AEC prefers the term 'geographical engineering' for its PLOWSHARE-type activities. ' "Geographical engineering" describes the use of nuclear explosives to change the geography of our planet,' it says in a booklet issued by its division of technical information, 'digging sea-level canals between oceans, stripping overburdens from deep mineral deposits, cutting highway and railway passes through mountains, creating harbours and lakes where none existed before, and altering watersheds for better distribution of water resources. Nor do proposals for peaceful uses of nuclear explosives stop with large-scale earth-moving. Also envisioned are constructing underground reservoirs, increasing gas-well productivity, and controlling subterranean water movement. Eventually, the energy from nuclear explosives may even be used for underground desalting of seawater, for producing steam, and for creating basic industrial chemicals directly from mineral deposits.' They also mention the kind of mining operations I have already described and add, 'The shattering effect and heat of nuclear explosions may one day enable recovery of vast oil reserves from sand and shale formations that are now uneconomical to exploit.'

The AEC does not give any indication of how much radio-activity all these various operations are likely to release, and probably does not know, but the assumption is that it would be considerable. It concedes that this would be a danger 'if not properly controlled' and also mentions possible risks from 'ground shock', 'base surge' and 'air blast'. It does not mention earthquakes.

The first nuclear explosion specifically for the PLOWSHARE programme was Project GNOME, which melted 2,400 tons of rock, leaving a cavity of nearly a million cubic feet capacity underground. The intention was to explore the possibility of using the heat developed as a source of power. Water would be pumped into the scorching hot cavity and turned to steam which could, in principle, be made to drive dynamos or do other work. GNOME was a mere 3.1 kiloton shot. It proved rather a disappointment. Thirteen thousand tons of colder rocks 'were blown or collapsed into the molten pool from the walls and ceiling. As a result the melted material was cooled suddenly and the heat distributed throughout a much larger mass. Thus it was not possible to recover any appreciable amount of the heat. Moreover, studies indicated that the steam produced was very corrosive.' It would not, the AEC concluded, be economic to use it.

Seven months after GNOME, a much more ambitious project, SEDAN, in which 200 kilotons (equivalent) were exploded, took place. Says the AEC, 'The effect of the SEDAN explosion was awesome.' Though the charge was fired an eighth of a mile below the surface, it excavated a crater 1,200 feet in diameter with a volume of 5.5 million cubic yards. The Defense Department helped out with two more shots in 1962, HARDHAT and DANNY BOY. HARDHAT yielded so little radio-activity that it was felt that industrial nuclear mining was 'on'.

In his book *Project Plowshare*, Ralph Sanders lists many specific ideas, such as blasting new harbours on the west coast of Africa or in South America. These could be so deep that much larger ships than any now in use would use them, which might reduce the cost of ocean transport. 'The imagination and effort devoted to the PLOWSHARE program must be great and relentless,' concludes the AEC with relentless fervour.

Meanwhile the idea came up of blasting a harbour in northern Australia, near Cape Keraudren. This region is rich in natural resources, such as nickel and iron, but they are hard to get out as there is no large harbour for a thousand miles. However, Port Hedland harbour, already equipped for ore-handling, is only 100 miles off, and could be enlarged. A feasibility study was launched jointly by the Australians and the Americans in 1966. The plan called for the explosion of five 200-kiloton shots buried offshore. All was going well, with early 1970 in view as the firing date, when the principal customers for the iron ore, the Japanese, indicated that they thought the price of the ore would be too high. This was as well, since the date set allowed little or no time for studies of the effect on the environment, or on people. No public announcement was made of how many people would be at risk, and how many people would have to be evacuated. There are no nuclear explosions without the release of some radio-activity to the environment, but nothing was said about the possible effect on sheep and cattle, on which Australia so largely depends. It would also be essential to discover whether any plants concentrate cesium or other nuclides in the way lichen does, and what of the danger that contaminated soil might be blown to great distances and there descend? In the dry, torrid climate of Northern Australia, this risk is far more serious than in the Arctic. Just before the Japanese pulled out the props, three Australian scientists from Sydney University, Professor A. E. Alexander, Professor L. C. Birch, a physical chemist and a biologist respectively, together with

N. A. Walker, the Associate Professor of Biology, issued an appeal for a two-year ecological study of land and sea areas involved, and for evaluation to be carried out by an independent body. Meanwhile the Australian and American atomic energy commissions have said that they will study the possibility of using nuclear excavation at other sites in the area.

Unwilling to abandon the rich iron deposits, the mining companies have now come up with another plan: to extract the ore itself with nuclear explosives. This time the plan is to place three to five 10-kiloton charges 800 feet down, which is about 450 feet below the ore body, spaced at intervals. It is hoped this would shatter some 45 million tons of ore. It would then be necessary to wait for up to six months for the radio-activity to subside somewhat. The hope is that much of it will have been trapped in a glassy mass of once-molten rock. The charges foreseen for this plan, known as the Wittenoom plan, are certainly much smaller than for the harbour, but they are large enough and ecological surveys should certainly be made and independently evaluated.

In the US, Kennecott Copper has been investigating a similar project with AEC co-operation, at Safford, Arizona, about 150 miles north-east of Tucson. In this case, after the blasts, the metal would be leached out chemically, thus limiting exposure of personnel to radio-activity.

Meanwhile, an even more grandiose idea had surfaced: to dig a ditch across the Isthmus of Panama, thus making a sea-level canal, which need have no costly and time-consuming locks to raise ships to higher levels, such as there are on the existing Panama Canal. When this was opened in 1914, its 110-foot by 1,000-foot long locks seemed big enough. Today they are too small for the world's 500 biggest ships, many of which are mammoth oil tankers.

In 1964, President Johnson established a Canal Study Commission to report on the need for such a canal and the cost of making it, and the best position. Though originally due to report in 1968, the date of the final report has been postponed until December 1970.

Meanwhile, the AEC began making test explosions, with soothing code names like SULKY and PALANQUIN. Since some thirty possible sites for the new canal have been suggested, it is impossible to be definite about the amount of nuclear explosive required, but for Route 17, the most popular candidate, a total of 166 megatons would be needed, according to a recent calculation. (For purposes of comparison, the San Francisco earthquake was equivalent to a 100 megaton explosion.) As the largest cratering test so far conducted is only 100 kilotons, one thousand times smaller, the AEC can only guess ('extrapolate' is the polite word) what the effects of this fantastic sequence of blasts would be. According to one authority, large explosions are less effective at earth moving than small ones, so that one 50-megaton and three 25-megaton shots might have to be fired together, with many smaller ones to fill the gaps.

A team from ESSA (Environmental Science Services Administration), sent to study the meteorological aspects, found a complex pattern of winds, and ESSA's E. A. Martell foresees an 'extended east-west radio-active cloud source for which the fall-out pattern would be widespread and unpredictable. Areas which may receive significant fall-out include Costa Rica, Panama, northern Colombia, and north-west Venezuela.' And he goes on to say: 'The fact that Central America is an active earthquake area further magnifies the difficulty of predicting effects. There is a real possibility that the nuclear detonations would trigger large earthquakes at great distances.' It would also be difficult, he says, to predict the effect of the waves which would be caused, while the air-blast might damage inhabited areas hundreds of miles away.

Professor LaMont Cole of Cornell University goes further. He calculates that the cesium fall-out from the explosions would provide 26.5 limiting doses for everyone on earth, since the radio-active cesium would enter the food-chains and end up everywhere. It might also affect the hurricane pattern, ruin the fishing and shift or destroy the Gulf Stream. This may be too pessimistic, but it does call in question the right of one nation to expose the rest of the world to such a risk.

This is no place to explore the engineering and other problems associated with this project, but something must be said about the people who would have to be evacuated. 'Preliminary evacuation plans anticipate that over 30,000 people from areas near Routes 17 and 25 would have to be resettled elsewhere for a few years.' Of course, if the radio-active cloud descended unexpectedly in some area supposed safe, there would have to be emergency evacuations as well. In the case of Route 17, people affected would be the Cuna Indians at the Caribbean end, the Choco Indians in the central and southern areas and various Colombian immigrants and colonists from central and western Panama. Martell observes that construction of the canal on Route 17 'would all but destroy the Cuna Indians and their culture'. Some would hide in the jungle and be killed by the blast, but those that did not could never return to their haunts, which would be taken over for defence areas and supporting communities.

Finally, there is the ecological risk. Since the tides on the Pacific side run to much greater heights than the Atlantic tides, strong currents would flow through the channel, carrying many species from one ocean to the other, and perhaps lowering the temperature of the Caribbean. Ira Rubinoff, the Assistant Director of the Marine Biology Department of the Smithsonian Tropical Research Institute at Balboa, says that only one fish is known to have got through the existing canal and to have bred. The fresh-water lake in the middle is the real barrier, not the locks; similarly in the Suez Canal, the salty Bitter Lakes constitute a barrier. He adds that when two species interbreed, the result can sometimes be extinction of both, if the 'crosses' which result are inferior to the parent lines.

When the Welland Canal to the Great Lakes was opened, the sea lamprey got in. Nearly a hundred years later, a lamprey population explosion occurred, decimating the white fish and trout in the lakes. The fishing industry lost millions of dollars, and the US and Canada chipped in $16m. in an attempt to solve the problem. Says Rubinoff: 'Spectacular as some of these cases may have been, they are minor by comparison with what would be expected to result from the construction of a sea-level canal in Central America. The mutual invasions of Atlantic and Pacific organisms should be much more extensive, numerous and rapid, and their ultimate consequences should be quite incommensurable with any biological changes ever recorded before.'

Seeing that this is only the first of many such proposals, I join with him in urging the appointment of an independent Commission for Environmental Modification, with adequate funds and power to review all alterations of the environment, on a world-wide basis. Late in 1969, following this and many other protests, the National Academy of Sciences set up a Committee on Ecological Research at the request of the Canal Study Commission to go into the problem—a step in the right direction.

When a Panama canal was first proposed, in the nineteenth century, some argued that such a project would be against God's will, as he had clearly intended the Atlantic to remain separated from the Pacific or he would not have left a strip of land joining the two Americas. Today western man is not troubled by any such scruples and he is sublimely indifferent to those, less arrogant, who prefer the planet the way it is. But his ambition does not stop at joining oceans, he would even abolish the ice-caps.

MELTING THE ICE-CAP

Man now has the power to alter the topography on a scale which could affect the whole planet.

One of the most ambitious of these schemes comes from Russia and proposes to change the climate of the Arctic and thereby of the whole northern hemisphere. The Moscow meteorologist P. M. Borisov proposes to put a dam across the Bering Straits, separating Russia from Alaska, and then to start pumping out the cold Arctic water. This will cause relatively warmer water to flow in from the Atlantic. He calculates that in only three years all the Arctic ice will have melted and the water temperature will have risen by anything up to 8°C. With the rise in air temperature which will follow, huge acreages of permanently frozen ground (permafrost) in N. Canada and N. Russia will become capable of carrying grass. Cattle will fatten on vast steppes which now are tundra. The basins of the Volga and Don will become sub-tropical. Britain will become warmer and damper, and the US perhaps too warm for comfort. Even as far south as Africa, Borisov thinks, the effect will be felt and grass will grow in the Sahara, as a consequence of the damper air fed by evaporation from Arctic water.

'We cannot precisely predict where and how the proposed human intervention will affect natural conditions,' he says with an airy insouciance which may well alarm the ordinary man. 'For theoretical computation is one thing and experimental testing is another.' So let's try it and see what happens.

One of the likely consequences which M. Borisov does not dwell on is that the N. Pacific and Bering Sea will become much colder. One can imagine what might happen to the rubber plantations of Malaya or the rice of Japan. Another is that the sea level will rise as a result of the melting ice. M. Borisov thinks this will amount to only 4 inches, but other calculations foresee a rise of many feet. The Arctic ice is predominantly floating, although some 20 per cent of it lies on Greenland and numerous islands. When floating ice melts only one-seventh of it goes to raise the level of the sea, whereas land-borne ice is all pure addition to the oceans. In contrast, the Antarctic ice is mostly land-borne. The question is, therefore, whether melting the northern ice cap would have any effect on the southern ice-cap. Such data as we have suggests that there is a certain symmetry in the global air circulation: certainly when bomb-tests are carried out in one hemisphere, part of the fall-out comes down in the other. It is therefore anyone's guess whether the Antarctic ice would melt. If it did, completely, it would raise the world sea level 400 feet, making Moscow a seaport and drowning uncalculated land areas. Since even a 20-foot rise would put London, New York and many other areas under water, the point is not without importance.

The alarming thing about this plan is that it is by no means impractical. Though the Bering Straits are 74 kilometres (46 miles) across, the depth is only 58 metres (190 feet). It is this natural underwater wall or sill which holds the cold water in. We know, also, that only 5,000 years ago the Arctic basin was ice-free all winter, which suggests that some comparatively small adjustment of water-circulation has occurred.

This scheme, as a matter of fact, is only the latest in a series of plans for warming the Arctic, mostly put forward by Russians, for whom the drowning of London and New York no doubt seems a small price to pay for making Siberia inhabitable. In 1963, V.N. Stepenov proposed to chip bits out of the Wyville Thomson Ridge, SW of the Faeroes, with underwater nuclear explosions. This, he felt, would enable cold water to drain out from the North Sea to the Atlantic. Several people, for example another Russian, G. Veksler, in 1959, have proposed dusting a black powder on the Arctic snow. This would cause it to absorb sunlight instead of reflecting it, and hence to melt. Presumably, however, the snow would tend to build up again, so that further dusting would be called for. Other proposals included dispersing the cloud cover over the Central Arctic basin by cloud-seeding techniques and diverting Arctic water into the Kara Sea. Recently, chemists have produced substances which can be spread over water surfaces in layers only a single molecule thick, termed monomolecular layers. These prevent evaporation: another Russian, M. I. Budyko, was quick to suggest their application to the Arctic. Fortunately, such layers seem to break up when the area to be covered exceeds a few hundred square yards, and they cannot yet be employed to reduce evaporation of irrigation water in desert regions. Obviously the stormy oceans would be even less suitable.

But, as J. O. Fletcher of the RAND Corporation has pointed out, this is by no means the whole story. The ocean ice-cover makes a tremendous difference to the behaviour of the atmosphere, since it prevents the ocean from supplying heat to the air in winter. Thus in the Arctic, the temperature averages $-30°C$. just above the ice, but is only $-2°C$. in the water just below it. In summer, the consequences are even more striking: the ice layer reflects two-thirds of the incoming sunlight. In the absence of ice, the ocean would absorb 90 per cent of it.

The upshot is that, when ice is present, the atmosphere cools more intensely in winter, warms more intensely in summer. Since the global circulation is driven by the difference in temperatures between the equator and the poles, the whole process would be affected.

Fletcher's interest in these calculations, it must be added, was not to warn mankind against meddling, but to argue that, if once the polar ice were melted, it would probably stay melted. The ice-layer is only 2 or 3 metres thick, and if it could be made to absorb all the solar energy available, it would probably melt. Fletcher's own suggestion was to spray aerosols into the stratosphere from aircraft. This would reduce the loss of heat by infra-red radiation, without appreciably reducing the incoming solar radiation.

Meanwhile, a professor of civil engineering at the University of California, T. Y. Lin, has calculated that it would be possible to build a bridge across the Bering Strait at a cost of approximately $1 billion. Professor Lin is a world authority on prestressed concrete and favours a bridge from the tip of the Seward peninsula across a chain of islands to Siberia. He reckons it would take five years to design and another five years to build. He suggests sinking piers similar to those used for off-shore oil drilling platforms. Then prefabricated sections of bridge would be towed into position and lifted into place. The bridge would have to be strong enough to withstand the battering of icebergs, so that unfreezing the Arctic would make a lighter and cheaper structure possible.

SPARE THAT TREE!

One very important way in which we shall, all too probably, be altering the environment on a massive and ultimately disastrous scale is by the wholesale felling of forests. Man has, of course, already made vast inroads on the forests, which currently occupy about 28 per cent of the land surface, mostly with disastrous results. When rain falls on forests, it drips gently into the soil, which is bound in place by the roots of trees and bushes. It goes to join the underlying ground-water, whence it will rise in springs in the dry season or can be tapped by pumps and wells. But when rain falls on open land, it washes the top soil away and carves great gullies, while in the dry season the wind, unbroken by trees, blows the powdery surface away, often at the rate of several inches a year.

In addition, forests serve as natural air conditioners: heat is collected by trees during the day and slowly released at night—anyone who has retreated into a forest on a hot day knows how much cooler it is there. The evaporation of moisture from the leaves exerts a cooling effect, since latent heat of vaporization is taken up.

The great floods of the Arno, such as that which bathed Florence in mud in 1967, have been experienced ever since the fourteenth century. When the woodlands round Florence were cut down and used as pasture for goats and sheep, these nibbled so close that the grass died and the ground turned to sterile baked clay. Brooks and wells dried up. By the eighth century, the woollen mills of Florence had to import wool and hair from elsewhere. The earliest flood on record was in 1333—there were doubtless others still earlier—when the city walls collapsed and so did three of the four bridges over the Arno. Three hundred people were killed. A local inhabitant, Vico del Cilento, urged a reafforestation project, but was ignored. Since then, there has been a flood in Florence every twenty-four years, and a major flood every hundred years. No reafforestation, even now, is being undertaken.

The Greeks understood about the importance of forests—at least Plato's 'Critias' did:

'What are now her mountains', he said, speaking of Attica, 'were lofty, soil-clad hills; her present day "shingle plains" were covered with rich soil; and her mountains were heavily tree-clad, a fact of which there are still visible traces. Now there are mountains in Attica which can sustain nothing but bees but which were clothed, not so very long ago, with splendid trees yielding timber suitable for roofing the largest buildings—roofs made from this timber are still in existence. There were also many lofty, cultivated trees, while the country boasted boundless pasture for cattle. The annual supply of rainfall was not lost, as it is at present, by being allowed to flow over the denuded surface into the sea, but was received by the country, in all its abundance, into her bosom, where she stored it in her impervious clay and so was able to discharge the run-off from the heights into the hollows in the form of springs and rivers of abundant flow and wide distribution. The shrines which still survive on the site of former springs bear witness to the validity of my present hypothesis.'

Three thousand years ago, China was covered with forest. Then the forests were felled to make agricultural land—hence the vast floods of the Yellow and other rivers, and the summer droughts. The eroded soil, washed down as silt, made the lower plains fertile, but, as it raised the river beds, increased the frequency of flooding. Many schemes of reafforestation have failed because of population pressure in the past: today the Communists are reported to be planting a forest belt all along the Great Wall.

The story is the same all over Europe: the forests of Scotland were cut to serve as fuel for ironworks. England, faced with the threat of the Armada, had to send to Norway for timber. The karst-lands of the Adriatic were created by felling. The new worlds were treated even more ruthlessly. New Zealand hacked down 15 million acres, while the unique forest empire of the United States is now only a memory. Many an island Eden has been ruined in the same manner, from the Cape Verde islands to the Seychelles. Even in Grand Canary the country was reduced to subsistence level by the same mistake. But the lesson is never learned. After the Second World War, the Americans urged the Japanese to convert forests to farmland. The Japanese had been through this one before: in the Meiji period the forests had been felled, causing disastrous floods. As a result the Japanese passed strict forest protection laws and concentrated agriculture in small plots, the yields of which far surpass those of Europe, still more the United States. However, in 1945 they were forced to fell, with the same result: floods and erosion. Before long, they re-enacted their forest protection code.

Currently, forests are being ruthlessly felled in many places—for instance, much of Brazil, especially in the northeast, has been stripped in a generation. In 1900, the area known as the Hump was 40 to 50 per cent forest. Today the figure is below 5 per cent. Not surprisingly, there are severe floods and $2,000m. is being spent to contain them for irrigation purposes. In the Congo, felling has had another consequence: soil temperatures become so high in summer as to kill soil bacteria and earthworms.

Britain, thanks largely to far-sighted landowners, avoided the consequences of felling by leaving copses, planting ornamental clumps and windbreaks, and above all by leaving hedges at the margins of her small fields, hedges which included many a tree. Currently some farmers are grubbing up hedges, in a pathetic attempt to imitate the methods of America, and the British Ministry of Agriculture, never very smart, is even encouraging this by giving grants for the purpose. It is reckoned that hedges are going at 10,000 miles a year. Erosion, especially uphill from the hedge-line, will follow. Meanwhile, heavy machinery is impacting the soil. In fifty years the consequences of this short-sighted policy will be all too clear.

Presumably the Ministry of Agriculture does not know that in Schleswig Holstein hedges have increased yields 20 per cent. In northern Europe generally, according to the chairman of the European Working Party for Landscape Husbandry, hedges and shelter belts have reduced evaporation by an amount equal to one-third of the annual rainfall.

Small wonder that East Anglian farmers who remove hedges soon ask for increased irrigation. In the case of shelter belts, he adds, the crop increase is 4.5 times the crop loss due to the ground taken up by the belt and its side-effects.

It has been shown in Germany that potato yields are 25 per cent higher where shelter belts are planted, while Russia has obtained a similar result with oats. Even pasture is improved. There is irony in the fact that man fells forests in his desire to grow more food and ends by being able to grow less food than ever.

As a kind of footnote to all this we note that forests are being destroyed by defoliants in Vietnam. Fred Tschirley, of the US Agricultural Research Service, who has made a study on the spot, reports: 'The defoliation program has caused ecologic changes. I do not feel that the changes are irreversible, but complete recovery may take a long time. The mangrove type of tree is killed with a single treatment. Regeneration of the mangrove forest to its original condition is estimated to require about 20 years.' No doubt over the next thirty years we shall see defoliants used elsewhere than in Vietnam.

Also on the horizon are such vast concepts as the Mid-Canada Development Corridor. The bulk of the Canadian population crowds near the southern border, where it is warmer and the growing season is longer. In area, Canada is the second largest country in the world, but sustains a population of only 20 million—89 per cent of them live in 15 per cent of the land area. The entire North-West Territories comprise only 23,000 people. The plan, put forward by Acres Ltd., a Toronto engineering group, is to develop much of the colder area for habitation by spending about $1.5 billion on a railroad to the Great Slave Lake and beyond, with a Trans-Canada Highway costing $1.75 billion. Docks, harbours, new town developments, etc., would bring the total to $5 billion. The new towns might follow the model of the proposed Russian 'all-weather towns' such as Yakutia, which are largely or wholly enclosed. Since the USSR supports cities of up to 250,000 population in Siberia and has Arctic cities in excess of 100,000 population, it is thought Canadians could be as tough. For the short-term exploitation of limited resources, 'plug-in' prefabricated dwellings coupled to a ser-vice-core (water, heat, sewage, air-conditioning) are envisaged. This is sometimes known as the 'disposable town' concept.

If those prove successful, no doubt the idea will be extended to the Antarctic also, and perhaps to Greenland and other inhospitable regions. The heat generated by such settlements will certainly melt the permafrost, if it does not alter the weather. Nuclear power sources will add their quota to the atmosphere, and solid pollutants will accumulate in the environment.

At present the world uses these remote areas as lungs, which purify or dilute the pollution produced by the more heavily populated areas, as far as they are able. What will be the position when the lungs themselves have become polluters? How much we need these 'lungs' I shall describe in Chapter 5.

To sum up, we are reconstructing the surface of the earth on a scale which is rapidly becoming so overweening that we risk shattering the natural balances between living organisms and between all organisms and the physical environment. We have only dangerously imperfect knowledge of these balances: what we do know I shall try to convey in the chapters which follow.

We will start with climate. For, while man dreams of altering the climate deliberately, he is already doing things which may be altering it unintentionally, and perhaps to an extent which could prove very disagreeable, not to say disastrous.

3 Ice Age or Heat Death?

As I FLEW across the Atlantic in April 1969 I saw icebergs as far as the eye could reach. In fact, ice coverage was more extensive than for sixty years past. This was not just chance: something peculiar is happening to the climate. Is it only the sun acting up or is man responsible?

With the advantage of hindsight, we can see that the world climate began to grow markedly warmer from a point in time about a hundred years ago, a trend which became quite obvious about 1900. Dr C.E.P. Brooks, an expert on the glaciers in relation to climate, reported in 1949: 'Since the beginning of the twentieth century glaciers have been wasting away rapidly or even catastrophically.' The Muir Glacier in Alaska has retreated as much as 2 miles in 10 years. Fifteen years ago another team of glaciologists, P. D. Baird and R. P. Sharp, described the retreat of Alaskan glaciers as 'alarming' and noted that on the Pacific coasts of America as also in Europe glacial melting 'appears to be progressing violently'. The year following, it was reported that the ice-islands which drift in the circumpolar sea were melting away and that the polar sea seemed to be becoming open. Rising temperatures also caused the snowline to retreat on mountains all over the world. In Peru, for example, it has risen as much as 2,700 feet in 60 years.

As a consequence of this the distribution of vegetation is shifting. The bare wastes of subpolar tundra in Canada and Russia are beginning to be dotted with trees. This has been noted in places as far apart as Alaska, Labrador and Siberia. In the Canadian prairies the agricultural cropline shifted some 50 to 100 miles northward, because the growing season is now some ten days longer than it was. Correspondingly, cool-climate trees like birches and spruce have been dying off over large areas of Eastern Canada and New England. Sweden reported that the timberline had moved up the mountain slopes by as much as 65 feet since 1930.

The distribution of animals has likewise been affected, many European species moving northwards into Scandinavia. In 1950 naturalists reported twenty-five new species of birds in Greenland, unknown there when the area was studied in 1918. In the United States birds like the cardinal and tufted titmouse, the turkey vulture and the blue-winged warbler have moved their ranges to the north. The opossum is a warmth-loving creature and is now found as far north as Canada. Tuna fish are found off the coast of New England and flying fishes are often seen off the coast of New Jersey.

Along the coast of Greenland, the Eskimos abandoned seal-hunting in favour of cod-fishing, as the cod replaced the seals. By 1946, cod-catches had reached a figure of 13,000 tons. In 1913 only 5 tons of cod were shipped.

The dry figures of the meteorologists confirm these tangible impressions. In the United States mean annual temperatures had risen 3.5°F. between 1920 and 1954. In 1953 the US Weather Bureau noted that 40 of the 48 states had annual temperatures above normal in most years over the period 1931–52. But the effect seems strongest further north: in Spitsbergen, situated only 10 or 12 degrees from the North Pole, average winter temperatures rose by as much as 14°F. since 1910. The ports there have been open to navigation seven months in the year. Fifty years ago, they were only open for three months yearly. Antarctic temperatures rose some 5° in the first 50 years of the century.

A warmer climate is agreeable to almost everyone except winter sports enthusiasts, but how much further could this trend go? The sea has been rising at a rapidly increasing rate, largely due (it is thought) to the melting of the glaciers. Between 1930 and 1948 it rose 6 inches. Erling Dorf, from whom I have copied most of these facts, calculates that this is four times the average rate of rise in the sea-level over the last 9,000 years, i.e. since the last ice age. And in the mid-1920's the rate of increase rose to *six* times normal. To measure the rise in sea-level is not always easy; how can one distinguish the land sinking from the sea rising? Satellites are making possible a more accurate type of survey which will bring more precision to such measurements. Still, for the moment, it looks as if here is a trend which, if it continued, could raise the level of the oceans several feet in a century—a phenomenon which would drastically change many coast lines and threaten major ports, such as London and Amsterdam, with inundation.

What is curious about this change is that it has not affected the tropics, while certain remote areas have actually experienced a cooling trend. These include the Hudson Bay region, Indonesia and north-east Australia, the central part of South America and also the most southern part, and the loneliest areas of central Asia. This contrast suggests that the cause is not increased radiation from the sun, which one would expect to affect the whole planet equally. And since the cooling areas are all remote from industrial development and thinly populated it gives colour to the idea that man is doing things which raise the temperature even in face of a general cooling tendency.

Actually, the answer to this question had been proposed by a British scientist, G. S. Callender, in 1938. Way back in 1861 the British physicist John Tyndall had argued that world temperatures depended on the amount of carbon dioxide present in the atmosphere. Carbon dioxide has the property of absorbing the longer wavelengths of heat radiation. So does glass, which is why we can have greenhouses. The heat enters in the form of relatively short-wave radiation and is absorbed by objects which emit it again at a longer wavelength which can't get out through the glass. So the greenhouse warms up. The carbon dioxide in the atmosphere exerts a similar 'greenhouse effect' so that changes in the level would affect temperatures on earth. What Callender proposed was that the general warming which I have described was due to the additional carbon dioxide added to the air by man.

As so often happens, no one paid much attention to the suggestion. That puny man could do anything which might affect the whole world at once was a notion which seemed too improbable in 1938. Twenty years later Gilbert Plass of Johns Hopkins University revived this idea on the basis of more information. He had been studying the effect of water vapour, carbon dioxide and ozone on the infra-red (heat) radiation in the atmosphere. Up to this time there had not been much in the way of measurements which would indicate to what extent the carbon dioxide level was rising. Now a new investigation indicated that it had risen at least 10 per cent since 1900 and maybe as much as 14 per cent, an increase from 290 ppm to 330 ppm if not more. This was startling, and scientists began to debate whether there was really a 'greenhouse effect'. The great scientific effort known as the International Geophysical Year was being organized at this time and careful world-wide measurements of carbon dioxide levels were made part of the programme. Over the next 5 years, 1958–63, they pinpointed the increase at 5 billion tons a year, a figure which showed that the rough early estimates for the period from 1900 were plausible. The measurements also revealed, what no one had suspected, puzzling local variations in the levels, a fact which might go far to explain the local variations in temperature which I just mentioned. The problem was to establish where the carbon dioxide was coming from. The first source which comes to mind is the burning of fossil fuels, notably coal and oil. These fuels have been used intensively for about a century and, in this time, it is calculated, we have poured an additional 360 billion tons of carbon dioxide into the air—from coal fires and furnaces, from motor vehicles and ships, from gas-making plants and aircraft. Recently the rate has been rising more steeply. If we reach double the normal level, the glaciers will begin to melt and the oceans to rise.

Others, however, said carbon dioxide was coming from the drying up of bogs and marshland. Edward S. Deevey Jr. calculated that bogs lock up about 366 billion tons of carbon dioxide which would be released if they all vanished—about the same amount which man has contributed by burning fuels. So far the evidence favours this origin for about two-thirds of the additional carbon dioxide. If so, the process is a self-stimulating one, for the warmer it gets, the more the bogs dry out and the more the bogs dry out, the more carbon dioxide is released and the warmer it gets. In the language of cybernetics, there is a 'positive feedback'.

Incidentally, every conversion of pasture to plough-land, and all felling of woodland, steps up the supply of carbon dioxide.

The difficulty in assessing levels of carbon dioxide is that quantities much larger than these are released into the atmosphere by the weathering of rocks, which contain an estimated 2.5×10^{17} tons—about a million times as much as the amount so far released by man. At the same time, plants take carbon dioxide out of the air, as one of the raw materials they need to manufacture plant-material. Presumably they do this at about the same rate at which it is fed into the atmosphere, since there is no evidence of any drastic build-up or depletion over long periods of time.

The harsh fact is that we can do no more at present than make intelligent guesses about these vast processes: we do not have the data to analyse them fully. Above all, we do not understand the transfers which we think take place between the sea and the air. The one thing which is beyond doubt is that the carbon dioxide levels are rising, and doing so at an increasingly rapid rate. Plotted on graph paper, the curve suggests that the average temperature of the earth would rise at least 5°C. by 1990. That may not sound much, because we are used to the 40° swings which take place between summer maxima and winter minima. But when we average these out, we find the annual average shifting only by a degree or two. A drop of 3° is enough to change the whole pattern of farming. The growing season for particular crops may be so much shortened as to make it impossible to grow them.

The warming which occurred between 1920 and 1950 in the US amounted only to 3½ °C. If this meant that ports, such as Spitzbergen, which used to be open only three months in the year were open seven, then by the end of the century they might be open the year round, and before much longer the entire Arctic Ocean would be navigable. The Alaskan and Siberian tundra would thaw out: trees would grow and cattle could be raised there.

But no sooner had scientists perceived this extraordinary possibility than the situation changed.

COOL IT, MAN

In the mid-1950's it began to dawn on people that temperatures, instead of continuing to rise, were beginning to fall. By 1958 Arctic pack-ice had begun to increase significantly. Colder winters were accompanied by colder and wetter summers. According to H. H. Lamb of the British Meteorological Office, perhaps the world's leading authority on long-term climatic changes, the growing season has become two weeks shorter since 1950 in England, and snow covers the ground twice as frequently in most inland districts.

A British student of climate as it affects agriculture, J. A. Clark, told the story in these words:

> The first four decades of the present century were exceptionally mild and had average winter temperatures about 1°C. higher than the figures available for an equivalent period of years at the end of the sixteenth and the beginning of the seventeenth century. However, in the last two decades, the average January temperature has already fallen 1°C. below that of the mild spell marking the 1920's and 1930's. Since 1940 there have been five winters which included a whole month averaging below freezing temperatures. No such winter occurred in the whole period 1896 to 1939, a fact which encouraged British housebuilders to leave the plumbing outside the house. While many people know that the winter of 1962–3 was the worst since 1740, they may not realize that equally severe winters occurred about every 20 years during the two preceding centuries. If the Thames did not freeze over—as it did eight times in the seventeenth century—it was because of the heat added by power-station cooling water. In 1963, ice-floes drifted in the straits of Dover and a small coaster was trapped in the River Welland for several weeks by ice.

By 1969, ice in the North Atlantic was more extensive than had been seen in 60 years. Between 1920 and 1965 drift ice was hardly seen in the neighbourhood of Iceland, but in the latter year it choked ports on the northern coast of Iceland and held up fishing. This happened again in 1968 and was still more marked in 1969. With the fishing industry half-paralysed, Iceland devalued her currency no fewer than three times, until it stood at half the former value. Crops were also disastrously small, and people began to talk of the possibility that the island might have to be evacuated. In Iceland, if the average summer temperature drops one degree, crop yields fall 15 per cent. A conference of scientists and others was called to discuss this catastrophic change.

The winter of 1968–9 was exceptionally severe in many parts of the United States, and England had its coldest February since 1909. Russian meteorologists pointed out that, from 1960, the pattern of polar air movement had reverted to a type which had prevailed in the opening years of the century. A further consequence of all this was increased rainfall in central continental regions—happily for India where very high rice yields resulted, in contrast with the famines of preceding years.

Some meteorologists believe that climate moves in complicated cycles, of many different lengths, and were ready to see this reversal of trend as just one more instance of an age-old process. In a moment, I shall discuss this view a little more fully. But even cyclic swings must have some explanation, and there were meteorologists who were more inclined to look for specific explanations than to write climatic changes off as due to general processes we do not understand. One of these was Professor Reid Bryson, head of the meteorological department at the University of Wisconsin. He had been making repeated trips to India, in connection with a study of the vast Rajputana desert. This once-fertile area of 250,000 square miles had become a desert as a result of human mismanagement, and it was hoped he could suggest means to redeem it.

Flying into India, he was struck by the uniform bluish haze which seemed to hang over the entire continent, running up to about 20,000 feet above the earth's surface. Visibility was about 7 miles and when he flew on down to Saigon visibility declined steadily to a mile and a half. Clearly it was not industry which produced it. It seemed to be due in part to agricultural burning, in part to desert dust swept up from areas where the earth was bare of plants. It was immediately evident that such a haze must cut off a good part of the sun's rays, reflecting them back into space. In so doing, it must make the earth below cooler. Aerial photographs revealed similar blue hazes over Brazil and Central Africa. The blue haze is so constant a feature that meteorologists take it for granted, and visibility in such areas is often no more than 3 miles. The haze generally lies between 3,000 and 9,000 feet above the ground, and contains 600–800 grams of material per square mile.

Intrigued by this, he began to look elsewhere. Another extensive source of atmospheric turbidity—to use the technical term—was the burning of wastes and natural gas at oil-wells. An extensive dark-brown pall spreads eastward from the Persian Gulf and other centres of oil production, notably in parts of China. The atmosphere is capable of carrying large quantities of fine particles for much longer than is usually realized. Busy with our earthly affairs, we usually ignore the haze above our heads, unless it happens to drop its particular contents on our heads. In 1968, a red dust settled on many parts of Britain. It proved to have been transported from the Sahara: the quantity was put at one million tons. During World War II, dust descended on the Caribbean which proved to have come from North Africa, where it had been stirred up by the tank battles in the desert.

Could it be, Bryson wondered, that man was putting such quantities of dust and grit into the atmosphere as to lower the temperature of the whole earth?

Not many places yet measure the turbidity of the atmosphere, but those that do show rapid rises since the 1930's. One which does is Washington, where levels were 57 per cent up on 1900 by 1964. Another is the Swiss resort of Davos, much visited by people with lung diseases: 80 per cent up. On the mountain of Mauna Loa in Hawaii measurements started in 1957. Ten years later the dust levels had climbed 30 per cent; this was especially sinister, since Mauna Loa is far from any industrialized area—clearly the phenomenon was global. But perhaps the most impressive and certainly the longest series of figures comes from Russia. By examining dust trapped in layers of frozen snow in the mountains of the Caucasus, Russian meteorologists can follow the trend as far back as 1790. They find a slow increase during the nineteenth century but a staggering rise after the Communists began to industrialize Russia. After 1930, levels rose an incredible 1,900 per cent.

Most of those who examine dust levels do so in towns where industry is producing preceptible pollution. Their reports also confirm the trend. Thus Chicago had twenty smoky days a year before 1930 but the figure had risen to 320 by 1948.

Bryson believes that this increase in turbidity has swamped the greenhouse effect and comments: 'There is no indication that these trends will be reversed, and there is some reason to believe that man-made pollution will have an increased effect in the future.' He reckons that a decrease of only 3–4 per cent in the transparency of the atmosphere would depress surface temperatures by 0.4°C.

Bryson's work inspired one of the Space Agency's British

advisors, Dr Jim Lovelock, to make some further calculations, designed to show how far the warming due to the carbon dioxide and the cooling due to the turbidity would balance out. The warming is proportional to the mass of the carbon dioxide, he believes, but the cooling is proportional to the *square* of the mass of the particles, and so rapidly exerts a more powerful effect. His predicted curve of temperature calls for a cancellation of the warming effect by 1963, a cooling of 1½ °C. by 1970, of 4° by 1975, of 5° by 1977 and so on—which suggests the start of an ice age well before 1980. (The last Ice Age is variously estimated to have been due to a temperature between 5° and 8° below the present norm.)

Actual temperatures recorded to date fall almost half a degree lower than his curve predicts, even though he uses the mean of summer temperatures, not of year-round temperatures.

Lovelock points out that there are various positive feedbacks which tend to intensify the situation. I have already mentioned one: the drying up of bogs. As the climate becomes colder and wetter again, bogs will spread again, locking up carbon dioxide as they do so. Another arises from the fact that ice and snow reflect more of the incoming solar energy than do land or sea. So, as it gets colder, and the ice-caps expand, less heat is retained.

Furthermore, resulting changes in weather patterns may make the effect particularly severe in some areas—notably the temperate zones in which most of the western world's population lives. In the northern oceans, there is rather a sharp division between the cold water which spreads southward from the melting ice-cap and the warm water flowing northward from the equator. Where they meet, the cold water, being denser, sinks and flows beneath the hotter water. In the southern hemisphere, of course, a mirror image of this situation is found.

It is an established fact that, when the climate is cooler, this junction moves southward, in the case of the northern hemisphere. (The reason for this lies in the balance which exists between the effect of salinity in making water denser and so liable to sink beneath less saline water, and the effect of higher temperature making it less dense.) It seems that this hot-cold junction in the oceans has now moved down as far as Iceland. A few more degrees' decline in the ocean temperature might bring it down to the latitude of Britain. Obviously any country which lies north of the junction will be markedly colder than one lying just south of it, even when the distance between them is quite small.

CLOUDY PROSPECTS

Dust particles do not only reflect incoming radiation, they also affect the weather because they provide nuclei on which water can condense, forming clouds. The effect of turbidity on the earth's temperature is therefore more complicated than I have so far indicated.

The focus of interest lies over the oceans, where such 'condensation nuclei' are normally few compared with land areas.

Clouds of course, reflect a lot of the heat radiated by the earth back again, as we notice on oppressive days when there is a heavy overcast. But at the same time, they screen off the incoming solar radiation. So the effects of dust will vary according to whether conditions favour cloud formation. Two US weathermen, Manabe and Wetherald, worked out in 1967 that a 1 per cent change in low cloud cover round the world could bring about a decrease in temperature of 0.8°C.— that is, four times the drop in temperature over the past 25 years. In case the significance of that little calculation is not fully apparent, let us project it further. At the present time, on the average, about 31 per cent of the earth's surface is covered with low cloud. Suppose that the cloud cover rose to 36 per cent—not a very startling shift at first sight—the average surface temperatures would drop 4°C. So, unless you are exceptionally keen on skiing, you want to think twice about contributing any condensation nuclei to the atmosphere.

The effect of dusty atmospheres can be seen on a small scale by studying how city climate differs from that of the country.

Following earlier British studies which had shown that industrial cities had more cloudy and rainy days than the open country upwind of them, Stanley A. Changnon Jr. of the Illinois State water survey made a detailed study of four mid-West cities, together with New York and Washington, in

1969. He found that precipitation and rainy days were increased up to 16 per cent, and summer thunderstorm days up to 20 per cent compared with the surrounding countryside. At La Porte, 30 miles downwind from the Gary–Chicago complex with its huge steel-making plants and other industrial installations, the increases ranged up to a staggering 246 per cent. Another consequence of the dust-laden air of cities is more frequent fog. A vivid illustration of the fog-making effect of these nuclei is provided at Morgantown airport, in West Virginia, which is frequently closed because of the fog generated by a near-by cooling tower. Again, in Edmonton, Alberta, you may see a fog-belt generated by the burning off of natural gas from a well.

Crystals of ammonium sulphate are often found in summer haze, which suggests that sulphur is an important contributor to turbidity. Combustion of coal and oil produces sulphur compounds, but world use of sulphur has rocketed, thanks partly to its incorporation in fertilizer as ammonium sulphate. This may help to explain why summer haze occurs in the country, even when the wind is not blowing from industrial areas.

Reid Bryson considers that an even more important climatic effect of rising turbidity than the change in world temperatures is the change in the temperature gradient which runs from the equator to the poles, and on which the wind circulation depends. Turbidity tends to reduce this gradient, thus weakening the westerly winds. Hubert Lamb has shown that during the 1960's the westerlies did in fact weaken.

One of the most important causes of turbidity is the exhaust of cars and aircraft, especially the latter since they place the particles high in the atmosphere. Bryson has made a blood-chilling calculation about this. He takes 3,000 as the number of jet aircraft in the air on an average day, and assumes that 50 per cent of them are making contrails; and that these persist for an average of two hours and spread to a width of half a mile. This would give you a 5 to 10 per cent increase in cirrus clouds in the area in which these aircraft mostly operate—the United States–North Atlantic–Europe zone. Or if the increase is averaged over the whole world, about one-twentieth of this.

Such a calculation does not pretend to accuracy but it indicates the scale of the phenomenon we are dealing with.

The prospect becomes even gloomier if we look ahead to the supersonic transports. It is claimed that at their intended operational height contrails will not be formed, but if for any reason they do not operate at this height, the situation is very different. And if they operate near the tropopause, that is the level at which the air temperature, instead of falling as you ascend, begins to rise again, they will produce contrails 1 per cent of the time. At this height they may persist for many hours and spread to a width of a mile or more. This would be sufficient to bring the cloud cover over the operational area to 100 per cent.

It is calculated that the cloud cover over the North Atlantic is already 10 per cent above normal, thanks to this phenomenon. Forecasts for the use of SSTs by the end of the century foresee 3,000 of them. So it is probable that long before this time the Atlantic, together with much of North America and Europe, will be permanently under cloud. As Bryson drily comments: 'We would like our grandchildren to experience blue skies more often than on rare occasions.' As far as I am concerned, that goes for my children too.

The National Climate and Atmospheric Research group at Boulder, Colorado, has recently made observations which confirm the fact that jet aircraft contrails stimulate the formation of cirrus clouds over large areas, and that this cloud cover can modify the radiation budget.

Bryson adds that he'd be glad to be proved wrong, but if his calculation is anywhere near correct, the problem seems too important to leave to half a dozen part-time investigators. But clearly there is little any one nation can do to reverse the trend, so we must prepare for a cloudy prospect even without the SSTs.

CLIMATIC FLIP

When I visited Professor Bryson, I found him studying the data published by a Danish-American team of researchers on temperature changes during the past 100,000 years. The layers of ice that form on the polar ice-caps contain a record of past temperatures, since the relative abundance of the two forms of oxygen—oxygen 16 and oxygen 18—trapped in the ice depends on the temperature of the rain or snow which formed it. This team from the University of Copenhagen went to the Century base in Greenland, and, with American co-operation, drilled down into the ice-cap and extracted a long core. The core was no less than 139 metres (440 feet) in length and embodied ice-samples laid down as long as 100,000 years ago.

When the temperatures are plotted against time, many rapid shifts are seen to have taken place, with others more gradual. One of the cyclic changes repeats every 13,000 years and is clearly due to the precession of the equinox—the small oscillation in the earth's axis. Others of 120 and 940 years can be shown to be due to changes in solar radiation, since this can be detected by other means. The point on which Bryson fastened was that the earth's atmosphere appears to exist in at least two relatively stable states and to switch rather rapidly between them. Having switched, it tends to stay in the new mode rather than to drift back, until some shock triggers a new flip. What could such a shock consist of? No one knows, but one can imagine a number of things which might suffice, from an outburst of volcanic activity to the impact of a large meteorite.

Bryson emphasized the extraordinary rapidity of these changes as indicated by the oxygen-isotope tracings. When the last Ice Age descended, at the end of the Pleistocene period, countless mammoths were embalmed or frozen, all over Europe, including England, and throughout Russia. Many are found, with skin and hair well preserved, standing on their feet. Some have undigested grass in their stomachs and fragments between their teeth. When one such mammoth was found in frozen soil early in this century, the fat was still yellow and the meat was in such good preservation that some bold experimentalists were able to cook and eat mammoth steaks. It would therefore seem that these animals were frozen instantaneously. Almost the only explanation conceivable seems a snowstorm so heavy as to bury them completely, with no subsequent thaw the following summer. This suggests a climatic change of incredible abruptness.

The inference from these facts is that the earth's climate can flip from one stable mode to another with undreamed-of suddenness, when once the trigger is pressed. We do not know what the trigger is, but we may be pressing it. It is hard to know whether to take such a proposition seriously and scientists themselves feel in a quandary, torn between the commonsense feeling that something so monstrous is not to be taken seriously, and their training which says one ignores the logical implications of one's data at one's peril.

Some meteorologists now think that not only an over-all reduction in incoming radiation but also small changes in the *balance* of short-wave and long-wave solar radiation can cause dramatic changes in the convective processes in the atmosphere, that is, the movement of warm air masses. But they know too little about the process to be able to predict whether a given change will put the temperature up or down. But they believe such changes are likely to be greatest in the temperate zones, and reckon that a 10 per cent reduction in the incoming energy would lower earth temperatures about 7½ °C.

It has long been preached as dogma that the oceans act as a kind of flywheel, damping out oscillations by absorbing heat at one time and releasing it at another. And it has been claimed that they also do this over longer periods, by such mechanisms as absorbing excess carbon dioxide and releasing it later. There almost certainly are such mechanisms at work, but they may be quite slow in responding to changes. Thus Gilbert Plass says the ocean would take about 1,000 years to absorb half the excess carbon dioxide which man has dumped into it in the past century or so. Then carbonates would begin to form, and the temperature would slowly begin to fall again, for plants increase their rate of respiration when the carbon dioxide level rises.

More orthodox meteorologists see the present cooling as the natural downswing after a warming period which, they say, started early in the nineteenth century. The Danish and American scientists who took the Greenland cores predict that the present cooling trend should continue until 1995. But as recently as 1960, many climatologists were saying that the general trend of increasing warmth should continue for at least two or three hundred years, and that the recent colder tendency would only last until 1965.

The course of variation during the last 10,000 years or so is now fairly well charted, recent studies of ice-melting by Dr Nils-Axel Morner of Stockholm University having documented the processes which followed the disappearance of the last Ice Age, about 12,000 BC, with unprecedented clarity. Dr Morner studied the pollen trapped in silts on the floor of the Baltic Sea, and the nature of the sediments, brought there by glaciers, in which the pollen and other plant remains were preserved.

Between 10,350 and 10,300 BC there seems to have been a brief cold snap, followed by a warmer period. The Baltic was largely filled with ice and Scandinavia was covered with glaciers. Not till 7730 BC did the sea rise enough to enter the Baltic. From 5000 to 2000 BC there was a period of higher temperatures, a so-called *hypsithermal*, followed by a fall which reached a minimum about 500 BC. The subsequent rise reached a maximum about AD 1000 and stayed around there until 1300. During this time, vines were grown and wine produced in England as far north as York, while Norsemen colonized Greenland and raised crops, cattle and sheep there. From 1600, however, the climate began to cool and the glaciers to advance. In the Alps several valley settlements were completely overrun. The 'Little Ice Age' of 1650–1850 followed. It was the failure of crops in Scotland and the deaths which resulted which were a main factor in Scotland's agreeing to union with England, though England did little to help her new citizens.

Between the 11-year and the long-term cycles lie others. The causes of these shifts are quite unknown: the sun's output is presumed to vary, but changes in the storage of heat in the oceans may also play a significant part. We do not even know what caused the ice ages. Both reduced and increased solar radiation have been suggested as causes. Increased radiation, it is thought, might suck up more water from the oceans which would come down as snow. This would imply that ice ages were wet rather than dry—but examination of lake-bottom sediments in Africa, now taking place, seems to suggest that ice ages were dry, since grass pollens are found rather than traces of tropical rain-forests.

Some of these changes are certainly cyclic: the influence of the 11-year sunspot cycle can clearly be detected, and there seems also to be a 22-year cycle. Some meteorologists, notably Mr H. H. Lamb, believe that almost all of them are cyclic. A majority, however, while conceding that some cycles are at work, think that many of these changes are random in character, being caused by such events as volcanic activity, changes in the output of the sun, the impact of bursts of high-energy radiation from space, and so on.

They point out that high-altitude recordings of solar radiation do not show variations of some 10 per cent to match recent climatic changes, while the carbon-cycle explanation of the burning process in the sun should, on the face of it, be perfectly steady.

On the other hand, some people have objected to the dust theory on the grounds that no cold spell followed the great Krakatoa eruption of 1883. Actually, measuring stations were too few and scattered at that time to justify such a conclusion. When Krakatoa ejected its 13 cubic miles of rock, dust and ash into the atmosphere it was three months before the dust pall reached Europe, causing the moon to look blue or purple and giving rise to the expression 'once in a blue moon'. Areas under the dust pall would be cooled, while others were normal, so the exact time and location of temperature observations would make all the difference. Similarly, when Katmai erupted in the Aleutians, in 1912, radiation fell 20 per cent in Algeria. In fact, it may be these differences which alter the global air circulation and so eventually affect the weather.

Today, too, we know more about how ice nuclei form on dust particles when the air is below freezing point, and Vincent J. Schaefer has shown that volcanic ash will provide such nuclei effectively, thus causing cloudiness. In the early 1950s Harold Wexler of the US Weather Bureau therefore revived the volcanic theory. It has been objected that at some known periods of cooling in the distant past, no traces of volcanic dust are found by geologists, but Wexler answers this by saying that the amounts would be scarcely detectable after falling. To the converse objection, that some known periods of volcanic activity were not followed by cooling, he replies that the particles may not have been thrown high enough or were too large to remain suspended.

Very recently, Dr J. Murray Mitchell of the US Weather Bureau has pushed this argument even further, claiming that the world cooling in the 1960s which I have described is due entirely to the series of volcanic eruptions which started in 1947.

The one thing all these observations show—and this is why I have detailed some of them—is that climate is nothing like as stable as we tend to think. Climate teeters, and to push it off balance is probably no great trick. As Walter Orr Roberts, President of the Universities Corporation for Atmospheric Research, recently warned a Department of Defense audience: 'a delicate balance of forces appears to exist which can be disturbed by a triggering action set off by any of several geophysical phenomena.'

THE HEAT DEATH

Increasingly, scientists are looking at the whole earth, with its land-masses, seas and atmosphere, as a single system in which energy and material are transferred from one part of the system to another at varying rates, which somehow balance out in the long run. The interesting thing is that they balance out at a level at which life can exist.

It would not take very large shifts of any of the variables to make life as we know it impossible. For instance, if the oxygen in the atmosphere were to fall, life would become impossible except for a few specialized organisms such as the anaerobic bacteria. But, equally, if it were to rise by only five per cent the fire-risk would be so increased that grass and forests would constantly catch on fire. The extraordinary way in which inflammability increases as oxygen levels go up is seldom realized, as was demonstrated when three astronauts died in January 1967, and in earlier, less widely reported, accidents. Furthermore, there would be other effects: if the vegetation burned extensively, this would raise the carbon dioxide concentration but also add to atmospheric turbidity, altering the temperature, though whether up or down, who knows?

As the physics of the whole earth has come into clearer focus, geophysicists have begun to ask themselves the most fundamental question of all: what is the rate at which energy is added to the entire system and the rate at which it is withdrawn? What are the dynamics of the heat-balance? Clearly these rates must match if the earth is not to get steadily warmer or colder. But there is a lack of reliable data.

The input from the sun is hard to measure, since it is partly reflected, partly absorbed by the atmosphere before it reaches instruments on the earth's surface which could measure it. Satellites are beginning to give us a more accurate idea of how much is reflected. Not until we have instruments on the moon shall we have an accurate account of the sun's output, which probably varies from time to time. And of course the earth moves closer to the sun and away again every year. However, in round figures, the energy arriving, which is known as the solar constant, is about 2 calories per square centimetre per minute at the surface of the atmosphere, when the earth is at its mean distance from the sun. About one-third of this energy is reflected; the proportion of energy reflected from a surface is known as its *albedo*, a term taken by nineteenth-century astronomers from the Latin for whiteness. The earth's albedo certainly varies seasonally: snow and ice are the most efficient reflectors and albedo rises in winter. But man is also altering the albedo in the longer term: concrete and asphalt have a different absorptive power from grass, and forest land or desert are different again. As we cut forests, or create dust-bowls, when we make artificial lakes and reservoirs, as we build highways or construct airports, above all as we create towns and cities, we alter the albedo.

In addition to this, man is adding heat to the environment every time he burns fuel, whether fossil or atomic. Towns and cities maintain the air several degrees above the air in the surrounding countryside. Nuclear power stations produce enormous amounts of waste heat—something like a hundred times as much as a coal-fired station of similar capacity. (Hence their need for large quantities of cooling water.) The fusion power which nuclear physicists hope to have available before the end of the century is even more wasteful of heat. And as population doubles, all these heat-making activities will double—or, rather, they will treble, if we take the growth of industrialization into account.

Some scientists have therefore begun to wonder whether we are not already adding heat to the environment faster than it can be re-radiated into space. If we are, the temperature of the earth will rise and this will cause the rate of radiation to increase (that is, the albedo will change) until a new balance is found. According to one calculation, the system will be appreciably disturbed if we add more than 1 per cent to the incoming radiation, and this could happen by 1975.

According to the great Russian meteorologist, M. I. Budyko, the 'thermal pollution' created by man currently amounts so far to only about one twenty-five-hundredth part of the total albedo. But another calculation suggests that the albedo is increasing at a massive 4 per cent per annum. Now a 10 per cent increase in the radiation balance would raise the average surface temperature of the earth by 10° to 20°C. and less than this, as I have already indicated, would completely change the climate. The poles would be as hot as the present tropics, the tropics would be uninhabitable by warm-blooded creatures, and would be the preserve of lizards and insects. Most of the fish in the sea would perish. According to this authority, it would take *only 26 years,* as things are going, to bring about a change of this order. In 70 years or so, the planet would be definitely too hot for life of any kind. This is the heat death. Others, more cautious, give us 150 years before we all perish in the heat death.

In a triumph of scientific understatement, Professor Gordon MacDonald of the National Academy of Sciences comments that thermal pollution 'will be of great significance in the coming decades.'

The trouble with this kind of projection is that the web of cause and effect is too complicated for our present levels of scientific understanding, and we have few reliable figures with which to compare one effect with another. I have described two processes which tend to raise temperature and one which tends to lower it: how are they going to balance out? Some of the things which man is doing tend to *increase* albedo—for instance building roads and cities does so. Since deserts have a much higher albedo than grassy fields the spread of the Sahara and erosion in other parts of Africa are increasing albedo, while the irrigation and farming of previously desert areas in India and elsewhere is reducing it. American Weather Bureau experts consider that a unit increase in albedo will produce a 1°C. decrease in average surface temperatures. And to make things more difficult, changes in roughness of the earth's surface affect the rate at which heat is transferred to the air. The plain fact is we do not even know whether, on balance, the albedo is going up or down. It may well be that the increase due to concreting the surface and building cities is roughly offsetting the thermal pollution caused by man's activities. If so, we are lucky and let us hope that they remain in balance.

Scientists know very little about the way in which the

oceans act as a regulator or balance wheel. Maybe the sea, with its vast capacity for storing heat, has been saving us from thermal pollution. But just as it takes a lot of effort to speed a heavy flywheel up, so, once speeded, it is hard to slow it down. If we find, too late, that we have altered the temperature of the ocean, we may well have to live with the situation. We do know that oil films perturb the transfer of heat from sea to air in several ways. They reduce evaporation and lower the radiative capacity of the water. They also reduce the turbulence. Professor Gordon MacDonald says bluntly: 'We do not know whether ocean pollution is a significant factor in climatic change. Data on the extent of oil pollution, the lifetime of an oil film on the sea surface, and the detailed effects of such a film are not available, so even the sign of the effect (i.e. is it causing an increase or a decrease?) of ocean pollution on the earth's surface temperature is not known.'

Again water vapour transports heat, but the comparative rate of water loss from bare and plant-covered soil is known only vaguely. As the meteorologist H. H. Landsberg says: in regard to the water cycle viewed as a process of atmospheric energetics, 'our understanding has barely begun'.

The one solid fact which emerges from all this is that man is now so numerous and so technologically powerful that he is affecting the entire environment. What those effects will add up to, we simply do not know, but we do know that they are so large that, in one way if not another, they could be catastrophic. They could even put an end to life as we know it.

Professor MacDonald, whose paper on these matters caused a stir at the meeting of the American Association for the Advancement of Science in December 1968, was emphatic about this. The vast increases in population, urbanization and agriculture have made 'what were once considered minor nuisances into global phenomena'. Furthermore, while we now know enough to spot these changes our understanding is 'far too primitive to predict confidently all the consequences of man's abuse of the planet'. It is shocking therefore that research in these areas is both unfashionable with scientists and treated as of low priority by government agencies with grants to distribute.

MacDonald does not leave the problem for others to cope

with but proposes a four-point programme of action, which seems to me so obviously sensible that one only wonders why nothing has yet been done.

First, he says, the significance of these climatic interferences must be recognized by nations throughout the world and within the United Nations. Second, world-wide programmes must be launched for monitoring turbidity, carbon dioxide and water vapour. We must have baselines to check future changes against, and we must monitor in the great ocean areas and high in the atmosphere, not just on land. Thirdly, we must monitor albedo continuously by satellites. Fourthly, the US government must foster studies of the thermal processes within the atmosphere, and the boundaries of the atmosphere with the land and sea. Most of the present computer-based model-building is directed towards weather prediction, in the sense of accurate forecasts for limited areas a few days or weeks ahead, rather than climate prediction on a global scale for years ahead.

While this chapter was at the printer's Dr Earl W. Barrett of the Environmental Science Services Administration made an even stronger statement, declaring that the total environment is being altered, perhaps disastrously and irreversibly, by human activities. Speaking before the International Solar Energy Conference in Melbourne, Australia, he said that 50 million tons of dust particles added to the atmosphere and retained there would cause the average surface temperature over the earth to dip from its present 60°F (15°C) to about 40°F (4°C)—a temperature at which most forms of plant life could not survive. He estimates that this is only some 10 to 20 times as much material as is now in the atmosphere. Thus it is essential to launch world-wide studies on the rate at which particulate pollution is increasing.

Meanwhile the Global Atmospheric Research Program includes no systematic measurements of dust densities and associated variables.

Mankind is not only altering the balance of the physical environment: he is also altering the balance between living things, which can also cause problems, some of which could be catastrophic. Let us look at these, which will eventually lead us back to the environment again.

4 Nature Hits Back

IF YOU SHOOT EAGLES, it is said, you may find yourself with a plague of locusts. For the eagles keep down the lizards. When the lizards increase, the frogs on which they feed decline. And when the frogs decline, the locusts on which they feed multiply. The study of such relationships is known as ecology.

This may be apocryphal, but a true story on these lines was told me by Professor LaMont Cole. In Malaya, an attempt to eliminate malaria nearly caused an outbreak of plague and certainly made a lot of roofs fall in. In spraying the malaria-carrying mosquitoes, they also reduced the number of roaches, which in turn reduced the number of geckos, and this in turn reduced the number of cats. With fewer cats, the rats increased and with them the plague-bearing lice. At this stage, the obvious—but fatal—thing to do was to put down rat poison. This would have caused the lice to look for new homes and they would have moved to human beings. Fortunately World Health Organization officers were on the spot: they did the right thing. They parachuted in more cats, and the plague was averted.

And the roofs? A side effect of all this was that a leaf-eating caterpillar which lived on the thatched roofs increased exceedingly, probably because the wasp which preys on it was also decimated by the DDT—though the geckos may have helped to keep it down too. Freed from their predators, the caterpillars munched away until they brought the roofs down. Doubtless there were other effects unnoticed by man but of interest to the animals concerned. All in all, a rather good example of what used to be called 'the balance of nature' but is now called ecology. For there is no single balance of nature, but many points of balance and they are easily disturbed, so that nature is always hunting to restore equilibrium. The dangers of disturbing the balance of nature are still little appreciated.

POPULATION EXPLOSIONS

In 1929 some African mosquitoes reached north-east Brazil, probably carried from Dakar on a French destroyer. There was a sharp outbreak of malaria, affecting nearly everyone in the local town, but this died down. For a few years the mosquitoes spread quietly along the coast and up the Jaguaribe river valley, until in 1937 an epidemic blazed up which continued into 1938 and 1939, killing an estimated 20,000 people, making hundreds of thousands ill, and nearly bringing the life of the countryside to a standstill. It was one of the worst epidemics Brazil has ever known.

The basic causes were simple. The local mosquitoes only bred in the forests and did not enter houses. The African mosquitoes bred in open sun and did enter houses. It took a $2m. campaign, supported by the Rockefeller Foundation, and about 3,000 trained workers, to exterminate the deadly visitor. One consequence of this was the institution of quarantine inspections of aircraft, just in time to intercept the African tsetse fly which carries sleeping sickness—at present still peculiar to Africa.

This is a population explosion, of a kind which the world is seeing more and more often, as a result of greatly increased travel and world trade, and the difficulties of supervision.

There are many other examples. The sweet chestnut disease reached the US from Asia about the beginning of the century, brought in on nursery plants. By 1911 it had spread to ten states and the damage was put at $25m. Today, the sweet chestnut has died out almost everywhere in the US and attempts are being made to introduce in its place the Chinese chestnut, which is immune to chestnut blight. Meanwhile the blight has got into Spain and into Italy, where the Chinese chestnut will not grow. No doubt it will soon reach Britain. The over-all cost is beyond estimation.

Or take the sea-lamprey, which reached Lake Erie about 1929; but Erie did not suit it. By 1937 it had got through the polluted St Clair river to Lake Huron and Lake Michigan, and by 1946 to Lake Superior. In these lakes it exploded. The lamprey is both hunter and parasite. It hangs on to a fish, squeezing into it a juice which stops its blood clotting, and then rasps and sucks the flesh and juices until the fish is dead, which may take as much as a week. Ten years after the lampreys got in, the catch of lake trout has fallen from 8,600,000 lb. to 25,000 lb. Other species of fish were also hit.

The great ecologist Charles Elton, who tells these and many other stories in his path-breaking book *The Ecology of Invasions by Animals and Plants*, notes that 'we are living in a period of the world's history when the mingling of thousands of kinds of organisms from different parts of the world is setting up terrific dislocations in nature. We are seeing huge changes in the natural population balance of the world.' And he asks: 'Will it be a Lost World?'

Though ecologists discovered why the African mosquitoes thrived in South America, more usually they are baffled by these population explosions. Why, Elton asks, has the Colorado beetle suddenly become a pest 300 years after the introduction of the potato? Why has the pine-looper started to attack Scottish pine plantations, though it has long been known there? Why did myxomatosis virus, which is not usually lethal in the Brazilian cotton-tail rabbits which it normally inhabits, prove deadly to the rabbits of western Europe? Going still further, why do epidemics of influenza and plague flare up and kill thousands, then die away again? The 1918 outbreak of 'flu is believed to have killed 100 million people, not sparing even the Eskimos. Who did what to which, to cause this?

Elton considers that nearly half the major plant-pests of the United States are introductions from abroad: some are still spreading, and others have only just got their feet in the door. Thus the golden nematode, first noticed on Long Island in 1942, so far affects only 8,000 acres of potatoes, but attempts to eradicate it have been unsuccessful.

As if the risks of accidental introduction were not enough, often it is deliberate attempts to introduce new species which cause the trouble. Thus when the Russians introduced a new species of sturgeon into the Aral Sea, it brought with it a parasite which did serious damage to another species of sturgeon there. There is now a growing belief that pests can be controlled by introducing their enemies, which is grandly known as biological control, as if the introducers knew exactly what they were doing. Sometimes this is enormously successful. When the fluted scale insect from Australia threatened the whole California citrus industry, it was completely controlled by bringing in 139 ladybirds, of an enemy species: their numerous descendants did the trick in a couple of years.

But it is not always like that. The giant African snail was brought from Japan to Maui, one of the Hawaiian islands, in 1936, while other specimens were brought to Oahu from Formosa and released in a garden 'for aesthetic reasons'. Soon it had become a pest and, in 1951, after various attempts to eliminate it had failed, it was decided to try biological control. But when you want to shift the ecological balance, it is a good idea to study the habits of the predator you wish to introduce first.

The two most significant snail-predators brought in to attack the giant snail were snails known as *Gonaxis* and *Euglandina*. *Gonaxis* flourished heartily, but did not attack the giant snail; so now there were two pests. *Euglandina* ate the giant snails all right, but did not stop there. It is a tree-climber and promptly moved out of the low limestone regions in which the giant snails dwelt, into the mountain forests where it proceeded to massacre the local tree snails. A competent malacologist (snail-expert) had advised against its introduction, but was ignored.

As Dr. Henry van der Schalie, Curator of Mollusks at the University of Michigan, from whom I have this story, comments: 'Eventually *Euglandina* may prove more difficult to control than the *Achatina* (giant snail) it is not likely to decimate.' But this is not all. The Hawaiian rats thrive on giant snails, and increased in number. But they are heavily infested with rat lung-worm, which it now turns out causes a serious human brain-disease known as eosinophilic meningoencephalitis. 'In Taiwan alone', says Dr van der Schalie, 'as many as a thousand people have been reported suffering from this disease.'

Undaunted, the authorities are launching an attack on another species of snail which carries the liver-fluke nematode which causes bilharzia or schistosomiasis. The predator which has been chosen is the sciomyzid fly. No one knows whether this fly can be relied on to attack the particular snail which carries the disease-agent, or even whether it will stay in the valleys where it has been put.

As the great naturalist, Dr Harley J. van Cleave, remarked, before his death, 'Man has meddled with everything. . . . Like an anarchist enjoying the protection and advantage of laws, his actions reveal a disregard for the very codes which prevent his destruction.'

But while man skates on thin ice by blunderingly shifting the ecological balance so as to cause population explosions, he also blindly tries to eliminate species he does not like, with consequences which are positively comic.

THE PERILS OF PEST CONTROL

When men try to grow a crop and obtain a maximum yield from it, what they are trying to do is to create an artificial ecosystem. But since it is out of harmony with the ecosystems surrounding it, it tends to break down, as the following story shows. It is reported by Gordon R. Conway, who is affiliated with the Agricultural Research Centre in the State of Sabah, Malaysia.

Cocoa is a rather new crop in Sabah: the first plantings were made in 1956. Large clearings were made in the forest, a few trees being left to shade the cocoa. Almost immediately several varieties of branch-borers, the larvae of moths, appeared, together with a tiny borer which attacked nearer the ground, ringing the tree. Among the trees under two years old, up to 20 per cent were killed. In 1959, dieldrin and DDT were applied at high concentrations. The borers looked a little pale, but persisted. Meanwhile various leaf-eating caterpillars, aphids, and mealy-bugs made their appearance. The sprayers returned to the attack, adding BHC, lead arsenate and a white oil (Albolineum) to their original armament. The coverage was 'very heavy'.

The branch-borers seemed to thrive on this: by 1961, one new tree in every six was attacked every month. Now two leaf-eating caterpillars showed up—one of them had been known only to attack coconuts before—followed by a planthopper. These all became 'extremely abundant', says Conway, 'the hoppers so much so that, on being disturbed, the adults, which resembled moths, rose in large clouds from the branches.' By July the most serious outbreak of all occurred: this time it was bagworms, of several species. Bagworms construct for themselves a bag of silk and sit inside, only their heads showing. When danger threatens, they retreat inside and close the top. This protects them very effectively from insecticides and, since they keep their eggs in the bag too, it also protects the eggs. They showed 'almost complete resistance to DDT, BHC, dieldrin, Diazon and dimethoate, all applied to run-off'. Victory for the bagworms. In addition to what they actually eat, they chew up large amounts of leaf to make the bags, so the damage to the trees is colossal. By late 1961, there were 70 acres of bare and dying trees, and it was spreading. Furious spraying knocked out one of the caterpillars but left the bagworms laughing. Picking them off by hand was tried in desperation. Verdict: ineffective and very costly.

At this point, someone had the brilliant idea of stopping spraying. Could it be that the broad-spectrum insecticides were knocking out predators on these pests more effectively than they were knocking out the pests?

Almost at once, the cocoa trees were covered with whitish cocoons, as scores of parasites attacked one of the caterpillars, which by June had declined to the point where it was negligible. In April and May it became evident that the plant-hopper was also on the way out. By August it was a goner, and in this month a decline in bark-borings was noticed. On opening some of the borings up, it was seen that a wasp was preying on the branch-borers. By the end of the year, they too had had it.

This released enough labour to treat the ring-bark borers by injecting dieldrin directly into their tunnels. At the same time it was found that the borers were coming from certain forests trees nearby which were heavily tunneled. These were then destroyed and the two measures together eliminated this pest. This left the smug little bagworms. A selective insecticide was found which killed about 75 per cent of them, and the trees began to put on new leaves. In 1963 it was possible to abandon this form of treatment, because a parasitic (tachinid) fly was now keeping them in check. In the five years following, up to the time of Conway's report, none of these pests reappeared. On the strength of this, the neighbouring commercial estates were urged to stop spraying also, with the same result. Only on one estate, where they persisted in spraying, has infestation continued.

As Conway puts it, with some restraint: 'My experience, and those of other entomologists in Malaysia, suggest that the increasing reliance on these pesticides has not been wholly beneficial.'

As this story shows, it is courting trouble to engage in cultivating large areas under a single crop: monoculture as it is called. If a pest gets in, it is liable to spread rapidly and cause widespread destruction. If the crop is an essential one, like wheat or rice, the result may be famine. It is simply a case of putting all one's eggs in a single basket. But we can express the moral in a more general, and more significant, form: don't oversimplify your ecosystems.

People still labour under the delusion that you can eliminate a pest—or a human disease—without causing adverse reactions elsewhere. They fail to realize the connectedness of the universe we live in.

Israel has recently provided a different instance of the same principle by creating oases in the desert, by means of sprinkler systems, and growing peaches, grapes and other such crops. Provided with a nice, damp environment, several insects of no previous economic importance have become major pests.

Before irrigation was introduced, onions were grown from seeds planted late in the year. Onion flies emerging from the pupal stage, found nowhere to deposit their eggs: only those emerging in December or January could find host plants. Following the introduction of irrigation, onions began to be grown from seeds sown in September and October. Result: the onion flies found nice soft seedlings to plant their eggs in.

Worse is the red pumpkin beetle: the larvae attack the roots of young cucurbits, while emerging beetles feed on the young leaves. Entire fields may be destroyed in this way, and often just before the fruit is due to be picked. Cucurbits are now grown under overhead sprinklers, which suits the pumpkin beetle, the eggs of which require moisture to develop. The larvae don't like moisture, however, so they migrate from the roots to the fruit and eat that instead.

The corn-seed maggot, once welcome because it eats locust eggs, also likes damp conditions to lay eggs in, and was no problem in the old days of dry farming. From being almost unknown, it has risen to the status of a major pest.

I cite these examples to show how touchy ecosystems are and how easily population explosions are caused among pests, for two reasons. The first is to show the risks involved in intensive food production, to which the world is becoming ever more committed; the second is to bring out how little able we are to predict the consequences of human interference with the environment.

It has been noticed that rain forests never have insect population explosions. The reason is thought to be that there are always a great variety of enemies and parasites ready to turn on any species which becomes unusually numerous. A case which appears to support this idea is found in Malaya, where a disease known as scrub-typhus has become a danger to man. The virus which causes this disease is carried in a creature which inhabits a grass used for thatching, named la-lang. Where the forest is felled, lalang becomes the dominant form of vegetation. In the forest, the organisms which carry the disease are kept to a low level.

Typical of a simplified community is the fruit-orchard, from which other plants are eliminated by weeding and spraying, as are insects, while animals are excluded by fences. As a result of the use of DDT to eliminate pests such as the codlin moth, the red mite has become a world-wide problem. Neglected orchards, in contrast, have practically none even now. Enquiry shows that this mite has no fewer than forty-five natural predators, which spraying eliminates.

The idea is now being put forward that one should deliberately restore complexity. Thus in California, where the scale-insect flares up in summer in fruit orchards, the dead-nettle on which it breeds, which had been carefully weeded out, is being experimentally reintroduced! The logic is this. With this plant to breed on, the insect starts to multiply earlier in the year, which gives its predators a better chance to get at it. In short, many of our pest problems are our own creation. If we simplify ecosystems, by removing unwanted species, it is at our peril. We may lose more than we gain. The environment is much more intricately and efficiently organized than, in our arrogance, we give it credit for.

VANISHING ANIMALS

There are a million species of insects, and no one would notice the elimination of a few, unless there were obvious ecological consequences. The position is different with larger animals, and especially the larger mammals. These can be eliminated relatively easily. In 1700, there were 60 million buffalo on the American plains. The Red Indians hunted them, but not to the point of reducing their numbers. Then came the white man, with his rifles, and by 1900 there were only a few dozen left. But it was not the rifles which were to blame, but rather the lack of any respect for the rest of nature. The Indian killed only when he needed, the white man killed 'for sport'. Battues were organized in which people tried to see how many they could kill in one day. Buffalo Bill got his name from his achievements in this noble activity, his finest performance being 250 slaughtered in a day. Sometimes the hides were taken, sometimes the tongue was torn out; but mostly the carcases were just left to rot.

When it came to catching birds, much larger bags could be achieved. In Michigan a billion passenger pigeons were taken in one year. On another occasion, 7¼ million were killed in one day at one spot. By 1914 the species was extinct.

Today, we do not operate on quite this scale. But the polar bear is in jeopardy, thanks to hunting parties; they are also shot when they come near human encampments in the belief that they are a danger, though it is unheard of for them to attack men without provocation. (Reports often speak of unprovoked attacks, but closer study shows the accusation to be unfounded: it is invented to justify the kill.) The turtle is threatened with extinction for another reason. It is too useful. The flesh, the shell, and the eggs are all sought after.

Vinzenz Ziswiler, a Swiss ecologist, in his book *Extinct and Vanishing Species*, lists about 150 species known to have vanished in the past three centuries. The list ranges from the aurochs (1627) and the dodo in the seventeenth century, to the Indian pink-headed duck in 1940. The reasons why animals vanish from the earth are various: the Tahitian parakeet went because its habitat was altered by drainage. The New Zealand quail succumbed to diseases introduced by settlers. The Tasmanian 'wolf' was hunted because it was ignorantly believed to be a predator—actually it is not a carnivore, but a marsupial like the kangaroo. The nocturnal kiwi or apteryx was wiped out by weasels introduced to 'enrich' the fauna of New Zealand. Schomburgk's deer was persecuted in Siam for religious reasons.

It is too late to do anything about these 150 vanished species, but we could do something about the 240 further species currently threatened with extinction. These include the Bactrian camel (400 left), the oryx (200), the Sumatra elephant (100), the Cape zebra (81), the cahow (50), the Manchurian crane (30), the Japanese crested ibis (12), the Everglades kite (4 or 5), the Bali tiger (3 or 4) and others for which the numbers are not known.

Not only animals but many plants are becoming extinct: about 300 species are in grave danger of being lost in Britain alone. The situation is most serious in islands where species exist found nowhere else in the world. In the Hawaiian islands, for instance, 95 per cent of the native plants are unique, and many are on the verge of extinction. It is now possible to spend a vacation in Hawaii without ever seeing a native plant. Philip Island in the western Pacific is now completely eroded, with only a few plants remaining in the valleys. When Capt. Cook discovered it in 1774 it was completely covered with vegetation. There were three unique species here, of which one, the glory pea, has not been seen since 1805; a couple of years ago only one of the other two species could be found, and of this there were only a few bushes left.

Collectors are probably the worst menace, especially in the case of orchids and succulents: many rare African orchids are on the point of extinction. In England, the lady's slipper orchid remains only in one secret locality. Unlike Czechoslovakia and Austria, Britain has no legislation to limit picking rare plants.

Does it matter that man is wiping out whole species from the planet? Evolution is capable of many quirks, and its variants are, some might say, of only museum interest. But apart from the aesthetic values of maintaining a richly varied flora and fauna there are practical reasons for doing so. Plants often turn out to have unique medical or other properties. Animals also still have much to teach. Thus the vanishing oryx can live indefinitely without drinking: hence it might become of great importance as a protein source in arid areas, as the growing world population expands into them. Who knows what future peoples will want? It is sheer folly to deplete the pool of genetic variation built up so painfully over millions of years.

LAKES AND MISTAKES

More complex chains of cause and effect also exist, and some of the worst examples of biological backlash have followed the creation of great lakes, such as Lake Nasser, and power projects, such as the Kariba Dam.

The most striking, and quite unexpected, consequence of the building of the Nasser dam has been the collapse of the Mediterranean sardine-fishing industry. The Mediterranean is poor in nutrients, except at the eastern end where the Nile used to discharge its rich burden of organic silt. The Egyptian sardine industry amounted to 18,000 tons, worth $7m.— sardines were almost half the total marine catch. Now the Nasser dam holds back the silts, and today the sardine industry runs about 500 tons, while the export of fish products generally fell to half in the 4 years following the completion of the dam.

A good part of Egypt's fish comes from five great shallow brackish lakes, separated from the Mediterranean by sand-bars. Here 19,000 people live, rearing fish in shallow basins to stock the lakes. The largest, Lake Burullus, yielded 15,000 tons a year. Catches have been declining, as herbicides, insecticides and copper sulphate seep into the lakes. Lately, a more serious threat has materialized: the sand-bars are slowly vanishing, now that the Nile no longer dumps its sediments in the area. Eventually the sand-bars will open and the lakes will disappear.

The sardine fleet is attempting to adapt by fishing for hake and lizard-fish, while the government, in desperation, has bought three ocean-going trawlers which will work off East Africa, but the eventual loss may be around $20m. a year. Early in 1970, however, it was reported that the increased salinity of the Mediterranean is adversely affecting fishing throughout its length, so that the final cost may prove more serious than is now thought.

. The loss of silt also means that the lower Nile Valley, once so fertile, now has to be treated with artificial fertilizer. The government therefore has to build fertilizer factories, and divert some of the electric power created by the dam to run them. The dam is intended gradually to bring into cultivation an additional 2 million acres. However, there is an enormous loss of water by evaporation from the 200-mile-long Lake Nasser, behind the dam, and from the irrigation ditches—more than the whole amount supplied by the pre-existing dam. It is considered there will actually be less water than was available before, quite apart from that lost by seepage. True, the water will be where it is wanted, though only the alluvium along the river bank is fertile: away from the river the land is completely desert. Dr A. A. Ahmed, a former technical consultant to the Egyptian Ministry of Public Works, has been quoted as saying that 'evaporation losses appear to be so great as to make the High Dam of doubtful benefit, if not hazardous.' Ahmed reckons that the whole of the Nile discharge could be lost by seepage during the first twenty years of its life, and about 70 per cent during the next ten years. Filling the Wadi Rayan would have been cheaper, he thinks, and just as effective.

But a still more serious consequence of this undertaking is the spread of the revolting disease known in Africa as bilharzia, and elsewhere as schistosomiasis. The disease is caused by a blood-fluke which is carried by snails but lays its eggs in man; the eggs are excreted into water, where they develop into larvae which enter snails. Here they develop into forked-tailed worms which attach themselves to people who enter the water; they bore through the skin and make for the liver, where they lay more eggs.

Now that malaria is largely under control, schistosomiasis has become the world's most widespread disease, afflicting an estimated 114 million people.

In Egypt the disease is already frighteningly common, owing to the general practice of excreting into the rivers and streams, and the lack of piped water. People also enter the streams either to bathe or wash, or to water animals, and become reinfected. It has been common since the time of the Pharaohs. Today it is reckoned that 70 per cent of the population of Lower Egypt are affected: in some villages the rate is 100 per cent. The life expectancy for women is 27 years, for men, 25. The rate at which the eggs are produced is fantastic. Dr. C. H. Barlow, who deliberately infected himself in the cause of science in 1944, produced 30,000 eggs a day. He became extremely ill, and was only cured after a year and a half, by means of a drug so unpleasant in its effects that most people refuse to complete the treatment.

The warm, slow-moving waters of irrigation ditches provide just the habitat that the host snails like, and favour the worst intestinal form of the disease; as irrigation spreads, so does schistosomiasis. Moreover the ditches are kept filled year-round. Formerly, they dried in winter, and the cold tended to destroy the hosts. Dr Henry van der Schalie considers that the spread of schistosomiasis may well cancel out all the benefits of this $1.3 billion dollar undertaking. The disease causes an extreme fatigue and lassitude which may have the effect of reducing agricultural output, rather than increasing it. At present there is no effective cure—the one used by Barlow is almost more dangerous than the disease—and it is extremely hard to eliminate the snail hosts. Copper sulphate can be dumped into the water to destroy them, but if only one survives, it will rapidly repopulate the area. Van der Schalie took part in one such attempt. Forty tons of copper sulphate were used at a cost of $13,000. Next year there were half as many snails, but just as many sites of infection. The following year the snails were back to the original density. One could not detect that the tract had ever been treated.

Though Lower Egypt has always been harassed by this disease, the Sudan has been relatively free; as the new irrigation canals are built, the disease will probably spread into Upper Egypt.

Willard Wright, a leading parasitologist, said in 1951: 'It is estimated that schistosomiasis is costing the country £20m. a year. The productivity of the population is decreased by 33 per cent. All the heavy labour is supplied from Upper Egypt where the disease has a very low incidence. Over a period of 20 years, 22 per cent of army recruits from Lower Egypt have been rejected for physical defects, whereas only 3 per cent of those from Upper Egypt failed to pass the examinations. The difference is believed to be due almost entirely to the high schistosome infection rate in Lower Egypt.'

And of course, Egypt is not the only area to be affected. Schistosomiasis is spreading in the Kariba area. A small irrigation scheme in the Zambesi valley reports 89 per cent infection with unusual symptoms, such as paralysis and cerebral abnormalities. In Rhodesia, the Umshandige irrigation scheme has been practically abandoned. 'The emerging countries in Africa face frightening increases in the incidence of bilharziasis', says van der Schalie.

These great dams are too often conceived in a spirit of technological over-optimism coupled with the feeling they confer national prestige. The effects are worst when they are one-purpose dams, intended simply to produce electric power, as in the case of the Kariba Dam, which created the largest man-made lake in the world.

The effects on local populations were disregarded, except where they exerted some political power. The lake flooded alluvial land on which local tribes carried out subsistence farming—but since this did not show up in the figures of gross national product, the loss of output was ignored by the planners. Yet, as Professor Thayer Scudder, an anthropologist who has studied the area, has pointed out, it was an actual cost and in the event of famine, lack of this output adds to the burden.

The flow of water from the dam was regulated by the engineers without regard to the attempts of these people to maintain themselves. For the first three years, while the lake was still filling, no water was released and people began to cultivate the low-level soils. Then in April 1962 their gardens were flooded ten feet deep in a single day. A local famine followed in the area where people displaced by the lake had been resettled. In the following year, the same thing happened, except the date was different. In 1963–64, the sluices were opened and shut repeatedly. In the dry season, when water would have been welcome, the river was made to fall and the crops were heat-struck. If the object had been to make a Keystone comedy, the effect would have been very amusing.

'It is hard to imagine how those regulating the flow of water through the dam could have acted in a way more detrimental to down-river agriculture,' comments Professor Scudder. The sudden floods are washing away the soil on the river banks and it is reckoned that in 10–15 years there will not be enough left to support the population. In any case, the relocation areas cannot support the existing population, and food shortages are developing.

The lesson is that the over-simple solutions offered by modern technology cannot successfully replace the intrinsically complicated natural systems. Disease and suffering for millions of people are the direct outcome.

THE GREAT CYCLES

The nexus of plant and animal interrelationships which we have been considering exists within a broad framework of soil, climate, water and atmosphere which also counts as part of the ecosystem.

Because the time-scale of change is very long compared with the human lifespan, we tend to think of air, water and soil as simply being 'there' for our convenience. In reality they are maintained by a complex series of transactions. Rock is heaved to the surface by volcanic action, disintegrated by the weather, added to by organic debris and finally comes to form soil. Soil is washed away by the rivers to the sea, where, in the course of time, it may become compressed into rocks of a new kind, and so on.

The two cycles which are of particular and immediate interest to us are those which maintain the supply of oxygen and nitrogen in the air, without which life would soon be extinct.

When we breathe oxygen we render it up again as carbon dioxide—that is, we have linked two oxygen atoms to each carbon atom. Similarly, whenever a fire occurs, including the burning of oil and gasoline in internal combustion engines, oxygen is consumed—or, more accurately, converted to carbon monoxide. Before the coming of technology, all the oxygen in the atmosphere would have been consumed in about 10,000 years, if it were not continually replaced. Now that all the oxygen is burned: part combines with minerals and metals, as we can observe when iron rusts. Rust is iron oxide; that is, oxygen atoms linked to iron atoms.

The only reason the world does not run out of oxygen is the fact that plants, unlike animals, breathe in carbon dioxide, retaining the carbon atoms but giving off the oxygen atoms. The drifting plant-life of the sea, the phytoplankton, provides 70 per cent of our oxygen, the rest comes from land plants, especially trees which process much more carbon dioxide than a similar area of grass would. (A little oxygen is made in the upper atmosphere, by the action of sunlight, which can cleave the oxygen from water, but the amount is inconsiderable.)

Thus the atmosphere is a biological product. If all life ceased, the oxygen would be gradually removed and the atmosphere would revert to its primitive state. The extraordinary fact is, the earth supports life only because there is life there—or rather, it is life which supports life. (Conversely, the reason planets like Mars do not have an atmosphere which supports life is that there is no life there to support: a curious paradox.)

As we shall see in the next chapter, man is interfering with this happy arrangement. But let us first consider the other element in the atmosphere, nitrogen, as important to man as oxygen though much less talked about.

Nitrogen deprivation is synonymous with human poverty. Much of the body is made of molecules which contain nitrogen: proteins, enzymes, hormones, vitamins and the nucleic acids which control growth and development. As the population of the world expands, the supply of nitrogen is becoming the critical factor, the lack of which is the chief cause of famine.

About four-fifths of the atmosphere is nitrogen, and this is very curious because nowhere else is nitrogen found in any quantity. It usually links with oxygen to form nitrites (which have two oxygen atoms per nitrogen atom) which turn into nitrates (which have three oxygen atoms). Or it combines with three hydrogen atoms to form ammonia. Ammonia, it is worth recalling, gets its name from the temple of Jupiter Ammon, where there was a strong smell of ammonia from the dung of the camels which brought his worshippers there.

The only thing which restores nitrogen to the atmosphere is the activity of certain specialized algae and bacteria, known as the denitrifying bacteria. They chew up nitrates and give off nitrogen. So this component of the air also depends on the presence of life.

Living creatures, whether plants or animals, require nitrogen to make the amino-acids from which they build proteins. (Crudely put, proteins are meat or muscle.) Plants obtain their nitrogen by virtue of another variety of bacteria, the nitrifying bacteria, which live on their roots and abstract nitrogen from decaying vegetable matter in the soil—or of course from nitrogen-containing fertilizers. Animals obtain it by eating plants or eating animals (including fish) which have eaten plants. Fortunately the nitrifying bacteria are numerous, or we'd all be dead.

When plants or animals die, another group of bacteria convert the remains into amino-acids and other residues. Then the aminifying bacteria convert these to ammonia (hence the smell at Jupiter's temple). Yet other bacteria convert ammonia to nitrites. Finally a sixth group of bacteria convert the nitrites to nitrates, in which form they again become available to plants. Nitrogen thus moves round a cycle from plants back to plants, dependent at every point on bacteria for its maintenance. At the same time the atmosphere acts as a reservoir to this process, both abstracting and giving up nitrogen, mainly through the agency of other bacteria. Yet we add hundreds of thousands of new toxic sutstances to the environment without testing whether they may be lethal to these humble servants of nature.

The turnover time of atmospheric nitrogen is much longer than for oxygen, probably around 100 million years, though this is not so long geologically. If life ceased, nitrogen would gradually combine with oxygen to form nitrates, and the quantities of both in the air would decline to a very low level.

There is also carbon dioxide in the atmosphere, mainly exhaled by animals, and water vapour. All these gases remain at remarkably constant levels, thanks to feedback mechanisms which are only partly understood. Thus both water vapour and carbon dioxide absorb the redder wavelengths of light, so that if the amount of these gases increases, light is cut off and plant photosynthesis is reduced, thus reducing the amount of these gases. But there are certainly many other regulatory feedbacks at work. Currently scientists are puzzling about the scavenging of carbon monoxide. Man is pouring enormous quantities into the air, yet the level remains constant. What he adds stays around for only a year or two, then vanishes. No one knows what removes it.

But ignorance does not breed humility, and the readiness of some scientists to intervene gives genuine cause for alarm. 'I am terrified to recall', says Professor LaMont Cole, 'that I have twice heard prominent chemists say, and have once read in a textbook, that it would be desirable to find a way to *block* denitrification because ammonia and nitrate are so important to agriculture!' But just because they do not understand all the mechanisms, and why they work so well, scientists are concerned that man's intervention may disrupt them. Any feedback mechanism can be swamped by too big an input. The thermostat which regulates room temperature cannot maintain the temperature if you open all the windows on an icy day, or keep you cool if the house catches on fire.

And what may be more important, these mechanisms respond very slowly: so even if they can absorb the effects of human activity, they may take centuries to do so, and in the meantime conditions may be adverse to life. Man has begun to intrude on this beautifully-balanced mechanism, as well as on the cycles which regulate the turnover of carbon, sulphur, phosphorus, carbon dioxide and other substances. No one knows how much overload they can tolerate.

The amount of nitrogen mankind is dumping into the ecosystem is truly enormous.

NITRATE JAG

Nitrogen is, in most cases, the limiting factor in the food-supply of man, animals and plants. Oxygen is present in abundance, and water usually so, but usable nitrogen as nitrates is generally short. The amount of living tissue which a plant can construct, i.e. its total growth, is usually limited by the amount of nitrogen it can acquire from the soil. So dumping on nitrogen is the farmer's first step to increase his yields. In arid lands, of course, water is important too, though water will do no good if nitrogen is short. After these two needs are satisfied, phosphorus is the next limiting factor.

Professor Barry Commoner has made a close study of the use of nitrogen compounds. He finds that in the US the natural turnover of nitrogen compounds is about 7 million tons a year, but that man superimposes on this cycle another 7 million tons in the form of fertilizers, plus a further 2–3 million tons coming from car exhausts and power-plants. This is a colossal intrusion. No one has worked out similar figures for any other country, as far as I am aware. But many European countries, notably Holland, use fertilizers much more intensively than does the US. 'This intrusion', says Commoner, 'has produced stresses which have already contributed to a serious deterioration of the environment. If continued they threaten to collapse important segments of the cycle itself. Correction of these trends will require us to solve very grave economic, social and political problems.'

What makes man's use of nitrogen especially significant is the fact that it is in the form of nitrates, which, as we have seen, are comparatively rare in nature, and the speed with which he has introduced them. In the US, use of nitrogen fertilizers has increased 14-fold in 25 years.

The immediate consequence of dumping nitrates on the land is that much of what is dumped is washed into the rivers and lakes before it can be absorbed by the intended crop. Here it successfully fertilizes the algae, which 'bloom' or, if you prefer, undergo a population explosion. When they die, bacteria destroy the remains, themselves multiplying and consuming enormously increased amounts of the other vital requirement, oxygen. This they draw from the water, leaving it anoxic (devoid of oxygen), with the result that fish, bacteria and other life-forms die. This then causes the algae to die—and very offensive the rotting masses are—the lake becomes abiotic (devoid of life). Algal 'blooming' occurs when nitrogen levels reach 0.3 ppm.

In natural conditions, lakes move slowly through this sequence of events, known as eutrophication, and 'die' after hundreds or thousands of years, depending on their size. Their tributary streams wash organic matter into them, which decays into a rich silt, and so releases nitrates. A disused canal or pond full of duckweed provides an instance of the process at work. Mountain pools remain clear because the melted snow which feeds them carries little organic matter. Rivers, likewise, normally remain clear as they wash the organic detritus down to the sea. Man accelerates hugely this natural process of ageing.

With no oxygen left, the capacity of self-purification is gone. A report prepared under Dr Athelstan Spilhaus estimates that, in the US, this process will consume the entire oxygen content of the summertime flow of every river in the country by 1980. Since nitrate-burdened water is unsuitable for drinking, this could mean a catastrophe. Already one small town in the US—Elgin, Minnesota—has had to find a new water supply for this reason, while other areas are at the danger-mark. Public health authorities have set 10 ppm as the acceptable level in drinking water. Decatur, Illinois, approached this level during the spring of 1967 and 1968, and it is reported that 25 per cent of the groundwaters from wells of less than 25 feet depth in Illinois exceed this level. A study made in California in 1960–61 showed, out of 800 wells examined, 88 above the limit, and 182 above 5 ppm.

Commoner made rather detailed investigations to make sure where the nitrates were coming from. In St Joaquin Valley, for instance, where fertilizer was being applied at an average of 167 lb. per acre, the sub-surface water averaged 44.5 ppm of nitrate-nitrogen, while another study showed that an average of 36 per cent of the nitrogen applied in fertilizer fetched up in the drainage water; over one-third—a startling amount. It has been argued in the past that nitrates in drinking water come not from fertilizer but from feedlots, and since these are usually near the homestead, they may indeed affect domestic wells. But investigation shows that, taking large irrigated areas, it is the fertilizer which is the main culprit.

The position is different in a case like that of Lake Erie, into which the sewage of many cities is dumped. The Report of the Federal Water Pollution Commission in 1968 estimated that the lake received about 37,500 tons of nitrogen a year from farmlands and 45,000 tons from municipal sewage. It is reckoned that the lake has aged 15,000 years in this century due to sewage. The southern end of Lake Michigan, of course, is dead, as is the south shore of Lake Ontario around Buffalo. Practically none of the sewage receives treatment to reduce its biological effect. Algal growths have become common, and the number of intestinal bacteria present in the lake-water has reached a dangerous level.

(Though much is heard of the condition of Lake Erie, probably Lake Michigan is in a worse condition. The amounts of DDT and other organochlorines are higher than in any of the other lakes, and in 1969 large quantities of coho salmon had to be destroyed because of the high load of DDT they carried.)

Many European lakes are already eutrophicated, as I noted at the beginning of this book, principally because of domestic sewage: these lakes are of course much smaller than the Great Lakes of the US. Eutrophication is also affecting San Francisco Bay, and the San Joaquin River which flows into it.

In 1968, a British research group, spurred by American anxieties on the subject, examined an 80-kilometre stretch of the Great Ouse, a river which runs through heavily fertilized agricultural land. It was found that 90 per cent of the nitrogen in the water came from fertilizers. The amount was enormous: equivalent to 46.25 kilograms per hectare (41.75 lb. per acre) over the catchment area. Farmers were applying, on average, 160 kg./ha. (145 lb. per acre). Thus one quarter of the fertilizer applied was ending up in the water. Apart from the waste, Britain needs her surface waters for drinking purposes. Several wells in Essex have been found to be above the WHO limits for nitrogen already.

Nitrates are relatively harmless in themselves. The reason nitrate-levels are regulated in drinking water is that, in the body, they may be converted to nitrites, which combine with the haemoglobin in the blood, destroying its power to convey oxygen. The result is asphyxia and possibly death. This risk has long been understood but it has only just emerged that foodstuffs may carry excess nitrates to the point of causing this condition, known as methoxyhaemoglobinaemia. In the past five years a number of European doctors have reported cases of infants affected with this disease after eating tinned spinach. Spinach is rich in nitrates, which airborne bacteria convert to nitrite, even when it is kept in a refrigerator. Enzymes in the spinach may also do this, both in fresh and frozen or tinned varieties. Various other baby foods carry nitrates at lower levels, beets being the next highest. Experiment shows that the nitrate level in spinach is directly related to the amount of nitrogen applied as fertilizer. In the US, where less fertilizer is used, there have been no cases of methoxyhaemoglobinaemia reported though potentially dangerous levels of nitrates have been found in samples of spinach and other vegetables. Nitrate poisoning of livestock, however, has been widely reported.

Studies sparked by these findings have also revealed that nitrates at 53–78 ppm are corrosive to tinplate.

NOXIOUS GASES

While nitrates are permeating the water and soil, two other

oxides of nitrogen (nitric oxide and nitrous oxide) are causing problems in the air, as is another nitrogen compound, ammonia. Cars emit nitrogen oxides, and the atmospheric burden seems to come partly from this source and partly from agriculture, since high levels are observed both at times when fertilizer is being applied and in areas where cars are much used. The correlation of car-use with inorganic nitrogen in rain is quite high. In the US six million tons of such oxides are injected into the air by cars every year. Except in the Los Angeles area, the new regulations do not cover them, but apply to carbon monoxide and hydrocarbons only. Fuel consumption by cars is expected to rise by 50 per cent in the next decade, while that used by domestic air transport may quadruple or more. The alert limit is quite low: 5 ppm. At 25 ppm the oxides act like war gases and cause lung-damage. But at much lower levels they diminish the capacity of the blood to carry oxygen, just as with nitrates. And at the moment we have no way of dealing with them. Moreover, in conjunction with hydrocarbons, and under the action of sunlight, they form smog.

There is even a suggestion that cancer-causing nitroso-compounds may be produced by oxides of nitrogen.

It seems likely that we shall have to restrict the use of fertilizers—a conclusion highly unwelcome to the light-hearted economists and agronomists whom we shall meet in a later chapter, solving the world's food problems by massive applications of fertilizer. The core of the problem resides in the fact that, when nitrogen is applied, it does not enter the organic humus which has been yielding nitrogen to the crops. Even when nitrogen is running off into the water, the soil is being depleted of its natural nitrogen. Simply cutting back on nitrogen, therefore, will lead to poor crops; it is necessary to restore the natural fertility of the land. This is also true in the sense that the porous structure of the soil depends on the presence of organic nitrogen, and unless the soil is porous oxygen cannot reach the roots. Heavy machinery is in any case compacting the soil; applications of inorganic nitrogen make matters worse.

The problem arises entirely because of the size of the population. This is true in the simple sense that fewer people mean smaller crops and less use of fertilizer; but also in the more important sense that small populations can afford to farm extensively, obtaining what they need by cultivating as large an area of land as necessary. It is only when land is scarce, that it becomes necessary to wring a high yield from each acre. The point is seldom grasped, and economists often point to the lower Russian yields as if this were a fault: equally they fail to see why European yields are higher than American ones. Europe just has less land per head.

Naturally, any attempt to bring about a reduction of the use of fertilizer would be bitterly resisted. As Commoner puts it, farmers have been on a nitrogen jag for so long that they become addicted. Even the use of police dogs and long terms of imprisonment would hardly deter them. Just as with radiation, the problem becomes a political one. How high a price are we prepared to pay to ensure the food supply? Obviously a high one. The fact that the Gordian knot can be cut by reducing the population is usually overlooked.

But changes in the physical environment do not simply affect plant and animal population. We are just beginning to absorb the alarming fact that these disturbances to the living ecosystems can react on the physical environment, as I shall now describe.

5 The Last Gasp

IT WAS ONLY IN 1969 that biologists became aware of the fact that a large starfish known as the Crown of Thorns had undergone a population explosion and a change of habits and was eating up, at a rapid rate, all the coral in the Pacific. A rumour that such starfishes were multiplying in the Red Sea had been heard back in 1963 but had not caused much attention. In 1966, reports came in that they were beginning to crunch up the Great Barrier Reef. But it was not until Richard Chesher of the University of Guam wrote to the internationally-read weekly *Science* in mid-1969 that the scientific community was shocked into attention. In Guam itself, he said, 90 per cent of the coral had been destroyed over a 38-mile shoreline in 2½ years.

The Crown of Thorns is a large sixteen-armed spiny sea-star, consisting of a 6-inch disc set with 2-inch spines. It eats twice its own area in a night, and destroys a square metre of coral in a month. In some areas Chesher reported the creatures are as thick as one per square metre. When they have eaten all the coral in one bay they move systematically on to the next. Normally, the Crown of Thorns (*Acanthaster planci*, to give it its zoological name) eats only at night, but the swarming populations of the Pacific have abandoned such leisurely methods and now, with a truly Protestant devotion to work, eat all day too. By the spring of 1968, Chesher noted, all the coral in Tumon Bay was dead; by autumn the creature had invaded Double Reef. Winter storms prevented observation of its progress between December and March, but when the scientists went out again, another 4 kilometres of reef was missing.

The University of Guam decided to counter-attack. Blanket use of powerful chemicals or pesticides was ruled out: it would have killed too many other creatures, including the coral. Divers were sent down with giant syringes and hot water bottles of formalin strapped to their arms, to inject the creatures with a lethal dose. Each man killed between 600 and 700 a day, but there were tens of thousands more, and the campaign had no appreciable effect.

Meanwhile reports came in that *Acanthaster planci* was besieging other Pacific islands: Truk in the E. Caroline Islands, Palau in the W. Carolines; Wake far to the north, Rota in the Marianas, and Saipan; and the Fiji Islands. Then it was reported from Borneo and New Guinea. On the Great Barrier Reef off North East Australia the situation became steadily more serious. As I write these lines, it is reported that a quarter of the 1,000-mile-long reef has vanished. Loss of the reefs spells economic disaster for Pacific islands, since they depend on the reefs for their economy and way of life, for the reefs contain the lagoons where the fish, which provide the chief source of protein, are caught. Lagoon fish cannot readily adjust to an ocean existence. *Acanthaster planci* may reduce the local populations to a state of protein deficency, and break up their pattern of culture, if it does not drive them away altogether. Such is the balance of nature: boom for one species spells bust for another.

CROWN OF THORNS

'These are not short-term population fluctuations,' Chesher warns, 'but population explosions.' What has caused them remains unknown. A fourteen-man team of specialists was hastily got together in the summer of 1969 and visited the area but returned substantially baffled. Their first thought was that shell collectors had overdone collection of the triton shell, principal predator of the Crown of Thorns, but triton shells seem to be present in their usual numbers; they just cannot cope with the demand. Another theory was that man, by blasting coral reefs in order to make military installations, had provided a favourable environment for the young to breed in. But the Crown of Thorns appears in places where no blasting has been done. Then it was observed that it was numerous wherever man was present. Is man discharging something into the ocean which actually gives this sea-star what it wants? Or has it just mutated, as a result of radiation?

Chesher reported, in December 1969, that 'Larger food and game fish were almost totally absent [in dead reefs] and even deep-sea fish populations may be affected by this breakdown in the food and life chains.' He also notes: 'Concentrations of organochlorines and other man-made pollutants have been increasing in the marine environment during the past few decades. These pollutants might either have eliminated planktonic predators, decreased the zooplanktonic standing population, or reduced the reproductive capacity of the zooplankters so that the zooplanktonic community can no longer expand rapidly enough to check the large influx of large swarms of *A. planci* larvae during the spawning season.... Another hypothesis suggests that predators of the adult. *A. planci* (i.e. tritons) might accumulate organochlorines in their tissues and that this might reduce the reproductive capacity of the predators. Subsequent release from predation might lead to the current population explosions.'

Chesher summed up his first report in these sombre words: 'If, however, the population explosion is due to a basic change in the life history of *A. planci*, control will probably not be possible.... There is a possibility that we are witnessing the initial stages of the extinction of madreporian corals in the Pacific.'

Such disasters are by no means unheard-of, he points out: 'The geological records clearly indicate that large groups of animals have become extinct within a relatively short time.' On the other hand, population explosions lead to population crashes. Perhaps *Acanthaster planci* will learn to control itself. Either way, something funny has happened; man is probably responsible; and the world has already got a lot less coral than it had, by an amount which will take centuries to replace. We must expect to see other ecological dramas of this kind in the next thirty years.

THE RED TIDES

The sinister behavior of the sea-star is not unique, but has parallels in the poisonous 'red tides' which periodically manifest off the coasts of California, Florida and elsewhere, killing millions of fish and sometimes killing human beings who are rash enough to eat shell-fish which have been in contact with them. The record of such deaths goes back to 1793; the tides themselves have been noted at least since biblical times. The author of *Exodus* (Ch. 7) describes how 'all the waters that were in the river were turned to blood, and the fish that was in the river died; and the river stank, and the Egyptians could not drink of the waters of the river.' The Greek Homer and the Roman Tacitus also refer to them. Darwin, when he was voyaging in the *Beagle,* noticed a reddening of the sea off the coast of South America not caused by the harmless organism which gives the Red Sea its name.

In modern times, the most serious outbreak occurred in 1946 off Florida. First the sea turned yellow; by the following June the water was thick and viscous with billions upon billions of tiny one-cell organisms known as dinoflagellates. Sixty-mile windrows of stinking fish lined the beaches: one naturalist estimated 50 million died. Schools and hotels had to close. Shrimps, crabs, lobsters, barnacles, oysters and turtles were also wiped out. Even the bait used by fishermen died on the hook.

The lethal agent, whose presence in trillions discoloured the sea, was a microscopic creature, a dinoflagellate named *Gymnodinium breve.* The red tides also manifest off the coasts of Peru and California, where the culprit is another dinoflagellate named *Gonyaulax.* These minute creatures, only a thousandth of an inch across, each contain a red 'eye-spot'. Normally they are present to the tune of a few thousand in a gallon of water. When the urge seizes them, they explode to a quarter of a billion per gallon, and the eye-spots give the water its reddish colour.

Eventually the red tides of 1946 subsided—the previous one in that area had been in 1932—only to reappear in almost every subsequent year: 1952, 1953, 1954, 1957, 1959, 1960, 1961, 1962, 1963, 1964. . . . Something funny had happened. On the west coast, though not as bad as this, *Gonyaulax* still claims victims and the sale and gathering of shellfish is prohibited in those months when they may have been in contact with this speck of dynamite. To consume such fish by mistake is no joke. A doctor gives this description of a woman who did so. 'She awoke quite conscious but helplessly paralysed—arms, legs and trunk. She could not move in her bed or stand when lifted to the floor. She was scarcely able to speak for numbness about the face and mouth; was violently sick but unable to vomit; had a severe headache and backache and extreme dizziness.' The cause of these dramatic and disagreeable symptoms is a nerve-poison which *Gonyaulax* produces—a poison as deadly as botulinus toxin, a few grams of which would suffice to kill everyone in the world, if fairly distributed.

It is obvious that a population explosion of toxic dinoflagellates which was not self-limiting could kill all the fish in the sea, not to mention quite a few people, and deal a crushing economic blow to large numbers of fishermen all over the world. It is therefore sobering to reflect that we have not the slightest idea what causes it to proliferate, or what normally limits it.

The curious thing about dinoflagellates is that they are incredibly choosy about certain heavy metals. There are numerous varieties of dinoflagellate, many of them harmless. They like, depending upon which one you are talking about, traces of zinc, copper, iron, magnesium and cobalt, and are exceedingly fussy about just how much. An alteration of only one part per million may be enough to determine whether they reproduce or not. (They're also fussy about other things: some insist upon being battered by waves, and refuse to live in the calm water of a laboratory tank, which ensures privacy from scientists.)

The best guess, at present, is that they proliferate when the level of cobalt is just right. It has recently been recognized that there are areas on land where cobalt is absent, and cattle sicken and die when kept on them. Traces of this metal are required to build the enzymes which regulate their life processes. S. H. Hutner and John J. A. MacLaughlin of the Haskins Laboratories, who know more about these dinoflagellates than most people, wonder if there may be cobalt deserts in the sea, as there are on land. If so, man's habit of discharging waste products blithely into the oceans may one day raise cobalt to the level preferred by these tiny creatures, and cause a worldwide dinoflagellate population explosion. The function of cobalt is to form part of Vitamin B-12, which dinoflagellates thrive on: alas, we have no way of measuring the amounts of B-12 present in salt water. (Even in fresh water, we are reduced to watching how *Eu-*

glena, the unicellular creature known as the slipper-animal-cule, makes out, as a basis for guessing the amount of B-12 present. And *Euglena* won't live in salt water.) Attempts to destroy them with copper sulphate or other chemicals may wipe out economically important species upon which fish depend.

Optimistically, Hutner and MacLaughlin also suggest that we could create nutritious tides of the non-toxic varieties of dinoflagellate, and thus bring into being sea-meadows in which fish would flourish. At the moment, our almost total ignorance makes it even chances which of these states we may bring about. We might even do both, in which case the mass of dead fish would be even more disagreeable.

Professor Paul Ehrlich, Professor of Biology at Stanford, has made the red tides the basis of a speculative forecast of a possible eco-catastrophe. In his story 'Eco-Catastrophe!' the red tides cause a failure of the world's fish catches; then a permanent change in the climate reduces agricultural food supplies; and finally a super-pesticide which slays all those insects which have chitinous horny exteriors, thus giving free rein to those they prey on, finishes the job off. Foreign aid programmes, which supply plants to manufacture the new pesticide to developing countries, are a major factor in accel-erating the final catastrophe.

THE FINITE SINK

Currently we dump into the oceans, or into the rivers which flow into the oceans, many thousands of products, the biolog-ical effects of which are in most instances unknown. These include oil, chemical effluents, heavy metals, trace elements, dry-cleaning fluids, radio-active wastes, chemical warfare gases and irritants, detergents, pesticides and innumerable other groups of substances. In fact, practically everything we throw away in liquid form reaches the sea, except a few things which decompose rapidly, while much of what we discharge into the air also descends eventually into the sea. It is reckoned that we now add half a million different sub-stances to the sea. In the vast majority of cases, we have no idea what their effect is, as it has never been investigated.

For instance lead, which is pumped into the atmosphere by motor-vehicles using fuels spiked with tetra-ethyl lead to raise the octane number, is now present in the Pacific—an area remote from those in which cars are mostly used—at about ten times the natural level, and comparable figures are being reported from many other sources. These levels have been rising ever since tetra-ethyl lead was first introduced 45 years ago; by the end of the century they may have doubled.

Again, the highly poisonous substance mercury is reaching the sea in ever increasing quantities. About half the world's total production reaches the oceans. Already the coastal waters of the Baltic Sea are polluted by it, and it is accumulating in the fish to the point where they are uneatable. Here I wish only to draw attention to the way we are changing the composition of the shallower parts of the sea—the parts where most of the fish live. And more than half the world's population depends solely on fish for a supply of essential protein.

Pesticides, such as DDT and dieldrin, are accumulating in the sea, as are various curious by-products of industry, whose very names are mysterious to all but the initiated—to take but a single example, the polychlorinated biphenyls.

The FAO points out that the combined effect of the numerous toxic substances working together may be far more harmful than tests of each one by itself would suggest. The implications could be serious, as I shall now show.

In addition to the invisible pollutants, there is so much assorted visible junk that Thor Heyerdahl, during his recent attempt to sail from Europe to America on a raft made of reeds, complained that he and his companions could not fill their toothmugs from the ocean, when they were hundreds of miles from the American coast, because of the filthy condition of the water.

Technological prophets tell us that well before the end of the century, the sea bed will be mined for ores, oil and other substances. Such factories will then be well placed to discharge their effluents directly into the ocean, instead of having to dilute them by river transport as now, a most efficient arrangement.

An even more serious threat may be that offered by radio-active wastes. Already it is the case that radio-activity can be detected in any fifty-gallon sample of sea water taken anywhere in the world. E. D. Goldberg told the AAAS meeting in 1968: 'Radio-active substances are found in all oceans and all organisms in the marine biosphere.' The United States Atomic Energy Commission has been mixing low-level wastes with cement in 18-gauge steel drums (little more than cans) and dropping them in the Atlantic. Recently Spain complained of such dumping taking place only 200 miles from the Spanish and Portuguese coastline. The British, more economically, run a pipeline a mere two miles out to sea and claim that it is safe to discharge up to 100,000 curies a month by this means. (As I argue in a later chapter, such reassurances are based on wholly unrealistic assumptions.)

The US Atomic Energy Commission justifies dumping in deep ocean water on the grounds that there is little or no mixing of the deeper water with the shallower waters in which fish, crustaceans and plankton live. Our knowledge of ocean movements is far too slight and based on much too short a period of investigation to justify claiming that no mixing will take place in a century or more. In such a period, who knows what unforeseeable natural disasters might not occur? A large meteorite might land in the oceans: meteorites have hit the earth often enough before; in 1908 a comet exploded over Siberia with such force that it blew flat every tree for 50 miles and the shock was registered on seismographs all round the world. Or again, underwater volcanoes might erupt. And apart from such infrequent risks, the Lamont Geological Observatory has very recently announced, on the basis of a recent voyage by its research vessel, that much more mixing does occur in the ocean than was formerly thought.

To add to the comedy, it is now seriously proposed that mining and other industrial operations shall be undertaken on the ocean bed where the effluents and 'tailings' can be pumped directly into the sea. Among other things, there are rich supplies of manganese there, and as we progressively exhaust our resources of coal, oil and natural gas, we shall have to look ever more intensively beneath the sea for new supplies. Apart from the fact that the underwater workers may be exposed to radiation as a result of our casual attitude to radio-active waste disposal, the heat developed in mixing operations will warm the circumjacent water which will then rise and ensure the mixing of deep and surface waters.

Nor do we know enough about sideways movements of the water, though we do know that deep ocean currents, moving very slowly, return the water carried in a contrary direction by surface currents like the Gulf Stream, the Peru Current, the North Atlantic Drift, the West Wind drift, the Equatorial Currents and so on. This no doubt explains the astonishing but little publicized fact that some of the steel drums containing broken test tubes and other laboratory junk dumped in the Atlantic by the AEC were later trawled up by startled fishermen off the coast of Oregon! By what route they had travelled from the Atlantic to the Pacific remains a nagging mystery.

As if this were not enough, in 1969 a rather thorough study made by Dr V. T. Bowen of Woods Hole Oceanographic Institute showed that radionuclides falling from the atmosphere after nuclear explosions penetrate the ocean depths 'much faster than had been predicted', at least in the North Atlantic.

Roger Revelle (formerly the director of the Scripps Institute of Oceanography) and M. B. Schaeffer claim that no less than 1,000 tons of fission products could be deposited in the deep oceans 'without serious danger'—though they do not say how much danger they regard as unserious—provided that the radio-active material remains on the sea bed for 300 years. They feel that we can bank on it staying down there this long, as they believe that it takes 1,000 years for the deep water in the Pacific to be replaced completely and 500 years for that in the Atlantic. However, I note that these comforting figures are arrived at by calculating the rate of surface evaporation; they do not allow for any mixing by thermal means.

The radio-active wastes accumulated by the year 2000 will, of course, greatly exceed 1,000 tons. (In the Pacific a mere half-ton released in a nuclear test caused marginal problems over one million square miles.) Even if there is no risk to man, it is obvious that there will be a risk of ecological damage: indeed Revelle and Schaeffer admit that much of the radio-activity which they claim would not involve 'serious danger' would enter food-chains.

It is often forgotten that, in addition to plankton, crustacea and fish, the ocean supports seaweeds, some of which are of industrial importance. The agar jelly which scientists use to support bacterial cultures is derived from seaweed: if it were radio-active it would be useless. Strangely enough, it turns out that sodium alginate, derived from seaweed, is able to purge strontium-90 from human and animal skeletons, while leaving the calcium in place. It would be ironical if, as a result of peacetime carelessness about radio-active wastes, we destroyed the only thing which could save lives imperilled by fall-out from nuclear weapons employed in war. Nor need we suppose that the kelp might be eliminated simply by direct absorption of radio-activity. For the kelp forests off the coast of California have been degenerating for a quarter of a century as a result of a population explosion among sea-urchins, which feed on kelp. The reason for the explosion is unknown, though it seems clear that it is not due to sewage outfalls. The workings of radio-active materials in sea creatures are still mysterious. Thus 'hot' clams were found in the Pacific two years after atomic tests—but their radio-activity was due to cobalt-60, a substance not produced in such explosions. The transformation which gave rise to it remains unexplained.

G. G. Polykarpov, a Russian scientist, has shown that quite low levels of radio-activity (0.2 microcuries) seriously affect the development of eggs of various species of fishes, causing developmental errors. Polykarpov makes no bones about the implications: '... further contamination of sea water is inadmissible.'

Discussion of ocean pollution would be quite incomplete without reference to a much more immediately alarming pollutant: fuel oil.

WHIFF OF OIL

Fred Singer, who, as assistant secretary at the Department of the Interior, is concerned with pollution, has calculated that the worldwide spillage of oil from ships, tankers and oil rigs amounts to about a million tons a year. But to this we have to add another million tons of waste motor oil, ten million tons of gasoline which has evaporated and which is eventually deposited in the seas, plus a million tons of assorted solvents, making some 13 million tons of this pollutant in all. Oil is, in some ways, the most damaging of all the half million pollutants we put in the sea, since it floats on the surface and is not diluted—until bacteria have managed to break it up. It also changes the evaporation rate and cuts off light and air from the sea below it, rendering the area uninhabitable; tars, of course, are even more persistent.

Crude oil is a complex mixture of products. The aromatic hydrocarbons are known to be acute poisons for man as well as for all other organisms. It was one of the tragedies of the *Torrey Canyon* oil-spill disaster that the detergents used by the British to disperse the oil had been dissolved in low-boiling-point aromatics—which multiplied the damage to marine creatures. The group of hydrocarbons which have low boiling points have until recently been regarded as harmless to the marine environment. But it has now been demonstrated that these hydrocarbons, even at low concentrations, produce anaesthesia and narcosis, and at greater concentration cell damage and death, in a wide variety of lower animals, and that they may be especially damaging to larval and other young forms of marine life.

Max Blumer, a senior scientist at the Woods Hole Oceanographic Institution, believes that the long-term effects of low concentrations of oil may be even more damaging and long-lasting than the obvious short-term ones. Many predatory fish find their prey by their sense of smell, while others escape predators by the same means; migratory fish certainly home by a fantastically delicate analysis of the smell of a particular body of water. The amounts of substances detected by olfactory means are incredibly small, a few parts per billion of water. The presence of oil and its associated aromatic fractions completely masks such smells—a thing as serious for the fish as being blinded would be to a man. The fish may also be misled by false cues. 'This', says Blumer, 'may have a disastrous effect on the survival of any marine species and on many other species to which it is tied by the food chain.'

Futhermore, we know little about the effect of oil on the creatures which inhabit the sea bottom. In the ordinary way, oil sinks very slowly, but the use of chalk to sink oil spills is often regarded as better than using detergents. We do not know whether the oil stays where it is sunk, but we do know that it will continue to exist for a long time before bacteria finally consume it. As man exhausts landward oil supplies, he will turn increasingly to under-sea sources, so that leaks (like that which caused disaster at Santa Barbara and which continues to flow) will become steadily commoner. Comments Blumer: 'If we do not take care of the present biological resources in the sea, we may do irreversible damage to many marine organisms, to the marine food chain, and we may eventually destroy the yield and the value of the food which we hope to recover from the sea.'

Blumer's complaint was sparked by a cruise of the Woods Hole Research Vessel *Chain* to the southern Sargasso Sea. The special nets which were towed to retrieve surface creatures always came up containing numerous lumps of oil-tar as large as tennis balls. After 3 or 4 hours of towing, the nets were so encrusted with oil that they had to be cleaned with a strong solvent, and sometimes tows had to be cut short for this reason. It was estimated that there was three times as much tar as there was Sargasso weed in the nets.

The emulsifiers used to disperse oil spills only make matters worse for shore creatures, since they wet their surfaces and enable oil to penetrate them. Winkles have an inbuilt mechanism for escaping danger, which is to relax their hold and fall into a crevice or pool. Unhappily, when there is oil pollution, this is just what not to do. Detergents disperse the oil over the beaches and into the rock pools, and instead of floating on the surface it becomes dispersed throughout the water, choking the starfish, seaweeds and shallow-water organisms which would otherwise have escaped. Many types of sea-creature of the kind known as gastropods hatch their young under stones on the shore or in the masses of jelly on the surface of seaweeds. Thus they suffer badly from an oil spill and may never recover.

When the *Torrey Canyon* ran aground, it was 15 miles from the shore, and the bulk of the oil was lost in the Bay of Biscay: it was detected 250 miles from Land's End. At this point the ocean deepens rapidly and it vanished. What would happen if a whole tanker load arrived on a single shore, or, worse, was spilled in an enclosed area like the Milford Haven estuary, beggars the imagination.

Dr A. Nelson Smith of University College of Swansea, who makes this comment, has studied the Milford Haven estuary, where there have been three major spills since it was opened as an oil port some 10 years ago. He found that many molluscs were totally eliminated in some areas, and decimated in others. When he returned after nine months, some species were showing recovery but others had gone further downhill. 'Most of the seaweeds of the upper shore were simply no longer there,' he says. The few large plants which could be seen 'were dry, blackened and obviously dead.'

The effect on sea birds is too well known to need describing. And as Lt.-Col. C. L. Boyle has said: 'The chances of a seriously-oiled bird making a complete recovery are still meagre.' The birds brought to the Slimbridge Bird Sanctuary after the *Torrey Canyon* incident died of enteritis, stress and pulmonary conditions, and many developed acute arthritis.

With the opening up of a north-west passage to the north shore of Alaska, where a huge new oilfield has been found, no doubt some of the ecologically most serious spills of the next thirty years will be in this area. It is substantially closed in by islands—it has even been argued by the Canadians that it should be regarded as inland territorial water. Spills will therefore be unable to disperse and will necessarily drift aground on islands and peninsulas, which are among the few large untouched habitats remaining on the planet. Already, during the exploratory voyages in 1969, two vessels have been crushed in the ice and oil has been spilled.

In theory, a system of control of oil pollution exists. The International Convention for the Prevention of the Pollution of the Sea by Oil, set up in 1954 and amended in 1962, attempts this. The body which administers the convention is the Inter-Governmental Maritime Consultative Organization and in 1969 it held conferences aimed at making control less ineffective: it urged governments to impose stiffer penalties and take other steps to reduce oil pollution. But governments are slow to fetter the freedom of oil companies, as everyone knows, and pollution is increasing rather than declining.

When the FAO discussed ocean pollution early in 1969, Dr Sidney I. Holt, of the FAO staff, sadly observed: 'Pollutants are increasing almost faster than our ability to get information on them.' So alarming was the situation revealed at this conference that the FAO has summoned another, more technical, meeting at which experts will pool their information as to the effects of marine pollution on living resources and on how to deal with the situation. The meeting is called for December 1970 and a hoped-for result is the establishment of a world monitoring system to spot pollution as it occurs and to give more precision to the scope of the problem.

As Dr Jack Pearce, a marine biologist from the Stony

Brook Marine Laboratory on Long Island, put it: 'Science cannot solve the problem.... It's time to introduce a subjective element—to speak out and say we need control—now!'

OXYGEN CRISIS

The late Dr Lloyd Berkner was a scientist of unusually broad qualifications. From being a radar engineer he passed to terrestrial magnetism and so to geophysics. He was for a time chairman of the President's Scientific Advisory Committee and also of the International Scientific Steering Committee. He won awards and honorary degrees from Britain, Sweden, India and countries round the world. At the time of his death in 1967 he was president of the Graduate Research Center of the South-West. Hardly the sort of man, one can be sure, to start a scare story for reasons of self-advertisement.

Yet in 1966, a few months before his death, he wrote a paper for the Population Reference Bureau drawing attention to the fact that the world's supply of oxygen comes largely from the diatoms, the small free-floating plants which form the basic food of most fish. Earth's oxygen would be used up in 2,000 years if not replenished by the photosynthetic activities of plants—that is, the process by which they make sugars from carbon dioxide and water in the atmosphere, a reaction powered by sunlight, giving off oxygen which they have split from the carbon dioxide. Seventy per cent of the new oxygen comes from diatoms, the rest from land vegetation. 'But if our pesticides should be reducing our supply of diatoms or forcing evolution of less productive mutants,' he pointed out, 'we *might find ourselves running out of oxygen.*' (The italics are Berkner's, not mine.) Since we know that fish are loaded with pesticides, it is absolutely certain that the diatoms are also, for this is how they get into the fish.

As scientists absorbed this shattering notion, it was pointed out that herbicides are effective at destroying phytoplankton, and a little calculation suggested that it would take the shipwreck of only three tankers the size of the *Torry Canyon* containing herbicide to produce a catastrophe of this magnitude. At present, to be sure, we do not move herbicides around the world on such a large scale, though rather large quantities have in fact been sent to Vietnam to defoliate the jungle. By the end of the century, when desperate attempts to meet the world's food needs may be in train, the transport of large quantities of herbicides may not be so unusual, while in the case of war, both the motive to transport herbicides and the desire to sink tankers would be operative.

However, it was not the risk of herbicidal action but of pesticides like DDT to which Berkner pointed. Just two years after Berkner's death, Charles Wurster, Jr., of State University of New York at Stony Brook, demonstrated that DDT does in fact impede the photosynthesis of plankton. And in spring 1970, marine biologists meeting in Edinburgh reported ominously that the numbers of a dozen species of plankton in the Atlantic have been declining for the last twenty years.

We are destroying oxygen today in far larger quantities than the world has ever seen. Every motor vehicle consumes oxygen. So do motorboats and snowmobiles. Every aircraft consumes still larger quantities: a 707 jet burns 35 tons of oxygen every time it crosses the Atlantic, and there are 3,000 jets in the air, around the world, at any one time. That's about 16 million tons of oxygen lost a year—and air travel is expected to grow steadily: the new 747's consume about half as much again. The oxygen demand of aircraft is expected to grow ten times by AD 2000. In addition, of course, every factory furnace consumes oxygen, as does every burning waste-dump and forest fire. The natural cycles of the ecosphere were evolved to cope with the oxygen demands of plants and animals—not with burdens like these.

At the same time we are cutting down the forests which provide most of the landward oxygen and replacing them with grass and cereals which provide far less, or asphalting and concreting over the land surface so that it provides none. It is reckoned that the United States now produces only 60 per cent of the oxygen which it consumes—for Britain the figure must be far lower—and relies on oxygen created largely in the Pacific by plankton for replenishment. In cities, the excess of consumption over production of oxygen is so marked that lowered oxygen levels can actually be demonstrated. In Los Angeles, for instance, oxygen is permanently about 6 per cent below the level in the surrounding country. Apart from longer-term effects, this already puts a strain on infants and anyone else suffering from respiratory defects and boosts the load on shaky hearts which may be near their working limits. In other industrialized countries, notably Japan, the position is similar.

Dr J. Lovelock, a British advisor to the National Aeronautics and Space Administration, calculates that the burning of fossil fuel—coal and oil—already absorbs 15 per cent of the biological production of oxygen. At the present industrial growth rate, he says, 'in three or four decades, fossil fuel burning may be the major sink of oxygen. We cannot be certain that the ecosystem will maintain a status quo favourable to us in the face of so large a perturbation.' And he adds the warning, 'Oxygen is only one of several atmospheric components similarly affected by industrial activity.'

We take oxygen so much for granted, that we do not stop to think that it exists only because of a slight mismatch in the amount created by plants and the amount absorbed by oxidation processes such as the formation of carbon dioxide and other oxides. Francis Johnson calculates this difference as being only one part in 10,000: thus a trifling perturbation of the balance could mean disaster.

He makes an additional point: 'A few ocean areas with anoxic bottom conditions and a few marshy areas in which peat is forming, are presumably the key-areas for maintaining our oxygen replenishment on a long-term basis. These limited areas are at least as susceptible to poisoning as are the open oceans. It is a matter of importance to man's future to recognize and preserve these areas.'

By the year 2000, with trebled or quadrupled ground and air traffic, and rather extensive deforestation, the safety margins on oxygen could be very narrow; in these circumstances, damage to plankton by pesticides or herbicides would not have to be very extensive to reduce man to his last gasp.

If all life were to be eliminated, the remaining oxygen in the air would steadily be removed, for there are non-biological processes which would combine it with the nitrogen as nitrogen oxides or nitrates, and with methane or marsh gas, while rocks exposed by weathering would also tend to lock up oxygen as oxides. 'The oxygen would eventually stabilize at some low level, due to its equilibrium between its production by water photolysis—the disruption of water by light energy—and the processes just listed.' Thus the earth's atmosphere would slowly revert to its primitive state in which oxygen-using life forms cannot exist, so that recolonization would be impossible except via the aeon-long processes by which life originated.

This provides an instance of the fact, so little realized, that life provides the environment it needs. Hence, any man-made change in that environment must automatically be, in some degree, unfavourable to life. It is a truth to which I shall return again and again.

Berkner's paper, which was entitled 'Truth and Consequences in a New Era', stressed that he only cited this possibility as 'simply one of many examples of how increasing populations might so pollute our economy that we would be brought to a sharp halt.' He continued by pointing out that our very attempts to grow food might be brought to a sudden halt because they would cause such ecological damage as to disrupt the very process they were intended to expand. With this aspect of the problem I shall deal in another chapter. Meantime, let me cite only Berkner's conclusion, that people will not change their ancient habits and beliefs unless they are moved by an irresistible force. 'I just fear that the only force will be hunger, disease, brutality and death. And when that time arrives, the ultimate catastrophe is upon us.'

In short, the basic significance of what we loosely call 'pollution' is not that it affects human health or looks terrible, important as these aspects are; it is that it imposes stresses on the delicate system of balances which we have been exploring—that is, on the entire set of planetary eco-systems, which we can call, for short, the ecosphere.

Thus the pollution problem about which Berkner tried to warn us deserves quite detailed treatment, especially since several new types of contamination are beginning to become noticeable and will unquestionably emerge as serious problems before the end of the century. But I warn you it is a horror story.

6 The New Look in Pollutants

THE GREY FLUFFY FIBRES of asbestos look innocent enough, as you crumble them in your hand. Asbestos is the stuff you make theatre fire-curtains of, and pads you can place your iron on when ironing. However, it is around us in myriad forms, insulating heating pipes, packing soundproof walls, used as filters in the making of beer, medicines and fruit-drinks, in conveyor belting and safety clothing, and a million other places. It is sprayed on electrical equipment, used as roofing, and embodied in floor-tiles. (In fact, floor-tile makers are the second largest users of this mineral.) And, above all, it forms the brake-linings of cars. Every train, car, plane, ship, missile, tank, tractor and truck contains asbestos somewhere in its construction. World consumption, which in 1910 was 30,000 tons, is now 4 million tons and rising. The USA alone imports nearly a million tons.

Nevertheless asbestos turns out to constitute a deadly threat to man. The story is worth telling in some detail because it illustrates in an unusually clear manner our amazing unwillingness to take action until tragic and extensive harm has been wrought.

Asbestos was first mined commercially near Quebec, as recently as 1789. In 1890 an asbestos weaving mill was established near Calvados in Normandy: fifty of the employees died during the first five years of operation. But before this fact came to light, a doctor in Charing Cross Hospital, London, Dr H. Montague Murray, observed the connection between exposure to asbestos and lung disease. He performed a post-mortem on a man who had died at 33, after working in the carding room of an asbestos-cloth making factory.

There had been ten men in the carding room: the other nine were already dead.

Neither Murray nor Auribault, the French factory inspector who reported on the Calvados experience, realized the massive significance of what they had found. It was not until 1924 that asbestosis was distinguished from pneumoconiosis, when Dr W. E. Cooke performed a post-mortem on a 33-year-old woman who had developed signs of lung trouble after 13 years' exposure, having started work at 13.

Now people started to investigate asbestos workers in earnest, among them Dr E. R. A. Mereweather, a medical inspector for the Home Office, who found that more than 25 per cent of the 363 men and women he examined showed signs of the disease. He also noticed that the longer that they had been at this work, the more severe the symptoms were. In 1931, asbestosis was at last recognized by Parliament as an industrial disease, for which compensation would be paid. But the story has several chapters yet.

When new drugs were introduced which cut the death-rate from infectious diseases, the victims of asbestosis survived longer—but developed cancer! Though this was spotted in 1935, it was not until 1949 that Dr Mereweather, who had now become Chief Inspector of Factories, felt ready to publish the review of data, from 1924 to 1946, which he had made. His figures showed that about 13 per cent of asbestos workers died of lung cancer, when the rate in the general population was only 1 per cent. But, as the cigarette manufacturers so often remind us, an association does not prove cause and effect, and Mereweather, anxious not to rock the boat, did not even formally claim an association. It was not until 1955 that the leading British medical statistician, Dr Richard Doll, published a study, based on 113 consecutive autopsies, which really convinced everyone that asbestos *caused* cancer. He showed that men who had worked more than 20 years in asbestos factories were eleven times as likely to get lung cancer as the rest of the population.

That was 15 years ago, and the story does not stop there. The scene now moves to South Africa, where a pathologist called J. Christopher Wagner found himself diagnosing no fewer than sixteen cases of a cancer so rare that most doctors meet it but once in a lifetime. Mesothelioma, as it is known, is a cancer of the membrane which surrounds the lung, the pleura, or that which lines the body cavity, the peritoneum. None of the victims had ever worked in the asbestos industry, but the first one examined had 'asbestos bodies' in his lungs. Checking on the others revealed that ten had come from an asbestos-mining district. Then Wagner got a mesothelioma patient who was the son of a mine manager and who had played on the asbestos dumps as a child. A mesothelioma hunt was launched and turned up eighty-nine cases—all came from the dusty asbestos-mining area. One, a woman who was born in this area but left it at the age of five, revealed that as a child she had enjoyed sliding down the asbestos dumps with her school friends. Two of these had already died of mesothelioma. Another patient had been exposed only up to the age of weaning, but developed the disease.

ASBESTOS AS A POLLUTANT

This put a completely new complexion on the matter: from being an occupational disease, it now emerged that the entire general public were at risk. Asbestos was a pollutant. Furthermore, exposures much smaller than would cause asbestosis, would, and do, cause cancer. It had long been known that asbestos fibres in the lungs may become coated with a yellow brown substance. These 'asbestos bodies' are numerous in the lungs of asbestos workers. Soon after this, another South African pathologist, Professor J. G. Thompson, stunned the medical world by finding 'asbestos bodies' in the lungs of people who were *not* asbestos workers. No less than 26 per cent of 500 consecutive specimens from Cape Town which he examined, bore them. Asbestos was now so prevalent in the environment that *anyone* could become affected, Thompson realized. As he pointed out, the average car goes through about four sets of brake linings and a couple of clutch linings in the course of its life. To this can be added increasing use of asbestos in many other spheres; and the particles, once inhaled, never dissolve or decay. Thompson predicted—and you who read this may see his prediction come true—that asbestos lung cancer will before long rival lung cancer from cigarette smoking as a cause of death.

One might imagine that, at this point, some government, somewhere, would have felt moved to take preventive ac-

tion. Or that asbestos manufacturers, who had notably failed
to pursue the problem up to this point, might now begin to
support intensive research. But no.

A wave of studies all over Europe and the US was now
launched and confirmed and reconfirmed the appalling diagnosis. Women who had washed the clothes of their asbestos-
miner husbands. . . . Women who had brushed their husbands
down after work. . . . A house-owner who had mixed and
applied asbestos cement to the boiler in her house. . . . A boy
who had helped his father saw up asbestos wallboard. . . . A
cheese-maker, whose 500-gallon vats were covered with flaky
asbestos. . . . All died of mesothelioma, the once-rare tumour.
This was the death-substance, a piece of fall-out from science
fiction. A powder so deadly that a saltspoonful could kill
you—after a lag of 20 years.

Did governments now act? No.

One of those who had become sucked into this drama,
quite as extraordinary as the threats from outer space which
were becoming current fare on television, was Dr I. J.
Selikoff, of Mount Sinai Hospital, New York. He, too, was
unconvinced—until seventeen patients, all of whom had
worked for an asbestos factory from 1940 until it closed in
1954, came to him with lung trouble. Today, eleven of them
are dead, all from asbestosis or cancers of one kind or
another; several of those still alive show signs of cancer or
fibrosis.

'I was forced', he says, 'to the awful realization of what
could happen to men who were occupationally exposed to
asbestos.' He approached several manufacturers for data;
they refused to co-operate. He, with another doctor, approached the US Public Health Service for funds for investigation. Request denied. So he went to the Asbestos Workers
Union, and brought in Dr Cuyler Hammond, a statistician of
unimpeachable standing who had investigated the cigarette-
lung-cancer question and the medical aftermath of the Hiroshima and Nagasaki explosions. The figures the union supplied revealed that, of 632 men who had been in this trade
from 1942, 45 had died from cancer of the lung, pleura, or
trachea (throat), where six or seven were to be expected.
Twenty-nine died from intestinal cancers, nine or ten were
expected. Further studies, supported by the Health Research
Council showed that those who smoked cigarettes regularly

were *ninety-two times* more likely to die of lung cancer than people who neither work in the asbestos industry, nor smoke. The figure is not exact—a larger sample may shift the ratio a little either way—but it is near enough. In 1968, Dr. Selikoff told a subcommittee of the House of Representatives that, if nothing is done, 'we may look forward to perhaps 6,000 deaths from lung cancer and to perhaps 15,000 deaths from cancer in general, among men in this single asbestos trade alone.' Since this union comprises 18,000 men, while there is a similar number not unionized, this is not something you can brush under the carpet. The battle is, at last, officially recognized.

Doctors are beginning to look narrowly at the ways in which asbestos is used. Is it really a good idea to filter beer and soft drinks through it? Surgeons have been sprinkling powdered asbestos on wounds in a belief that this may promote healing. Asbestos is used to make imitation snow: the powdered form of asbestos is of course the easiest to breathe in. Asbestos powder mixed with water is even given to children, in some schools, as play-dough.

There are scores of heart-rending, absorbing individual stories here, and much research is being done which I have no space to describe. One day someone will write a book about the asbestos story, and it will be a best-seller. I have only gone this deep into the subject because I am determined to make the point that we practically never take action in good time. We always believe the soothing words. Back in 1906, when Dr Murray testified to a Committee on Compensation for Industrial Disease, did it call for action? It said 'one hears, generally speaking, that considerable trouble is now taken to prevent the inhalation of dust, and so the disease is not so likely to occur as heretofore.' In 1930, the Home Office Report to Parliament said, soothingly: 'In the space of a decade, or thereabouts, the effect of energetic application of preventive measures should be apparent in a great reduction in the incidence of fibrosis.' Dr Selikoff, speaking at a Symposium on Unanticipated Environmental Hazards, acidly remarked, 'I do not know if it is entirely appropriate to consider our current problems with asbestos an "*unanticipated* environmental hazard". As I look back, it would seem that we should have had some premonition.'

So when you read, in the pages which follow, briefer

accounts of some other 'unanticipated hazards' about each of which soothing words have been and will be said, remember that official reassurances are often painfully unreliable. One thing you can bet on—asbestos is going to be in the headlines from now on. Five per cent of the US employed population works in shipbuilding or constructional industries: 99 per cent drive cars or walk in streets where cars are driven. Who knows what the cancer/asbestosis rate will climb to? Who will be the first to take decisive action?

DDT: THE STATE OF PLAY

It was 1963 when Rachel Carson's *Silent Spring* burst upon the world. In it she indicted the new pesticides, and in particular DDT, for the effect they were having on birds and other forms of animal life. At the time she was told, in outspoken words, that she was making a fuss about practically nothing. Her whole thesis was attacked as unscientific. Now, seven years later, there is pretty general recognition that the danger was a real one, and several governments, among them the USA and the UK, have taken steps to limit the use of the organochlorine pesticides, as the group which contains DDT is called. (Sweden's one-year total ban was imposed in order to reveal how much of the DDT contamination was arriving on the wind from other countries, and how much was produced by Swedish use of the substance.)

But there are indications that the DDT story, like the asbestos story, is a serial and there may be several chapters still untold. However tough DDT may be for birds and small mammals, says the petro-chemical industry, it has never yet killed a human being. That is certainly untrue, as I shall show, added to which there are risks to health which, though not lethal, may be sufficiently serious. Among them is the effect on fertility.

Meanwhile, it has become apparent that DDT has become the most abundant pollutant in the global ecosystem. Scientists were shocked when it was found that DDT was present in the fat of Arctic seals and penguins, at a distance of 50 miles from the McMurdo Sound research station—presumably from the wastes thrown out by the personnel there. But a more recent study suggests that there are thousands of tons of DDT in Antarctic snow, which must have reached it from the air. DDT was recently identified high in the air over Barbados and is found as high as 21,000 feet over India.

Because DDT persists in the body, any new intake is simply piled on top of the existing burden; hence a treatment which causes no harm the first time it is used may cause serious harm if it is applied year after year. Persistence also allows the DDT to undergo 'biological concentration'. Thus the plankton of the ocean—the invisibly small organisms on which fish feed—absorb one part per million, the fish that live on the plankton will slowly build up 10 ppm or more in the tissues. If bigger fish eat the small fish, this will concentrate it further, and they will end up with 100 ppm or more in their tissues. If man now eats the predator fish, a further concentration takes place, perhaps to 1,000 ppm—depending on how much fish he eats and whether there is DDT in other items of his diet. Since for about half the world fish is almost the only source of protein, this can be serious. Eskimos depend largely on fish, as do the peoples of many Pacific islands, fishing communities in North Borneo and so on. A sequence, such as plankton–fish–predator–man, is known as a food chain. Another food chain, which we shall meet in the next chapter, is algae–insects–birds–man.

It is the existence of biological magnification which makes it almost impossible to define a safe level of treatment of crops or trees.

DDT persists in many unexpected places, for instance in the organic detritus such as leaf-mould or the rich silt in slow-moving rivers. In 1969, Charles Wurster and various associates tried the experiment of feeding detritus containing 10 ppm of DDT to fiddler crabs. After only 10 days of this diet the crabs' behaviour became unco-ordinated and sluggish. Killed, they proved to have trebled their DDT levels in this short period. This doubtless explains why these crabs vanished 10 years ago from such areas as the Carmans River marshes.

Entomologists at the University of Maine, trying to find out how long contamination persists after forests are sprayed with DDT, looked at the small creatures living in the northern Maine forests which had been sprayed for spruce budworm. The areas they examined had been sprayed once only either in the year 1958, or in 1960, 1963, 1964 or 1967.

This enabled them to measure DDT levels at various periods of time after spraying. Shrews, which are carnivorous, and therefore concentrate the DDT more, started with levels of nearly 16 ppm, which fell away to 1 ppm after 8 or 9 years. However, the figure of 16 is an average; some shrews had over 40 ppm, others as little as 0.25 ppm. Since 30 ppm is known to be a toxic level in birds, it is a good guess that a large number of shrews died and just weren't there for the investigators to examine. They reckoned that while the herbivores had got back to pre-treatment levels by the end of the period, the carnivores would take 15 years to do so. Since shrews don't live that long, several generations would be required.

If this was what happened when a forest was sprayed once only, it is obvious that where areas are sprayed repeatedly many carnivores will rapidly become extinct and even the herbivores will be affected.

In the body, it should be explained, DDT tends to convert into similar substances known as DDE and DDD, the three being known in scientific parlance as 'DDT and its metabolites'. In general DDE is as undesirable as DDT, while DDD is, at least in some cases, less toxic. In what follows, where DDT is mentioned, the culprit at the site of the trouble is often DDE.

In Rachel Carson's day it was thought that DDT either killed you, by interfering in some way with the brain and nerves, or it didn't. Then it emerged that DDT was reducing bird populations because it did something to their ability to manufacture shells for their eggs.

In the past 15 years there have been great population collapses among many species of carnivorous birds, notably the peregrine falcon. But many others have been affected: for instance there was an almost total failure of reproduction of the brown pelican in California in 1969. Their eggs just caved in.

Examining birds' eggs in museums for 50 years back showed a pretty uniform thickness up to the late 1940's, then a sudden reduction. It also turned out that the amount of DDE in the egg was beautifully correlated with thickness, but inversely; that is, the more DDE the thinner the shell. As I write, comes the news that Lucille Stickel, of the Patuxent Wildlife Research Center, has been feeding DDT and its metabolites to mallards at 3 ppm. Not only were the shells 13.5 per cent thinner than normal, but six times as many eggs were cracked or broken, and fewer than *half* the expected number of ducklings survived. DDT and DDE were equally damaging, though DDD did not have this effect.

It was thought until quite recently that grain-eating birds were less affected, except perhaps where they were in the habit of eating seeds which had been predressed with dieldrin or similar pesticides. This conclusion was based on an experiment with quail back in the 1950's which had been fed as much as 200 ppm of DDT without apparent ill effect. Quail lay eggs all the year round and so are not entirely comparable with other birds—in any case it has just emerged that though the parents survive this dose all right, the offspring do not.

Actually 1969 was quite a black year for DDT manufacturers. It also emerged that DDT reduced the reproductive rate of fish, at levels equivalent to 1 ppm, which is about the level in the Coho salmon in the Great Lakes. Fed to brook trout, the parents survived but the fry died from the DDT accumulated in the egg yolk. Everybody was congratulating themselves that the attempt to restock Lake Erie was working, when considerable mortality of these salmon was reported and some stocks were condemned as unsuitable for human consumption. Risebrough showed that fish in the Pacific are carrying similar levels of DDT, which suggests that, all over the world, major marine fisheries may be nearing the point of collapse.

In the previous year, the newly-formed Environmental Defence Association in the US filed suit against the Michigan Department of Agriculture to prevent a proposed application of dieldrin, and against numerous Michigan municipalities which were still using DDT in an attempt to control Dutch elm disease. While the MDA was ruled immune from suit, injunctions were obtained against fifty-five municipalities. The Michigan Department of Natural Resources decided to take a stand against DDT, which led to prohibition of its use in Michigan. A further attempt to sue the MDA led only to a brief hearing. Finally two bodies, the Citizens' Natural Resources Association and the Izaak Walton League, found a means to bring the issue squarely before a judicial forum. They requested the Department of Natural Resources in

Madison, Wis., to rule whether or not DDT is a pollutant of the state's waters under the unique Wisconsin water pollution laws.

Backed by the EDA, and with the support of a Scientists' Advisory Committee with more than 200 members, it conducted a hassle which lasted almost six months. Industry set up a special task force to fight back. Some of the cross-examinations lasted three days. DDT, said one of the task force's witnesses, was 'completely harmless'. Another witness declared that opposition to DDT and pesticides came from people who were preoccupied with sexual potency. (It wouldn't be a bad reason, actually, as I shall shortly explain.) Others contented themselves with stressing how useful it was. The hearings were adjourned after 27 days of testimony from 32 witnesses.

While DDT is currently the central villain, we should not ignore the increasing sinister reports concerning dieldrin and aldrin, the terrible organophosphorus twins. In Britain, for instance, dieldrin and aldrin were placed under a voluntary ban in 1962. A voluntary ban means that farmers were asked not to use them as seed dressings unless they really felt they had to. In 1965 they were banned absolutely for some purposes, left voluntary for others. But in 1969 workers at the Monk's Wood Field Station reported on the strange behaviour of badgers in Britain. They were seen bumping into walls as if blind. They squealed frequently as if in pain and gnashed their jaws. Their muscular co-ordination was poor: they shambled about as if drunk. They were ravaged by thirst and lapped frantically at any liquid. Finally they went into convulsions and died.

Completely healthy badgers don't behave like that and the biologists suspected something must be amiss. Examining the corpses they found from 17 to 46 ppm of dieldrin in the liver, as well as up to 36 ppm of DDT derivatives. In contrast, badgers killed in road accidents carried a mere 0.446 ppm of dieldrin. The conclusion was inescapable: dieldrin is bad for badgers; the facts also suggested that the voluntary ban on the use of this delightful substance was not working very well. Three months later the Ministry of Agriculture, unimpressed, renewed the voluntary system for another year. Dieldrin may not be used against carrot fly but may be sprayed on potatoes to control wireworm; a variety of bulbs and seeds may be dipped in it.

DDT, SEX AND CANCER

When Rachel Carson wrote, not much was known about the effect of heavy loads of DDT in man. The classic case was that of a British laboratory worker who, in 1945 with the heroic curiosity of a Haldane, soaked his hands in water containing DDT for some minutes. Since nothing happened, he tried kneading an inert dough, to which some DDT had been added, for a few minutes with his hands. The results were described by Sir Vincent Wigglesworth:

> From one to ten days after, a feeling of heaviness and aching developed in all the limbs, with weakness in the legs. There was also what the subject described as 'spasms of extreme nervous tension'. There was some improvement during a holiday taken at this time; but, on returning to work, the condition deteriorated and some three weeks later the perpetual aching in the limbs confined the patient to bed. Sleep became almost impossible, the feeling of extreme nervous tension became more frequent and a state of acute mental anxiety developed. About six weeks after being confined to bed involuntary muscular tremors occurred over the whole body. After 10–14 days the patient got up, although the aching in his limbs was still severe. His recovery was very slow. He was away from work for 10 weeks in all, but even at the end of a year his recovery was not quite complete.

It did not strike either the man himself or the neurologist who treated him that the DDT he'd handled might be the cause of the trouble.

After this report, no one felt much like repeating the experiment. True, there was a spare-time gardener who collapsed and was found to have 23 ppm of DDT in his body-fat, thanks to over-enthusiastic use of pesticide on his little plot. And in 1959, a New Zealand doctor reported that an obese patient of his had developed signs of DDT poisoning after going on a slimming course. As he gradually worked off his fat, the DDT which had been sitting in it was left behind, concentrated in the remaining tissue. And at least one child died in convulsions from drinking some—one fluid ounce of 5 per cent DDT, to be exact.

The impressions given by these and by animal experiments was of a substance which acted on the brain, affecting the higher motor centres, perhaps through the cerebellum. DDT, we now know, does more: it stops the transmission of nerve impulses. And the effect is irreversible. Confusion, delusions, loss of memory, attacks of mania. . . . these are the symptoms of mental disease. DDT, it is not too much to say, can drive you mad, permanently.

But that is not all it can do.

In 1957, it was shown, to the astonishment of scientists, that DDT induces the formation of liver enzymes (substances regulating bodily processes), and these enzymes regulated the sex hormones oestrogen, progesterone and testosterone (progesterone is the key constituent of the contraceptive pill). Richard Welch of the Burroughs Welcome Co., who proved this point, stumbled on an even more startling fact: DDT can itself act like an active oestrogen. The reproductive failure which this evokes in birds could, at suitable doses, be evoked in man. DDT was thus not only a direct nerve poison, but had less obvious effects on fertility.

And as if this were not enough, it is now pretty clear that DDT is a carcinogen, or cancer-producing substance. As early as 1947, a study made by the American Food and Drug Administration showed that when DDT was fed to rats they suffered an increased rate of liver tumours, but the finding was quietly brushed under the carpet. At that time DDT was the wonder-weapon against malaria and no one wanted to hear an unkind word about it. Just twenty years later, an American team came up with the news that trout receiving DDT in their food displayed an unusual rate of liver tumours. Two years later—once more 1969 emerges as the critical year—Hungarian scientists reported the results of examining more than 1,000 mice, spread over five generations, all of whom had received 3 ppm of DDT in their diet. Nearly 29 per cent of these mice developed tumours, against fewer than 4 per cent of the mice on clean food. Moreover, the leukemia rate in the first group was five times that in the latter. By this time the prestigious National Cancer Institute had joined in the fun and, on the strength of a large-scale definitive study, reported quadrupled frequency of tumours in liver, lungs and lymph-glands. The cancers were of the same kind and at about the same frequency as those caused by known carcinogens. The conclusion was inescapable: DDT was carcinogenic to mice.

But this does not prove that it is carcinogenic in man, said the inveterate optimists. Well, you can't feed DDT to volunteers and see what happens, you can only examine people who didn't volunteer but ingested DDT anyway. So at Miami University School of Medicine, doctors made biopsies of human beings who had died of cancer and compared these with biopsies from an assortment of people who had met death by accident.

The DDT levels in the former were twice as high as in the latter. The accident victims carried some 10 ppm, which is average for Americans; the cancer victims had 20–25 ppm. Of course it was still possible to argue that cancer caused increased pesticide retention, and not that pesticides cause cancer. It was just possible. But the optimists began to look a little wan. (The figures also showed links with hypertension and cirrhosis of the liver.)

In October five pregnant or nursing American women, backed by the Environment Defence Fund, petitioned the Food and Drug Administration to lower the limit of permissible DDT in human food to zero—for the law says that human food may not contain carcinogens. That leaves the FDA holding the baby. Where does it leave the rest of us?

Americans are not fit for human consumption, since they average over 10 ppm of DDT in their body fat, double the amount permitted in food by the pure food laws. Nor is American mothers' milk free to cross state lines (except, of course, in the original container) for similar reasons. The Swedish ecologist G. Löfroth points out that people with such levels of DDT in their fat are actually consuming about one-tenth of what the UN agencies call 'acceptable intake'. He concludes that the maximum acceptable intake should be about one-twentieth of what is currently regarded as the danger level.

The British are rather more edible than Americans, with about 5 ppm of DDT, while the Swedes are little higher, around 7. But in Israel the figure rises to 19 ppm, and in India to a terrifying 29 ppm. Since these are averages, it must be concluded that some Indians at least are carrying 50 or 60 ppm of DDT, an amount which may well be lethal. It is sometimes asserted that no one has yet died from absorbing DDT: such figures indicate that this is almost certainly untrue. I predict that before long evidence of human mortality from DDT will be provided, and at a guess the place it will come from will be Israel, since in India autopsies are rare and deaths could occur without the cause being closely investigated.

Moreover, although the adult population consumes one-tenth the amount now reckoned dangerous, on the average, there are groups which take in much more, notably babies. Swedish human milk (according to the Swedish National Institute of Public Health) contains 0.117 ppm. This means that breast-fed babies consume 70 per cent above the permitted amount of DDT every day, English babies much the same, American babies quite a bit higher.

And the situation becomes more horrifying if we bring dieldrin into the picture. Löfroth calculates that 40 per cent of the babies in Sweden ingest at least twice the amount of DDT maximally acceptable, while a British scientist has shown that British breast-fed babies consume at least ten times the recommended maximum. Since Western Australians carry about three times the amount of dieldrin in their fat that the British do, their babies may be getting thirty times the maximum thought desirable.

It is estimated that about a million metric tons of DDT have been distributed around the world so far. Last year (1968) the US made about 114,000 tons, worth about $20m. and of this two-thirds was exported, much of it to countries with primitive or non-existent methods of regulating its application. The total level in the environment is higher than people imagine, because the levels found in animals and man only reflect the current position. Even if all DDT manufacture were stopped overnight, the DDT in man would continue to rise for several years, as he absorbed more and more from his environment.

Let us supplement these generalities with a few specifics, and for various good reasons let us consider the Baltic Sea. Swedish soil now carries some 1,250 tons of DDT; it is found even in areas which have not been treated with DDT—the bulk of it is in the rural areas where food is grown. From the land the pesticides are washed or blown into the sea. The Baltic is now 'grossly polluted'. A survey of DDT levels in Baltic creatures published late in 1969 showed that one seal

had as much as 56 ppm of DDT in its body fat. The DDT
levels in guillemot eggs were ten times those in the eggs of
British guillemots. The levels in seals were ten times those in
British seals or Canadian seals. Worse still was the case of
the white-tailed eagle, now dying out. Of ten pairs in the
Stockholm archipelago only two pairs succeeded in breeding
last year. By way of experiment, DDT was fed to bald eagles
until they died: they proved to have 56 ppm of DDT in their
fatty tissue. Two dead white-tailed eagles which were recovered contained a staggering 190 and 230 ppm in their pectoral muscles. A seal was found with an even more staggering
310 ppm. They also contained mercury and a substance
called PCB, to which we shall come in a moment.

The Baltic is a shallow sea, the gateway to which is only
18 metres deep. Biological activity is low because temperatures are low: much of it is iced over in winter. The water
sits in layers, mixing very little. The central parts are devoid
of oxygen and devoid of life. High levels of hydrogen sul-
phide make life doubly impossible. Thus the Baltic provides
the paradigm which other bodies of water are due to follow.
Is it any wonder if Löfroth asks despairingly: 'There is at
least the possibility of a human tragedy of global proportions
occurring if our present practices continue unrestrained.
Must we demand the evidence of catastrophe before we act?'

By way of a coda to all this, comes a report from Britain's
Association of Public Analysts. They say that lard now contains a higher proportion of pesticide residues than any other
food they tested. Next worst, were apples, brassicas (i.e.
cabbage, brussels sprouts, etc.) and potatoes, all of which
exceeded the recommended limits. The survey, supported by
233 local authorities, continues.

I imagine that the next few years will see a progressive
tightening of controls on DDT, dieldrin and similar substances, with the western countries making these controls
fairly effective and many underdeveloped countries paying
lip-service but taking very little in the way of effective measures to ensure the rules are obeyed. Already in the US consumption in 1967 had fallen to half that in 1959.

Ways will be found to get DDT out of the systems of
people who have absorbed it. Preliminary studies at the
University of Miami indicate that phenobarbital and a substance used to control epilepsy, selling under the name of

Dilantin, may have the effect of removing DDT from the body. Dr John E. Davis found that people taking these drugs had low or zero levels of DDT in fat. Whether they can remove it from the brain is another question.

BIOLOGICAL CONTROLS

The best hope lies in the use of biological methods of control of pests, and these may be forced on us by the increasing development of resistance to organochlorines in insects. The Anopheles mosquito, which carries malaria, is now completely resistant to DDT, while the protozoon which also acts as host to the malaria bug during part of its life is becoming resistant to anti-malarials. The outbreak of plague in Vietnam was due to the fact that the local fleas have become resistant to pesticides. Some insects not only adapt to DDT but become addicted to it and can be fought by depriving them of DDT!

Here is an expert opinion: 'In general the synthetic organic pesticides are ecologically crude and engender serious problems: resurgence of target pests, outbreaks of non-target species, and pest-resistance to pesticides. These have contributed to a steady increase in the use of pesticides in recent years. For example, in California pest-control costs, for two of its major crops—citrus and cotton—have risen sharply over the past decade. A critical analysis nationwide would reveal a similar pattern: bollworms in Texas cotton, spider mites in deciduous fruit orchards, cabbage loopers in vegetable crops and so forth.' That was the voice of Robert van den Bosch of the Division of Biological Control at the University of California at Albany, Calif. Van den Bosch used to consider DDT less harmful than its alternatives. After the evidence presented at the first Rochester Conference on Toxicity in 1968 he reversed his opinion, he now holds that the use of organochlorines should be cut down and eventually stopped altogether. 'The chemical alternatives to DDT are disturbing,' he says, 'but until better things come along, these appear to be the safer materials.'

The fact is, insects cannot be eliminated, as farmers tend to think. Eliminate one lot, another flares up; eventually the first lot develops resistance and returns. The best one can hope for is to preserve the ecological balance among them, so that these flare-ups are eliminated. A low continuous level of pests is much better than an alternation of somewhat bigger harvests and serious disasters.

The new development in pest control is the use of hormones, such as those which prevent larvae from metamorphosing into the adult form as a caterpillar metamorphoses into a butterfly. These juvenile hormones also kill eggs and have been hopefully christened the 'third-generation pesticides' (arsenates, nicotine and so on were the first generation, DDT, dieldrin etc., the second).

But these substances also have their dangers. There are a million species of insect and only 3,000 of them are harmful to man. But the third-generation pesticides act on good and bad insects indiscriminately, killing 1,000 good ones for every bad one. They are immensely powerful. For example Czech workers have managed to extract from the natural oil of the *Cecropia* moth one of the half-dozen hormonal components. This is so powerful that an ounce would clear ALL insects from 2 or 3 acres. The original oil, with its several ingredients, is far more potent. Soon man will be able to synthesize all these components. Professor Carroll Williams, the acknowledged leader in this field, warns us that 'any reckless use of the materials on a large scale would constitute an ecological disaster of the first rank.'

The origin of the pesticide problem lies not in pesticides, so much as in mankind's increasing use of monoculture—the growing of vast acreages of a single crop. It is the availability of unlimited quantities of their favourite food that enables pests to multiply enormously. The denouement to which this always tends is the total destruction of the crop and a population crash among the pests. Come to think of it, that is what that superpest, man, is up to also.

WHAT BECAME OF THE EAGLES?

In the years that followed the publication of Rachel Carson's bombshell of a book, populations of various predatory birds fell sharply—the peregrine falcon was the one which attracted most public attention—and in many of the cases studied the levels of pesticides in the tissues were far too small to account for their deaths. Simultaneously, however, scientists investigating DDT levels began to notice, in the tracings of their instruments, irregularities which were certainly not the peaks which indicated the presence of DDT or its breakdown products. They ascribed them, in their notes, to 'unknown organochlorine products not corresponding to any known pesticide or its metabolites' and speedily forgot them.

It was not until 1966 that a Swedish research worker at Stockholm University, Mr Sören Jensen, stumbled on the explanation. In 200 pike taken from different parts of Sweden he found unusual levels of a class of substances known as polychlorinated biphenyls, or PCB for short. PCB is not a pesticide. It is a component of paints and varnishes, it helps to colour plastics and improves electrical insulation. It is present in high-temperature lubricating oils. Other workers had commented, without much interest, on the fact that it was present in the air over London and Hamburg. Other cities had not thought of looking. Then some was found in seals off the coast of Scotland.

Mr Jensen, worried by what he had found, extended his researches. He looked at fish and fish spawn from all over the country. They were contaminated with PCB. He examined a dead eagle found near Stockholm. He tried his own hair. It too contained PCB. He looked at the hair of his wife and baby daughter. PCB. As the baby was only five months old, he deduced that she had got her burden of PCB from her mother's milk. He then approached the Swedish National Museum of Natural History with an odd request. Could he have snippets of the tail feathers of eagles in their collection, with the date of the bird's death? The earliest PCB he detected was in an eagle from 1944. Before this eagles, at least, were PCB-free.

Now PCB is not the kind of thing anyone of sense wants to absorb. Experiments with mice had already shown that it was particularly harmful to the liver, where it induces enzymes, the regulatory substances which control biochemical activity. It was also known to be equally harmful to the skin. Whether it had other effects was not known at this time. Unfortunately, like the old man of the sea, PCB is easy to acquire and hard to get rid of. It cannot be destroyed by incineration, which merely wafts it into the air. It can enter the body by being breathed in, or concealed in food, but it does not need these aids: it can pass directly through the skin. It is much more stable than DDT (itself a rather stable substance) and hence much harder to convert into innocuous breakdown products which can be washed out of the system. The PCB which Mr Jensen found came, he suggested, from industrial smoke, from burning rubbish dumps and the like. From the air it passed into the water, and thence into fish and so into man. Mr Jensen took the view that this was a matter for some concern. A careful check with a more sensitive device, the mass spectrograph, was made and confirmed Jensen's diagnosis.

At the end of 1967, two scientists at the Freshwater Fisheries Laboratory in Pitlochry, Scotland, who had been analysing the tissue of seals and porpoises for traces of DDT, reported, with some irritation, that the readings in their experiments were being confused by PCB, which was not destroyed by the process which removed another contaminant, BHC. To make quite sure they knew what they were talking about, they ran a separate experiment to separate the PCB from the DDT and daughter-products. Their aim being to report on DDT they paid no further heed to the PCB, though what they had to say about DDT I shall come to in due course.

They had obviously not been keeping up with the scientific literature, because only two months before in the same magazine, *Nature*, three workers at the Laboratory of the Government Chemist in London had come forward with confirmation of Jensen's work, based on a possibly more accurate technique; what they said, in effect, was that the various unidentified peaks 'not corresponding to any known pesticide' noted by those who had examined seal's blubber, human flesh and various fish and birds, were all due to PCB. This being so, why was it the case that PCB seemed to stack up much more readily in birds, seals and fish than it does in man and his domestic animals such as cows and sheep? In some birds, they added, PCB outweighs the DDT.

Two weeks later, Dr D. B. Peakall, an American of whom we shall hear more in a moment, wrote in to say: maybe this explained the fact that the widespread decreases in various birds of prey had occurred where pesticide residues were far below the toxic dose.

Meanwhile Jensen had been studying levels of DDT and PCB in creatures living in the Baltic. One seal, which had 56 ppm of DDT in its body fat, had 13 ppm of PCB. The eagles which, as already noted, had up to 310 ppm of DDT in their pectoral muscles averaged 190 ppm of PCB in muscle, with 240 ppm in the worst case.

Simultaneously, in America, Professor R. W. Risebrough, with various colleagues of the Institute of Marine Resources at San Diego, triggered by the rapid decline of the peregrine falcon, was carrying out a rather massive survey of the DDT position in living creatures throughout the world. Like the Pitlochry team, his group also found unidentified bumps in the tracings made by their analytical equipment, which they had no trouble in ascribing to PCB, having read about the Swedish work. Peregrine falcons trapped in late 1968 were carrying up to 98 ppm PCB in breast muscle, up to 34 ppm in their brains. Risebrough found significant amounts of PCB in Arctic peregrines only a few months old. A bird trapped in California showed exceptionally high—probably fatal—levels in the brain and was almost devoid of reserves of fats (lipids). Black petrels, shearwaters and other birds were studied: high PCB, high DDT, and shells one-third thinner than normal—and this was in a wild region of Baja California, remote from industrial pollution and human interference.

Risebrough noted that the few surviving pairs of peregrine falcons which were still breeding in California were, like those in Britain, living in relatively uncontaminated regions and were wisely confining their menu to relatively uncontaminated animals, such as doves and sparrows. Of the creatures they investigated, only the fish-eating bat was reasonably clear of both PCB and DDT. Risebrough now really got going. He analysed the Caspian tern and the red phalarope; the common murrelet and the ancient murrelet; the mourning dove and the meadow lark, the merlin and the barn-owl, the cormorant and the frigate bird, the cinnamon teal and the brown booby, the black-crowned night heron and the American kestrel, the golden eagle and Cooper's hawk, the white crappie and the black crappie, the sooty shearwater and the pink-footed shearwater, the bluegill and the brown pelican, not forgetting the Adelie penguin and the elegant tern. Everywhere the story was the same, all had DDT or its breakdown product DDE (about equally unpleasant) and most had PCB. The white-tailed kite, which lives mainly on voles, showed up pretty well, but only the eggs of the Adelie penguin, which came from Cape Crozier in Antarctica, were wholly free from PCB. But let us not build too many hopes on that: unless we find no PCB in the body fat of Antarctic organisms, we should not infer that PCB has not yet reached the Antarctic. Risebrough concluded that PCB is mostly carried to remote places in the air, where it is to some extent broken down by ultraviolet light, when it is present. The unusually high levels in San Francisco Bay, San Diego Bay and Puget Sound are presumably due to PCB entering the water directly in the form of industrial waste. He summarized his findings with a dry 'The presence of PCB in the few land birds and fresh water fish analysed indicates that it is also distributed among the continental ecosystems of North America. Peregrines could therefore acquire PCB, as well as the other chlorinated hydrocarbons [meaning primarily DDT] over all their global range.' Tough on the peregrine falcon, a species long revered and respected. The naturalist G. H. Thayer has described it as 'the embodiment of noble rapacity and lonely freedom'. 'An irony therefore exists in the fact', says Risebrough, 'that the peregrine may be the first species to be exterminated by global contamination.'

Meanwhile scientists had been learning things about PCB which suggested that the lonely peregrine was not the only organism which needed to worry. In 1967, D. B. Peakall, a Cornell ecologist who was a collaborator in Risebrough's global study the following year, had shown that DDT and dieldrin affect the production of the sex-hormones progesterone and testosterone, closely connected with fertility. This work was now extended and it emerged that PCB was approximately *five times* as potent in inducing the enzymes which control the amounts of these substances. Moreover, only 40 ppm of DDE was enough to cause a significant effect. From which it followed that the danger mark for PCB was a paltry 8 ppm. Both substances therefore are capable of rendering the creature that consumes them infertile, even when they do not cause its death.

Note that figure of 40 ppm, for there are already human beings who carry that amount of DDT in their bodies. How much PCB they carry is something scientists have not yet got around to determining.

In short, the identification of PCB as a threat to animals and hence, perhaps, to man may prove only the first chapter in another of these sinister serial stories, which start with reassurances and denials and end with the institution of controls after endless avoidable harm has been done.

What must strike the layman as extraordinary is the cheerful assumption made not only by the public but by many experts that if a substance doesn't kill you pretty promptly it is harmless. The normal method of rating a pesticide is to feed it in increasing doses to rats until they begin to die. The amount which humans can take is then calculated on the assumption that a small fraction of what will kill rats, with some allowance for difference in body-weights, will be OK for man. No consideration is given to the effect on fertility, or on the health of the offspring. Examinations are not made for chromosome breakage or genetic damage. The possibility of reduced resistance to infections is ignored. The possibility of a very long decay in action is not considered, nor is the possibility of a slow build-up. A prime example of this is monosodium glutamate, the cause of the 'Chinese restaurant syndrome' and widely added to baby-foods, believe it or not. Yet another is the Thalidomide story.

I have related how the unpleasant effects of DDT were slowly discovered, but here is one more story which shows how deviously such substances may work. Normally trout adapt themselves to changes in temperature. DDT interferes with their ability to do this. More than this, it blocks their ability to learn to avoid danger, and it does so at the fantastically low concentration of 20 parts per billion.

In coming years countless new substances will be devised by chemists and some will prove, like Thalidomide, to be potentially dangerous in the extreme. Thalidomide is a most useful drug, provided it is not taken by pregnant women. DDT is useful too and may sometimes be the logical thing to use. The extreme of a total ban is only one degree less silly than the extreme of unrestricted use. Cannot we find a rational middle course?

There is at least one group of substances known, which will soon be killing people off if it is not doing so already, which has not even reached the point of general recognition: metals such as lead, mercury and cadmium. Mercury has begun to cause concern in Sweden, but lead and cadmium are still in the early phase in which public health authorities deny that there is any problem. Let us see if this confidence is justified.

7 Breathe Only Out!

IN THE LAST CENTURY hat-makers dressed the fur used in beaver hats with a substance containing mercury. The fumes from this gave them mercury poisoning, which caused a curious mental disturbance, described by a toxicologist in these terms: 'The psychical or emotional disturbance is characterized by self-consciousness, timidity, embarrassment with insufficient reason, anxiety, indecision, lack of concentration, depression or despondency, resentment of criticism, irritability or excitability; these appear sometimes to cause a complete change of personality. Headache, fatigue, weakness and either drowsiness or insomnia are frequent complaints; in advanced cases there may be hallucinations, loss of memory and intellectual deterioration.' This would seem enough, but there is also slurring of words, hesitancy in beginning sentences and difficulty in pronunciation, while the hands tremble and the handwriting is altered. Excessive perspiration, attacks of blushing, ulceration of the gums, loosening of the teeth and diarrhoea round out a charming picture.

This is why hatters are proverbially mad and why a Mad Hatter appears at Alice's tea-party. It was not a source of fun to the hatters, nor to the miners who produced the mercury: there are vivid eighteenth-century accounts of this 'most cruel bane'. Mercury is readily absorbed by man through any mucous membrane, such as the lining of the mouth or stomach, and will even pass through the unbroken skin. Students using mercury in chemical experiments have been known to develop mercury poisoning from the fumes. When I remember the pride with which, as a schoolboy, I husbanded a small bottle of mercury and how I once spilt the contents in my tuck-box, my blood runs cold.

Today mercury is no longer just a threat to some industrial workers. It is being diffused into the environment in a big way and may already be a global pollutant.

What makes this especially serious is the recent discovery (1967) that mercury can be converted into a far more toxic form, methyl mercury, by unidentified bacteria when no oxygen is present—a state of affairs which exists in the silt of lakes and oceans, where decaying organic matter provides the methyl groups of atoms which convert the mercury to this even more sinister substance. Animal experiments show that it concentrates a hundred times more than mercuric chloride, and 10 per cent of it lodges in the brain.

Mercury is used increasingly in industry—as a catalyst in making polyvinyl chloride (PVC) and in the paper-making industry; as electrodes in the manufacture of caustic soda, by laundries, as phenyl mercury acetate to prevent moulds growing, and so on. It is also used to coat seeds to prevent fungal attack.

All was calm until about ten years ago when fishermen in the huge, almost enclosed, Minamata Bay in Kyushu Island, Japan, began to show the numbness, tunnel-vision and other signs of nerve-damage which I have described. At first doctors were baffled, especially when it was observed that cats were also displaying these symptoms. Then it was discovered that the local shellfish were full of mercury, as were many fish. All fishing in the bay is now banned, but this was too late for several of the fishermen, who were permanently disabled or died. The mercury was traced to a local factory making vinyl chloride, which had recently stepped up output. Most of the mercury in the effluent was metallic but there were small amounts of methyl mercury. This was concentrated in the marine organisms and the fish which ate them concentrated it still further.

In 1965, an exactly similar incident occurred in the Agana River in Niigata, but, alerted by the Minamata incident, the trouble was diagnosed in time. The Japanese authorities have now banned fishing in two more rivers and have launched a wide-ranging investigation of industries using mercury—of which there turn out to be no fewer than 194.

In 1967 they awoke to the realization that Japanese rice contained 0.1 ppm mercury. As a result, the use of organomercury compounds by farmers was banned throughout Japan.

Not long ago, shellfish in Galveston Bay, Texas, were found to be loaded with mercury, again from industrial effluent, but speedy precautions were taken.

The scene now shifts to Sweden, where methyl mercury seed dressings had been in use since the 1940's. In the 1950's, dead birds and animals were noticed which proved on examination to contain high levels of mercury. 'By the early 1960's, the very existence of some seed-eating and predatory bird species was claimed to be threatened by mercury poisoning,' says Dr A. Jernelöv, head of the Swedish Air and Water Pollution Research Laboratory in Stockholm. Moreover, Swedish eggs were found to contain an average of 0.029 ppm mercury against an average of 0.007 ppm in the eggs of six neighbouring countries: four times as much. Two eggs a day at this level would bring you above the 'acceptable daily intake' suggested by the World Health Organization. The hens got the mercury from fodder, grown from mercury-treated seeds. There is thus a food chain: fodder, hens, eggs, man.

When the feathers of museum specimens of birds were analysed, low levels were found in birds taken throughout the period 1820–1940, but there was a rapid rise in the 1950's. The situation was different, however, in the case of birds which eat fish, rather than seeds. In these birds the levels of mercury started to rise from 1890, and the mercury was almost entirely in the methyl-mercury form. What is more, while the mercury in seed-eating birds began to decline after the Swedes banned the use of mercurized seed-dressing in 1966, the mercury in the sea birds did not. They were getting *their* mercury from the effluent of paper-mills and chlorine factories. Swedish fish carry up to a lethal 101 ppm mercury, fifty times the normal amount. The Swedes have been obliged to prohibit the sale of fish from all lakes where specimens show more than 1 ppm and to recommend that fish containing below 1 and over 0.2 ppm should not be eaten more than once a week. My Swedish friends put it more bluntly: 'When in Sweden, don't eat fish.' They add that the level should have been set at 0.5. It is the fact that fish is a major article of diet in Sweden, one may suppose, which constrained the authorities to accept fish above that level for intermittent consumption. The limit is, in any case, provisional and investigations are proceeding. They have already shown that not only the lakes but the coastal waters of the Baltic are dangerously laden with mercury.

Sweden is a large user of mercury, consuming about 44 lb. for every inhabitant annually. Finland and Norway are equally heavy consumers. But probably the champion is Japan, which uses 1,600 tons a year against America's 400 tons and England's 20. What this is doing to the Pacific no one knows. There is at present no organized monitoring of mercury levels anywhere.

Nor is it all clear what would be a tolerable level. Hitherto, official levels have been based on the assumption that if no obvious disease develops all is well. But it is known that alkyl mercury can pass through the placental barrier in mammals. In the Minamata tragedy, nineteen children were born with congenital mercury poisoning to women who themselves showed no sign of being affected. In rabbits, comparable doses cause the foetus to be resorbed or to be born dead. In mice it certainly increases sterility in both sexes at doses appreciably below the lethal level. Mercury can also cause chromosomal abnormalities, certainly in lymphocytes —cells which protect the body against infection—and many of the deaths at Minamata were from secondary infections. This raises the possibility of a genetic effect, but the matter is not yet investigated in man, though there is certainly such an effect in plants and fruit-flies.

In fact it is not known whether there is any threshold below which no damage occurs. Mercury seems to destroy individual cells and so may use up the body's cell-reserves for a while without noticeable effect. So it may cause earlier onset of senility, or lowering of intelligence, or shortening of life. Absence of obvious symptoms is no reason for complacency.

In addition to the effect on humans, the effects on animals must be considered, apart from those used for food. Bird populations in Sweden have been seriously affected. But since one of the ways in which mercury is excreted from the body is via feathers or fur, it may be that relatively hairless animals, such as pigs and men, are more vulnerable.

A Swedish scientist, S. Tejning, who showed that the offspring of randomly chosen mothers had 28 per cent more mercury in their blood corpuscles than the mothers did, recommends that the acceptable dose be reduced to 0.2 ppm.

In view of this the English tolerance level of 0.1—which is double that suggested by the World Health Organization and more than three times that which the Benelux countries allow—is almost certainly too high. And perhaps Britain, America and other countries should now follow the example of Sweden, Germany and Japan in banning the agricultural use of mercury. As I write, the state of Montana has announced that, while sportsmen may still shoot partridges and pheasants, they must not eat the game: it contains too much mercury!

The mercury story illustrates the usual history of official unwillingness to face the facts. When conservationists asserted that mercury seed dressings were poisoning seed-eating birds and their predators, industry and agricultural experts dismissed these allegations, adding that crops would decline if the dressings were not used. That was in the 1950's. In 1965 the mercury content of seed dressings was ordered to be reduced to half the former level and the dressing was only to be used on infected seeds. No decline in crop yields followed these measures. In the same year a scientific conference showed beyond cavil that a drastic decrease in wild bird populations *had* occurred.

Again, when the mercury content of Swedish eggs was noted, it was maintained that the amount was toxicologically insignificant, and that in any case it came from the natural mercury content of Swedish rocks rather than from seed dressings.

Similarly, when methyl mercury was found in fish, the fishing industry objected to the regulations made, saying that no instance of human beings harmed by mercury in fish had been reported in Sweden. Subsequently, it turned out that the standard of 1.0 ppm set by the National Institute of Public Health was based on a misreading of the facts. In examining the Japanese data, the fact was overlooked that the figures were for amounts of mercury per kilogram, dry weight—i.e. after water had been extracted—whereas the Swedish calculations were based on wet weight. If this had been understood, a figure of 0.2 to 0.4, rather than 1.0, would have followed from the calculations. Covering up, the Institute of Public Health announced that it was basing its recommendation on the case of a single man reported to be healthy after consuming a milligram of mercury a day for a long time.

Though mercury will, I make no doubt, be brought under some degree of control—whether we shall ever get back to pre-industrial standards of purity is another matter—there is another metal, equally dangerous, which is not yet generally recognized as a threat and which will prove far more difficult to regulate. I am thinking of lead.

THE MENACE OF LEAD

The American people walk around with 20 tons of lead in their bodies, not counting any old bullets. Lead is a more dangerous metal than you may think. Birds which have been shot by sportsmen but have recovered from their wounds usually die of lead poisoning. Marshes which have been heavily shot over for years contain so much lead, in the form of pellets, that the duck who breed there develop lead poisoning. Indeed, cases are known of human beings who have retained a single piece of shot in their appendix, after eating a game-bird, and have developed symptoms of lead poisoning. Some authorities even claim that lead poisoning caused the collapse of Rome, for the Romans lined their copper drinking vessels with lead as well as using lead pipes.

In recent years the production of lead has zoomed to nearly 4 million tons a year, forty times the pre-industrial level, but it is not the lead used by industry or the building trade which currently presents a real danger to man: it is the lead pumped into the atmosphere by cars, ever since tetra-ethyl lead was first added to motor-spirit in 1923 to improve its anti-knock rating. Air samples taken in remote areas of the Pacific show traces of lead, while over large cities the concentration is ten thousand times the natural level, and rises and falls twice daily as motor traffic varies. In the soil of these cities it is present at ten times the normal level. Says Dr Clair Patterson of the California Institute of Technology, there is now 'intense, widespread pollution' from lead.

But health authorities claim there is no immediate danger. Thus the US Department of Health, Education and Welfare declares that present body-burdens 'are well within the currently-accepted range of lead levels for humans and are not significant in terms of a threat for the occurrence of lead intoxication.' Doctors and local health authorities often issue similar reassurances. In this chapter, nevertheless, I propose to show that, on the contrary, it is virtually certain that large numbers of people are already being poisoned by lead and that well before the end of the century this will have become an agonizing problem.

The complacency of the health authorities derives from the fact that their experience has been almost entirely with what they call 'classical lead poisoning' in an industrial context. It is termed classical because it was recognized in lead miners as early as the sixteenth century, when Paracelsus described it. It was studied in some detail by the doctors of the early nineteenth century.

The early symptoms of lead intoxication are fatigue, disturbance of sleep and constipation. The blood count will already have fallen and soon anaemia will become apparent, with colic and neuritis. Then general weakness and loss of weight are seen. Usually the victim will be in the hands of a doctor by this time, but if exposure to lead continues, or when the exposure though short is very severe, mental symptoms follow, the lead having now broken through the barrier which protects the brain from poisons in the blood. The hands tremble (tremor of intention), there is mental confusion, excitement and the patient has hallucinations. He has difficulty in hearing and suffers from double vision. His speech becomes slurred. In children such attacks, when not fatal, are followed by permanent mental retardation.

According to the accepted accounts, 90 per cent of lead which is ingested in food and water is excreted again, the balance being absorbed in the tissues and bones. The blood level represents the amount dissolving out of the tissue again. Thus, according to the orthodox account, the body is well organized to deal with a brief increase in the amount of lead ingested, even if it is a large one. The excretion rate simply rises, and little remains in the system. It also follows that the amount in the urine is a poor indicator of the degree of poisoning, and especially since people vary widely in their ability to excrete lead. Other signs, such as unusual blood cells, are also a poor guide: the best indication is the level of lead in the blood.

I trouble the reader with these medical details because, as

we shall see in a moment, this is a wholly inadequate account of lead poisoning as we know it today.

The level at which the symptoms of lead poisoning are first noticed is put by some authorities at 0.5 ppm in the blood; others say that it is all right to go up to 0.8 ppm. Even on these assumptions, the safety-level seems to be set unexpectedly high. It is regarded as quite all right for a person to have 0.25 ppm in their blood, and a survey of the US population shows a range between 0.05 and 0.4 ppm in healthy persons. Now the usual practice with pesticides and the like is to set a permitted level at least one-tenth of the danger-level, to give a margin to cover individuals who are exceptionally sensitive, particularly pregnant women, and children, and to guard against local variations such as high lead content in the soil, and hence, perhaps, in drinking water. So the 'safety-level' for lead, which is only half the danger-level, is rather extraordinary, and many people in the US are undoubtedly well above this so-called safety level. Obviously, they are all set for trouble, if anything happens to push their lead burden a little higher. For the moment, I say nothing about the position as regards children. And the situation in the UK is closely similar.

Now surveys show remarkable variations in the lead content of food and water. A British survey showed that the lead content of lettuce could range from 0.3 to as high as 50 ppm; potatoes ranged from 0.2 to 17 ppm, carrots from 0.2 to 11 ppm. A check in British Columbia showed similar variations. The average was 2.7 ppm. The British Ministry of Agriculture assumes that food will not contain, on average, more than 0.5 ppm, so that a person who eats 2 lb. of vegetables a day will take in not more than 4 milligrams of lead. The Ministry was therefore taken aback at these results, which implied an intake double what they supposed.

Similarly, the level approved for British drinking water is a maximum of 0.1 ppm. And a survey in 1967 showed that most (not all) water supplies were below this limit—in some cases only just below. But after water has stood in lead pipes for 16 hours, the level may be as much as 0.3 ppm. So anyone who is away from home for a day or two, or who only draws water to drink once a day, could be consuming water with far too much lead in it. None of this suggests a very high standard of control, especially as these facts could have been ascertained any time in the past hundred years and have only just been discovered.

It is the fact that existing standards are rather marginal, and are based on experience with, on the one hand, small doses received from food and water over a long period, or, on the other, with large doses received through the lungs in an industrial situation, which creates the problem. For today we are faced with small doses, received over long periods, absorbed through the lungs. Moreover, the lead which is now being breathed in is of a previously unfamiliar kind: tetra-ethyl lead from the exhausts of motor vehicles. It was already known that the absorbability of inorganic lead compounds varied a good deal—the oxides and chlorides being easier to absorb than the chromates and sulphides, for instance—but little was known about organic compounds of lead, of which tetra-ethyl lead is one.

But, before the peculiar dangers of tetra-ethyl lead were realized, the cat was put among the pigeons by another discovery.

It was in the early sixties that Dr H. Schroeder of Dartmouth Medical School published the first of a series of papers which cast a sinister new light on the whole problem. He placed rats in cages supplied with elaborately filtered air, from which every possible contaminant had been removed. His quarters were at the top of a remote hill 1,500 feet high, a mile from the nearest public road, the air intakes to the cages being placed in a nearby forest, with electrostatic precipitators. All nail-heads in the cages were covered and the staff even removed their shoes on entering the laboratory, among other precautions. Then he introduced traces of specific contaminants, such as lead, in known amounts and waited to see what happened. He found increased death rates at all ages. Moreover, in all rats which survived the first three months of life, the median life span was reduced by 200–250 days, those rats with the highest concentrations of lead in their systems dying first. Since three years is the average life span of a rat, a cutback of some eight months is nearly a quarter of its life span and would correspond to a shortening of some seventeen years in man. Post-mortem examination showed that the levels of lead in the tissues of the animals were similar to or less than those found in adult human beings. *There was no sign of lead-poisoning* nor any increase in tumours.

The significance of this, of course, was that the whole practice of judging the safety level for exposure to lead by the point at which obvious disease sets in was completely destroyed. More than this, it strongly suggested that human lives were and are being shortened by such exposure. And since the United States, despite its high standard of medical care, has such poor life expectancies—it is thirty-second on the world list—the suspicion is reasonable that this may be due to the fact that so many Americans are exposed to lead and maybe other pollutants.

This important study, which was repeated with variations in subsequent years, nevertheless received little attention. It was still maintained that man's exposure to lead was 90 per cent due to what he ate, and public health authorities clung to the comforting fact that there had been no significant change in the statistics of gross lead poisoning for thirty years or more. Atmospheric lead, they claimed, was unimportant.

THE LEAD YOU BREATHE

Gradually, however, figures were accumulated which made this claim untenable. Studies by Professor Eli Goldsmith, a biologist of wide experience, known for his discovery of insect chemisterilants in California, showed that people living in cities had much higher levels of lead in their blood than people living in the heart of the country, while men working in garages, guards in tunnels under rivers and traffic-control police had still higher levels. In the mountains of California, men had 0.12 ppm and women 0.09. This was rather better than the rural population of the US as a whole, who had 0.16 and 0.10 ppm respectively. But people living in downtown Philadelphia had 0.24 and 0.18, while the urban average for the whole country was 0.21 and 0.16— nearly twice as much as the mountain people. But the traffic cops and heavily exposed men had 0.3 or 0.31—nearly three times the mountain dwellers and twice the level of the rural population generally. Such figures completely rule out the proposition that atmospheric lead provides only one-tenth of the amount coming from food and water. Goldsmith drew the logical conclusion, that long-term increases in atmospheric lead are certainly going to put up the levels in the blood of exposed populations.

Another study, this time by H. V. Thomas and his colleagues, shows that men living within 250 feet of a freeway averaged 0.227 ppm of lead against 0.16 ppm found in men living near the coast in the same city. For women the figures were 0.167 and 0.099. Thus men living near this freeway carried nearly 50 per cent more lead than the control group, while the women were two-thirds worse off—perhaps a reflection of the fact that women, many of whom stay at home or shop in suburban areas, tend to be less exposed than men who drive to work or work in areas where traffic is dense. Supporting evidence came from roadside vegetation, which is heavy with lead.

Quite recently, another fact has come to light which changes the whole character of the controversy. It appears that tetra-ethyl lead, which is much more volatile than many other forms of lead, concentrates by preference in fatty materials (lipids, to be technically accurate) and hence in the brain and nervous system, which inorganic lead seldom reaches.

Serious and fatal illness struck men after they had spent a few hours cleaning out the sludge from gasoline tanks, about one per cent of the sludge consisting of tetra-ethyl lead. The symptoms were acute mental disturbance with delirium and mania. The victims experienced hallucinations. After a few days some of them went into convulsions, followed by coma and death. The less severe cases showed 'mental confusion, sleeplessness, excitement, agitation and disorientation'. Some had abdominal pains and nausea, with vomiting. Between the attacks of mania and delirium there were periods of acute depression and apathy.

Now the extraordinary thing is that in many of these men the blood-levels were completely normal, while in others they were only slightly raised—from 0.6 to 0.7 ppm. Now these were acutely sick men, who had been exposed to heavy concentrations. Obviously less exposed individuals, whose symptoms might be only fatigue and depression, would in all probability have only normal levels of lead in their blood.

Unlike inorganic lead, tetra-ethyl lead is readily absorbed through the skin.

There are substances, known as chelating agents, which will pick up atoms of metals such as lead, immobilize them and carry them out of the system. One of these is known as EDTA, for short, and it is highly effective at clearing the system of inorganic lead. Attempts to use it to remove tetra-ethyl lead, however, have been unsuccessful, owing, no doubt, to the fact that lead which reaches the nervous system is not available to the bloodstream.

Some of those who have resisted the idea that tetra-ethyl lead constitutes a risk have declared that the particles are of such a size that they are unlikely to reach the lungs, being 20 microns or more in diameter. But investigation has shown that more than half the particles of lead emitted by a cruising car are very much smaller than this, being 0.3 microns or less in diameter.

When Dr Clair Patterson, a geochemist at the California Institute of Technology, wrote a paper declaring that the US population was exposed to 'severe, chronic lead insult' (insult being a technical term in medicine) and that the currently accepted 'safe' level of 0.25 ppm was at least ten times as high as it should be to provide a safe margin, he was criticized severely by toxicologists, who employed just such arguments as: lead was only absorbed through the intestinal tract; the particles were too large; the blood levels were normal anyway. Patterson pointed out that if the safety margins applied to insecticides and food additives were applied to lead, 'lead would necessarily be considered toxic at present environmental exposures.' And, as he noted, although unaware of the peculiarities of tetra-ethyl lead, animals show brain and spinal nerve damage at levels similar to those of current human exposure.

Mueller, of the University of California, who came to his support with figures of actual particle sizes, made another vital point. In setting 'safe' levels on the assumption lead reaches people from food and water, it is assumed that children, being smaller, will eat and drink less and so receive a smaller dose. But children can be exposed to lead-polluted air and thus acquire lead in their still developing brains. Children are especially at risk, for if their brains are invaded by lead, permanent damage and mental retardation may follow. At a meeting sponsored by the Lead Industries Association and held in Chicago in 1958, Dr R. K. Byers, a neurologist specializing in children's illnesses, told colleagues: 'I originally got interested in lead because of children, who had had lead poisoning and had been sent home from the hospital cured, who then turned up in my neurological clinic because they were misbehaving in one way or another or not learning in school. One kid set the schoolroom on fire, another nice little girl danced around on the desk.' Though these children all had signs of lead poisoning, none of them had the obvious signs of brain deterioration which doctors call encephalitis. 'The point I am trying to make about these children is that though none of them, at two or three years, had an acute encephalopathy with their acute intoxication, when they reached six or seven they showed evidence of injury. . . . I think that lead does something to the growing brain which is different from what it does to the adult brain.' He also made the comment: 'I can't believe that this isn't in some way related to interference with the brain enzyme systems through amounts of lead which may not in themselves be impressive.'

In stressing the underrated importance of atmospheric lead I by no means wish to play down the importance of the lead in food and drink. One threat is superimposed on the other.

The level of lead in British food is far higher than in the US at 1.4 ppm against only 0.2 ppm. Much of it used to come from lead arsenate sprays used in agriculture. These are being replaced by fancier, though not necessarily safer, pesticides. Meanwhile people are eating a growing proportion of canned food. Anyone eating an average of a can a day, and absorbing 0.3 per cent of the lead used to solder it, could acquire a typical body load from this source alone.

It seems clear that the complacency of the health authorities is unjustified.

One of the smoke-screen devices used by those who pooh-pooh people like Dr Patterson as alarmists is to write of the level typically found in the blood of modern man as the 'natural' level. It is not natural. The level of lead in the blood of pre-industrial man, deriving from soil-lead compounds only, was about 0.0025 ppm, or 2.5 parts per *billion*. That is about a hundred times less than the currently typical level.

But the million tons of lead a year which are pumped into the atmosphere by the vehicles in the United States alone do not stay put in the air. Much of this lead drifts down on to soil, vegetation and also fruit and vegetables. This lethal dust is joined by lead from smelting plants and other sources, such as the manufacture of batteries. (Children who ate wild fruit near a smelter died in convulsions and proved to have lead burdens of 2.14 ppm in their blood.)

But the smaller lead particles stay airborne for indefinite periods. In 1969, a research vessel set out from San Diego carrying on the bridge equipment for measuring atmospheric lead, carefully screened from possible contamination by lead on the ship itself, and sailed to Midway Island and on to Samoa, making continuous measurements. The scientists, three oceanographers from the University of California, found between 1.5 and 2.5 milligrams of lead in every cubic metre of air near San Diego. As they sailed on the levels slowly declined until in Samoa they reached 0.0003 milligrams per cubic metre. In other words, the air off San Diego had at least 5,000 times as much lead in it as the Samoan air. But even this was hundreds, perhaps thousands, of times higher, they believe, than would have been found a century ago. The conclusion is painfully clear: a fine mist of lead is slowly spreading out from every industrialized country. Already there is no part of the planet which remains completely uncontaminated. Even in the snows of Greenland, the lead level is a staggering 500 times above the pre-industrial level. Man can never hope to remove this contamination. The most he can do is stop polluting the air, and leave the task of cleaning up to nature. How long that would take, no one knows. Lead is accumulating in ocean sediments at 430,000 tons a year in the northern hemisphere. This is forty times the historic rate.

So far I have written only of the threat to man directly. But lead also enters plants and so reaches man and animals in food. You cannot eat food containing even one-tenth the average concentration of lead in the soil—that is, about 1 ppm—for very long without becoming ill, from classical lead poisoning. Plants have evolved mechanisms for limiting their uptake of lead from the soil, but have not evolved filters for atmospheric lead because they never needed to.

It is quite possible to make high-octane fuels without adding lead, but they come slightly more expensive. Indeed, one US company marketed such a fuel recently, but there was no demand for it. And unfortunately these high-octane fuels produce more of the smog-forming contaminants.

By the end of the century, the number of motor vehicles in the US will, it is believed, have reached 150 million—some say over 200 million, about double the present figure. The average length of journeys will have risen by 50 per cent. The amount of gasoline burnt, therefore, could rise by a factor of three. And while the introduction of electric vehicles may have begun to act to counter this rise, the increasing number of motor boats, snowmobiles and light aircraft could well push the figure even higher. We can contemplate, if nothing is done, exposures to lead three or four times those now usual. Such exposure would certainly lead to an increase in classical lead poisoning and perhaps when that happens something will at last be done.

But long before classical lead poisoning emerges, shortened life and brain damage, especially to children, will, I greatly fear, be widespread. Lead poisoning, in this wider sense, will become one of the more important medical pandemics. And it will not be in the US only, nor confined to highly industrialized countries. The miasma will be affecting their less 'progressive' neighbours too.

There is a third metal which, though by no means so widespread as lead, deserves attention for its effect on sexual fertility and potency, and because, according to Christiansen and Olsen, two Swedish researchers who have made a special study of it, it 'has probably got more lethal possibilities than any of the other metals.' This is cadmium.

MOST LETHAL METAL

Cadmium, with its silvery sheen, is an attractive-looking material. It has become popular for plating containers, giving them a smooth rustless finish. Many outbreaks of poisoning have been reported from using them—usually because fruit-juices have been served in them, the acid dissolving the cadmium. The immediate effects are damage to the kidneys and the central nervous system. Anaemia follows and if the dose is large enough complete loss of sexual fertility or potency results. When injected into animals experimentally, a single injection causes death of the cells in the testes and damage to the seminiferous tubules.

It also has the unpleasant habit of remaining in the body a long time, in some circumstances, before exerting its effect. Swedish workers making accumulators, none of whom had worked with cadmium-containing materials for from 3 to 9 years, suddenly developed cadmium poisoning of such severity that they died. How cadmium manages to lurk so long is completely obscure.

If cadmium is swallowed it causes intense vomiting, and when inhaled it is a lung-irritant. But it was not until after World War II that anyone realized that, at low doses over a long period, it could affect the entire system. Like lead, it causes fatigue and a pale appearance, but has the additional peculiar property of causing dental caries and destroying the sense of smell, while there is a watery discharge from the nose.

So little is known about it that one British investigator concluded that it was impossible to recommend safe working conditions, a finding which did not deter people from working with it.

Up to this point in the story, cadmium has not appeared as a threat to the population at large, vicious as it is in individual cases. But recently it was noticed that patients dying of hypertension (high blood pressure) often carried unusually large amounts of cadmium in their kidneys. Investigators, trying to understand this, administered traces of cadmium to rats in their drinking water. They developed a form of hypertension strikingly similar to the human variety. Moreover, when the rats were fed cadmium in amounts comparable with those in the average American diet over a long period, their blood pressure rose and their kidney cadmium reached approximately the same level as is found in the average adult American. To clinch the argument, the rats were given EDTA which, as already mentioned, has the capacity of picking up atoms of metals, such as cadmium, and immobilizing them. Given EDTA, the rats slowly got better.

The doctors then tried giving EDTA to human hypertensives: the effect was not so marked or consistent, though in some patients there was a small fall in blood pressure. It did, however, cause them to excrete zinc, and the current idea is that it is not so much the cadmium as the ratio of cadmium to zinc which is the crucial factor. The atoms of these two metals are similar in several ways, and enzymes which normally incorporate zinc may, it it thought, take up cadmium instead, with dire consequences. However, the EDTA also caused increased excretion of lead and manganese, so that the picture is by no means clear.

Despite this, experts on industrial cadmium poisoning deny that it has any such effect, in the workers they have studied, and query the whole idea.

However this may be, it is now pretty certain that cadmium, just like lead, shortens the life span when absorbed in doses too small to cause detectable poisoning. Dr Schroeder, who did the lead experiments which I have described, also exposed rats to traces of cadmium, with closely similar results. At less than the concentrations found in human kidneys, life was shortened significantly, with the curious difference that cadmium was more powerful than lead in the case of males, while the reverse was true for females. Incidentally, titanium was as life-shortening as lead in females and worse than cadmium for males. The life of males was shortened more than that of females, a fact which curiously echoes the human sex-difference in life expectancy.

Whatever the mechanism, this discovery has focused attention on cadmium as a potential menace to the population at large. As the Heart Information Center at the National Institutes of Health cautiously puts it, 'Thus the presence of cadmium in the environment may be of considerable importance.' The worrying fact has come to light that most Americans accumulate more than 10 milligrams of cadmium in their bodies before the age of 20. This cadmium is concentrated almost entirely in the kidneys, where it combines with zinc in a special protein. Looking round the world, investigators find that while Africans have less cadmium in their systems than Americans, as one might expect, some eastern peoples have more. Top of the list, so far, are the Japanese, where the obscure disease itai-itai is now suspected to be cadmium poisoning.

Where all this cadmium comes from is something of a mystery. The unevenness of the body-burden around the world suggests that it comes, at least in part, from human activities. Does it enter the body from the air, or from the water or, via food, from the soil? Perhaps a mixture of all three. Measurements in city air show levels of 1 microgram per cubic metre in London, about the same as zinc but far less than lead. But an American study, made in nineteen locations, showed wide variations from place to place.

I suspect that biological magnification is at work. Cadmium is present in US oysters, known for their concentrating ability, at anything up to 3.66 ppm, and in lamb and chickens at almost 4.0 ppm. Kidneys are also loaded. Certain types of phosphate fertilizer have been found to be rich in cadmium, which is readily absorbed by crops. But the primary source is the flue-dust from zinc, lead and copper smelting plants. We need to know where it goes from there, but our ignorance is immense. It is thought that the presence of zinc may intensify the effects of cadmium.

What makes the situation worrying is our total uncertainty as to what is a tolerable level. For industrial purposes it is usually set at 1 milligram per cubic metre. This is probably a good deal too high even for industry, in the light of the new facts I have just described; it is certainly too high for the unprotected population, which includes pregnant women. For very recent work has shown that it is teratogenic—that is, it induces monstrous deformations of the foetus. Drs V. H. Fern and S. J. Carpenter injected female hamsters on the eighth day of gestation with cadmium sulphate at 2 milligrams for each kilogram of body-weight. This was a far smaller amount than the 145 milligrams per kilogram found in the Swedish workers who died after several years of not using cadmium-containing materials. But it caused a total disruption of the embryo, the details of which it would be morbid to describe.

SHORT LIVES AND GAY?

I have described some of the problems created by three metals, which we are currently dumping into our environment in quantities which appear far too large for comfort and which are shortening many lives. By the end of the century, at this rate, they will be affecting everyone. But there are many other metals of equally menacing character, and no doubt we shall find good reasons for exploiting some of them widely between now and the year 2000.

Take beryllium. A silvery metal lighter and stronger than aluminium, it has great attractions for use in aircraft and spacecraft. Indeed, as long ago as World War II attempts were made to use it for aircraft engines, but cost and lack of suitable techniques for working it caused it to be dropped. A change in the availability and cost of electric power could put beryllium back on the map in a big way. It is also important in the atomic energy industry.

An epidemic of obscure illness broke out in beryllium-using industries during the years 1942–47 in America. Since so little was known, a file of cases was established, known as the Beryllium Case Registry. Many of these cases came from the fluorescent lamp industry, since traces of beryllium are used to alter the quality of the light given by these lamps. Of the nearly 800 cases in the registry, over a quarter proved fatal. Some of these were not beryllium workers, but neighbours who had been poisoned by contaminated clothing.

Beryllium poisoning is sometimes mistaken for tuberculosis and other diseases, which may cause under-reporting. It is not yet known whether it is a cause of cancer. In fact, the mechanism of the disease is still unknown. To understand the nature of beryllium poisoning is 'of world-wide importance' to use the words of Dr Harriet Hardy, who operates the Beryllium Case Registry.

The investigation of beryllium poisoning has been made most difficult by commercial secrecy. 'Because the exact composition of phosphors in use was a jealously guarded secret, it was difficult to be certain of the dose of beryllium that was causing the poisoning,' says Dr. Hardy. 'In addition, financial problems associated with launching a new operation are great, and recognition of job-related disease leading to compensation claims is a consequence that hinders accurate study of industrial disease.'

There are many other toxic metals coming into use. Titanium, which shortens life more than lead or cadmium, is extensively used in supersonic aircraft. The story of selenium —currently fashionable as a preventive of dandruff—is rather like that of cadmium: a prolonged failure to recognize the danger it presents at low doses. Then there is thallium, which is used to coat seeds because it is so unpleasant that the birds decline to eat them. A family which unwisely mixed thallium coated seed-corn with its ordinary corn died to a man. Thallium is also used in ant-destroyers. Being very stable as well as highly toxic, it accumulates in food chains. Birds die after eating as few as four mice which have accumulated thallium sulphate. Whether it is getting to man is not known. But it may be significant that it causes alopecia (a form of baldness). After it was used extensively in Hawaii, young rats were found to be completely hairless. They must have received their load of thallium through their mothers' milk.

All in all, the heavy metals are an unpleasant lot. Breathing in minute amounts can cause heart and lung damage. Eating small amounts causes liver and kidney damage. And some at least are linked with cancer.

The conclusion cannot be avoided that the environment is much less safe than is commonly supposed. But metals and pesticides are only the most obvious of the contaminants we are pouring into the environment. It is estimated that more than a quarter of a million different substances are released as wastes, effluents or gases. Practically none of them have been tested for their possible effects on the ecosphere. It is high time that we stopped regarding the obvious illness as the only sign of environmental contamination. Our whole method of setting 'acceptable intakes' is hopelessly naïve and remains unchanged from the nineteenth century.

The story is always the same—fatuous confidence that all is well, followed by a long rearguard action in an attempt to justify the earlier complacency. Only a confirmed optimist would assume that we shall not continue to repeat this immature pattern in the years ahead.

But while the pollutants just considered are little recognized as threats, there is another kind of pollution which is widely recognized, and assumed to be fully under control: ionizing radiation. Recently, scientists of great reputation have begun to question that assumption.

8 The Fifth Factor

WHEN MARIE CURIE, in the early years of this century, slowly refined a ton of uranium ore donated by the Joachimsthal pitchblende mines, she ended up with a thimbleful of a strange substance which would blacken photographic paper, even when not in contact with it, make glassware fluoresce and alter the conductivity of gases. Evidently it was emitting energy, and in such quantities that it remained permanently warmer than its surroundings.

The substance was radium, of course. Like other radioactive substances, it emits energy because individual atoms are exploding, or, to use the proper term, decaying into lighter atoms, the weight lost reappearing as energy, thus confirming Einstein's famous assertion that matter is simply energy locked up in some mysterious manner. In radio-active substances, it becomes gradually unlocked of its own accord. The manner in which it does so is inexplicable. After a given time—in the case of radium it is 1,620 years—half the atoms will have decayed. After another 1,620 years, half the remaining atoms will have decayed, and so on. Not until there is only one atom left to explode will it become inert. The rate of decay, therefore, is expressed as a 'half-life.' The half-life of radium is 1,620 years. The point is important because it means a radio-active substance does not become harmless, even for practical purposes, until many times its half-life. The half-lives of radio-active substances range between seconds and billions of years, and the reason for this is completely unknown. It is also unknown, and very puzzling, how atoms 'know' when it is their turn to explode. Why do they conform to this strange rule?

Radium decays into another radio-active substance, radon

(a gas), and this in turn decays: after a series of such decays, you are at last left with an inert substance, which turns out to be lead. Each decay has a different half-life. Other radio-active substances, like thorium and uranium, also have their own decay sequences, each of which is unique. Finally, these substances have the property of making anything which they are put in contact with somewhat radio-active also, and this activity persists after it has been removed from contact.

The energy produced is strong enough to damage or destroy living cells: it was for this reason that radium was placed in malignant tumours. Unfortunately, if the amount was powerful enough to destroy the tumour rapidly it was also powerful enough to create new ones. People who handle radio-active materials without protection are liable to develop tumours later. This fact first came to light when girls painting luminous watch dials with radium developed tumours of the lips, because they had moistened their paint brushes by putting them to their mouths.

One more fact must be mentioned: radio-active substances emit three kinds of radiation, christened alpha, beta and gamma. The gamma form is much the most powerful and will pass through several inches of lead before being stopped. For most practical purposes, therefore, we need only consider the gamma rays, for if these are adequately shielded, the others will be shielded more than adequately.

I have summarized these well-known facts to emphasize that we are dealing here with something unlike anything we have known before. To the familiar elements of earth, air, fire and water we have, so to say, added a fifth: ionizing radiation, so called because (unlike light, heat and other forms of radiation) it knocks electrons out of atoms, a process known as ionization. There is no method, it cannot be over-emphasized, of rendering such radiation inert. You can change the substance chemically—say, from a liquid to a solid—but it will still be as radio-active. There is nothing to do but put it where it will do least harm and wait. In some cases you may have to wait billions of years.

THE PROBLEM OF RADIO-ACTIVE WASTES

The simplest way to measure radio-activity is to compare it

with a single gram of radium: the amount of radiation this emits is termed one curie. Before World War II, the total stock of radium was about 10 curies, and if a radium needle containing a few microcuries (millionths of a curie) were lost, the fact made headlines. Today we think more often in terms of megacuries, i.e. millions of curies.

How much radio-active material will the world have to cope with by the end of the century?

There will be increasing use of radio-active materials in industry. Already steel furnace linings are coated with such materials, as a way of indicating (by release of radio-activity) that the linings are wearing thin. Radio-active 'moles' are sent crawling through underground pipes to reveal the whereabouts of a blockage—they can be followed from above ground, thanks to the gamma-radiation they emit. Hospitals and research laboratories use radio-active versions of various chemical compounds for analogous reasons. The fate of the compound in the body can be traced by monitoring the radiation. And no doubt we shall see the use of nuclear explosive for large-scale excavation, as is currently being studied for the sea-level Panama canal and other projects (pp. 43–45).

It may well be that the biggest source of serious individual accident will arise from the industrial uses. The history of radium needles shows that people can be incredibly casual in handling such materials. (In the fifties, large numbers of people were contaminated in Mexico in this way. In the sixties, a number of people suffered burns from gold wrist-watches, because radio-active gold from radium needles had been used in their manufacture.) The gamma sources used for pipe-tracing comprise a whacking fifty curies of activity each. One has already caused the death of several members of a family who found it, and 'grave concern' is felt at the possibility of these hot 'moles' going astray.

But all these sources will be minor in comparison to the nuclear power industry. The size this industry may attain depends on the growth of demand for electricity, and estimates of this are constantly being revised upwards. In 1967 the AEC estimated a total installed capacity, worldwide, of 1,556,000 megawatts (MWe) by the year 2000, of which 734,000 MWe would be derived from nuclear sources. This is about 100 times the amount so produced today, and assumes world demand for electricity will be 8,000 billion kilowatt-hours (KWh), but admits the figure could be 25 per cent lower or higher. Back in 1952, the AEC had expected that by 1970 we would have only 5,000 MWe of nuclear power; in fact, we are nearly at 7,000 MWe already and by 1975 the figure will be 140,000 MWe. Some people think these estimates too low: Dr William Webster in the US has estimated the nuclear share in the world's electric power requirements by 2000 at 3–4 million MWe—constituting nearly half of the world's electric power requirements.

What this will mean in terms of radio-active wastes depends on how far the demand is met by building light-water reactors (on which the US is currently concentrating), heavy-water reactors (which are being developed in Britain and elsewhere, as being more efficient) or thermonuclear processes. The radio-activity evolved is greater in heavy than in light-water reactors, and much greater in thermonuclear devices. At present the latter are not practical, but the Russians have recently reported success with this method in the laboratory and their claims have been fully substantiated by a British team which went out to investigate them. Thermonuclear power may thus be practical before the end of the century.

According to a 1967 report issued by the Oak Ridge National Laboratory, and making due adjustment for the somewhat higher demand for electricity now expected—but not to Dr Webster's estimate—the following amounts of radioactive waste are to be anticipated by the year 2000 in the US alone. On the assumption that only light-water reactors will be in use, the amount of spent fuel which will have to be processed, which today is 300 tons, will amount to over 21,000 tons. The accumulated volume of liquid wastes will be 60 million gallons; or if converted to solid form will occupy 600,000 cubic feet. The total beta activity will rise from 1,000 megacuries in 1970 to 155,000 megacuries. But in March 1970 it transpired that there are *already* 75 million gallons of radio-active wastes (a figure which may include military wastes), which suggests these figures are greatly underestimated.

All these estimates are little more than guesses, since no one knows what types of reactor will be in use by the end of the century, or how much liquid waste will be converted to solid form. Merril Eisenbud, another expert in the field, foresees a million megacuries of wastes stored in 1,000 million gallons of waste solutions. The risk which this represents to man and the environment depends, naturally, on how effective the containment and disposal of wastes is, and the answer may be different for different types of radio-activity. Much smaller quantities than this, notes Eisenbud, could create real problems. In the US most high-level wastes are stored in tank farms. Estimates of their life range from 10 to 20 years. At Oak Ridge, 5 acres a year were being used up in this way; at Hanford the rate must be much higher—the plant has 500 square miles of land.

Since this cannot go on indefinitely, major efforts to find alternatives are being made. Three are thought to be particularly promising—to run the wastes into disused salt-mines; to fracture shale or other rock formations and run the wastes in; and to convert the liquid to a glassy mass which can be buried. For purposes of calculation, the active life of these wastes is taken as 600 years, and they must not leach out of the mines or rocks during this period—especially not into drinking water.

Since 1959, solid wastes have been stored in reinforced concrete vaults with walls up to 17 inches thick and weighing up to 10 tons each. It is known that in April 1963 a special train hauled 240 of these assorted units to Oak Ridge for burial. Such trains might be a rather common sight by the year 2000.

At Hanford, rather alarmingly, the majority of wastes can be stored in a sixty-metre deep layer of silts *above* the local water table. Some early attempts at waste disposal were not too successful. In 1959, about 280 megacuries of waste was released into three soil seepage pits, but in the same year and again in 1961 the sides of the pits collapsed, releasing nuclides into neighbouring White Oak creek.

The long-term safety of tank storage is difficult to predict, says Belter of the AEC, because of lack of data. Most of the tanks now used are from 15 to 26 metres in diameter and hold up to 5,000 cubic metres (a million gallons) of waste. There are, or were, 200 such tanks in the US containing over 280,000 cubic metres (55 million gallons) of waste, at up to 10,000 curies per gallon—'more than enough', as Sheldon Novick remarks, 'to poison all the waters on earth'. The vicious liquids within them boil furiously from their own radio-active energy and the tanks have to be cooled continuously. A failure of the cooling arrangements would cause a disaster. They also have to be watched for leakage. The contents are of course intensely corrosive. In some cases seepage through welds has been detected after only a few months. The risk of earthquakes shattering such storage tanks and trenches has been overlooked until recently.

Because of these difficulties, conversion to solid form is increasingly favoured, and may reduce the amounts requiring to be handled, by the year 2000. The total investment in waste management facilities was $230m. (say £100m.) in 1967, 70 per cent of it for the tanks. Operating costs amounted to over $6m. (say £2½ m. p.a.). Belter suggested that storage and treatment costs in 2000 would not exceed $240m. (£100m.) per year in the US, but this is evidently an underestimate.

These figures are all for the US alone, other countries being less forthcoming with their data. The working rule is to double American figures to get a world figure. In all this nothing has been said about gaseous wastes. They are often ignored but may prove the most awkward pollutants of all.

KRYPTON AND TRITIUM

The indications are that the most serious nuclear contaminants in the years ahead will not be those with which fallout has made us familiar, such as strontium and iodine, but two unfamiliar gases, krypton and tritium. Both are emitted in large quantities in fuel processing and in power production and are released to the air, thus affecting the atmosphere of the whole world. Either one may become the first nuclide to make the subject of international control, since it is much cheaper to dump them in the atmosphere than to eliminate them. From the atmosphere, they descend into waters and so affect drinking water. They also dissolve in body fluids. Krypton is a stable gas, with a half-life of 9 years; tritium, which has a half-life of 12 years, is a form of hydrogen with a nucleus three times as heavy as normal.

Within two or three years the concentration of krypton is expected to match that of the natural radio-active gas, radon: by AD 2000 there may well be a million megacuries of accumulated krypton, equivalent in activity to 1,000 tons of radium. The total body dose rate may be 1.8 millirems* per year. Professor Otto Haxel, of Heidelberg, as long ago as 1963 pointed to this danger and called for: (*1*) the setting up of a world-wide network of monitoring stations to detect the sources of the gas; (*2*) the curtailment of purely military uses of fission; (*3*) development of storage methods, and (*4*) initiation of research to establish a maximum permissible concentration. Seven years later, none of these steps has been taken, as far as I can determine.

Professor Haxel thinks that 10 per cent of the observed concentration comes from bomb-tests, 20 per cent from civilian reactors; he deduces that the remainder, much the greater part, comes from military reactors.

In view of the seriousness, in the long term, of this threat, a projection has been made as far ahead as 2060 by when, if no steps are taken, the concentration would reach 50 microcuries per cubic metre of air: Sir John Cockcroft has suggested that the standard should be set at 0.6 microcuries per cubic metre, so this would mean that by 2060 atmospheric krypton would be present in roughly 100 times the recommended amounts. Cockcroft's criterion, I reckon, will have been passed by 2000. Moreover, krypton dissolves in body fluids, and the dose from this source alone would be 25–100 millirads in the northern hemisphere—about half of what is currently regarded as the maximum allowable from *all* sources. Unfortunately krypton, though it can be removed from liquid effluents, is very difficult to remove from flue gases, and even harder to store after you have removed it.

Tritium may prove more of a problem than krypton, since the molecule is so small it is very hard to control. It leaks out of aluminium and stainless steel fuel canisters by actually diffusing through the metal, and it passes most valves and seals. It is expected that by 1975, man-made tritium will have accumulated to the point where it equals the naturally produced amount (69 megacuries) and by 1995 it will surpass the amount produced, so far, by nuclear weapons testing (7,000 MC). But this calculation assumes that only light-water reactors are being used. So-called heavy-water reactors produce much more: if only 10 per cent of the installed

*Millirems and millirads are units of radiation dosage. For an explanation, see p. 173.

capacity is in this form, it would double the tritium inventory, while 20 per cent would triple it, and so on. The position becomes far worse if thermonuclear reactors become practical: they are expected to produce more than 100,000 times as much, per megawatt of power. This may even rule out their use. It is known that about half the tritium released in bomb tests has come down between 30° and 50° North latitude, owing to the way in which the atmosphere dumps what it contains. Therefore most of the tritium from a nuclear economy will come down on 10 per cent of the earth, the 10 per cent which includes most of Europe and the US.

In current technology, 20 per cent of the tritium released goes into the air, 80 per cent into cooling water. Since it requires 18 million gallons of water a day per ton of fuel to dilute it to acceptable levels, this method is of 'limited applicability'—as J. O. Blomeke, an expert on radio-active wastes, drily puts it. Only the largest lakes will serve and then only if the number of power stations is limited. It is expected that 7 MC will have accumulated in Lake Michigan by the year 2000, when there will be about 180,000 MW of nuclear power around the lake. Each large reactor will produce 2,000–3,000 MC per year. How long the water stays in the lake is only guessed at, but one calculation suggests that anyone drinking this water for 25 years would absorb the entire permissible dose, on present standards. So, despite the assurance that levels in the lake will be thousands of times lower than what the AEC regards as satisfactory, the prospect seems rather dim and suggests that the AEC's standards for water purity are totally unrealistic.

Incidentally, tritium is also widely used in luminescent paints, for scientific tracer purposes and so on, which will add to the burden.

Up to date, no recommendation has been made by the International Commission for Radiological Protection (ICRP) for permissible exposure to tritium at low levels for large populations, though there is a recommendation concerning the genetic effects in large populations. 'It is to be hoped that a comprehensive, internationally acceptable recommendation may emerge before this world-wide contamination becomes much greater,' as A. W. Kenny of the British

Ministry of Housing observed at a seminar, held by the International Atomic Energy Authority in Vienna in 1969.

The biggest risk will exist near fuel processing plants, and D. G. Jacobs, in a survey of tritium problems for the AEC, speculates that their size may have to be limited by safety considerations.

K. E. Cowser and colleagues calculate the probable dose to an Oak Ridge resident from both krypton and tritium, if there were a 6-ton-a-day plant at work there—the size foreseen for 1990—as 160 millirems a year.* Since the permissible dose for average populations is 170 millirems, such a large dose from one source would not be acceptable. By 2000, he thinks, the release of these two gases may impose 'inacceptable radiation exposures to man and his environment'.

ARE THERE SAFE LEVELS?

With these amounts of radio-active material about, the question arises, what is a dangerous level in the environment? This naturally depends on another question: what is an acceptable dose to the human body and to animals and vegetation? The short answer is that, as far as we know, all radiation does damage and the only safe dose is zero. The arguments by which various official bodies have arrived at figures for 'acceptable doses' are quite devious and I doubt very much if the public would regard them as acceptable if it understood the position. Conspicuously little effort has been made to explain the complexities to the public as a whole. There should have been a major educational effort to explain this completely new problem; it should be part of the educational curriculum in every school. I shall therefore now attempt to summarize this matter, despite the fact that it is quite involved, because of its extreme importance.

Radiation differs from familiar pollutants in three main ways. First, as I have already indicated, it cannot be used up or inactivated. It just decays away in its own good time, which may be a very long one; one cannot really say it becomes weaker, since, though fewer and fewer 'explosions'

---

*The forecast is for 219 megacuries a year and an accumulated load of 1,540 megacuries assuming 675 gigawatts, but Cowser puts this higher, at 520 MC a year and an accumulated total of no less than 3,150 MC. (This assumes 700 GW nuclear capacity.)

occur, each one is just as powerful as any other, and as capable of causing damage to its immediate surroundings. Second, it exerts its effect on living tissue at a micro-level. A single molecule of the most vicious pollutant imaginable would not harm a fly. But a single atomic explosion of a carbon atom which happened to be in a crucial position, e.g. in the genetic material (DNA) of a sperm or egg-cell, could cause a mutation which might be transmitted from offspring to offspring for an indefinite period. Everything depends on precisely where the radio-active atom is when it blows up. Thirdly, there is this curious element of chance. It is as if you were about to fire a machine gun at a crowd. You could say with certainty that some people would be killed and others would be injured, but you would have no idea at all which ones. In the same way, if you spray the environment with the miniature time-bombs known as radio-active atoms, you can be sure some people will be hurt, but it is purely a matter of luck who is hurt and who escapes.

Though this is similar to other cause-and-effect relationships with which we are familiar most people find it difficult to embody it in their thinking. Thus, when we are told that cigarette smokers have an increased chance of dying of lung cancer, there is always someone who protests: 'I know a man who has smoked heavily all his life and he's over 90.' In living our lives, naturally we have to accept many such risks: the question is whether we want to add to them. If you are being shot at with machine guns, it is healthier if there is only one rather than five or six.

Apart from these basic differences, there is the fact that there are many different radio-nuclides, with different half-lives and different effects in the body. Radio-activity is not one pollutant but a whole group, and acceptable levels are different for different nuclides. Thus the general rules which the authorities lay down are only rough guides, which have to be interpreted in the light of knowing the particular combination of nuclides released in a given accident or operation—if you do know them. In addition, we may have to consider alpha, beta and gamma emitters separately.

In measuring the effect of radiation on living tissues, we are primarily interested in the amount of energy absorbed by the tissue, which will depend on how far the tissue is from the radiation source and whether anything (air, clothing, bricks etc.) lies between. So the curie is no good to us. The dose unit used is the *rad*, defined as the amount of radiation depositing 100 ergs of energy in one gram of tissue. But even this does not quite pin it down, as alpha rays are roughly ten times as effective as beta and gamma. So, when a mixture is involved, we use the *rem*, defined as one rad of alpha or ten of beta or gamma rays. However, different tissues absorb differing amounts, so even these units are not precise measures of the biological effect.

Before we can proceed to the question of what is an acceptable dose, I must say something about the differences between the more important nuclides. There are four which have so far proved particularly significant because the atoms, having entered the body, get built into its structure, for the body cannot distinguish them from non-radio-active forms of the same atom. They therefore stay there until they finally explode, whereas many other nuclides are excreted, so that the period of risk is much smaller.

Iodine–131 accumulates in the thyroid gland, which requires iodine. As this is a very small organ, any active atoms are concentrated in a small space. They eventually cause cancer of the thyroid. The half-life is relatively short: 14 days. *Iodine–129*, produced in much smaller but not negligible quantities, has a half-life of 17,250,000 years.

Strontium–90: the body mistakes this for calcium, to which it is chemically similar, and builds it into bone. When it explodes, the daughter product is *yttrium–90*, which tends to lodge in the gonads (ovaries and testes) and may cause damage or mutations in eggs or spermatozoa. The half-life is 28 years.

Carbon–14 can be built into any type of living tissue, all of which contains carbon, but constitutes a serious risk if it should get built into the genetic material (DNA), especially the rapidly dividing cells of an embryo or infant, and above all if it gets into the DNA of egg or sperm, in which case it may cause a mutation affecting all future generations derived therefrom. The chance of this is small; on the other hand carbon–14 is around for a long time. Its half-life is 6,000 years, so that, as atomic tests continue, the amount around is constantly increasing.

Where the half-life of a nuclide is short—a matter of minutes or days, say—obviously we can create new amounts every month or so without building up an accumulation. But when the half-life is long, as with carbon, much of the first lot we created is still around when we create some more, so that a stock builds up in the environment, much as with DDT. When the period is in thousands of years, quite small additions, made regularly, will eventually build up disastrous levels. Since carbon–14 can be so dangerous genetically, any addition is most undesirable.

Cesium–137, with a half-life of 33 years, resembles strontium in being concentrated in living tissue, but goes to the soft tissues rather than the bones. After 20 years of storage, the wastes from reactors consist as to more than 99 per cent of strontium and cesium, the other nuclides having decayed.

Our main information about the effects of radiation on living creatures comes from the explosions at Hiroshima and Nagasaki, and from accidents in research centres, and concerns short but massive doses. This knowledge is relevant to what would happen in the event of a serious accident at a power station, but we are concerned here mainly with the effect of low doses spread over a long period, about which much less is known, since we have not had people exposed to small but significant amounts of radiation under observation for long periods. The fact that 300 rads to the whole body will kill 50 per cent of the persons exposed, whereas the same amount spread over 70 years (it is said) may produce no perceptible effect, may or may not indicate that damage is repaired. But there is also a 'delayed action' effect. This was noticed long ago with uranium miners, who developed cancers in more than the expected numbers many years after retiring from the industry. This latency period is commonly 20 years or more. It probably represents the gradual using up of the body's spare capacity to deal with damage. Ageing is believed to involve a similar process—and it is significant that exposure to radiation also shortens life, by an amount directly proportional to the amount of radiation received. Cancer-producing substances also frequently show a latency effect (as in the case of cigarette smoking) and it is significant that radiation also causes cancer.

The medical effects of low dosages of radiation are known to include the production of leukemia (500 additional cases in every million persons, p.a., for every 300 rems of exposure, and proportionately), cataract, and skin or bone cancers. Leukemia results from the radiation reaching the bone marrow, where blood cells are formed, and thyroid cancer results if it reaches the thyroid.

BIOLOGICAL CONCENTRATION

It follows from the fact that some nuclides get built into tissues that biological concentration can occur. When iodine–131 falls on grass and is eaten by cows, it is concentrated in the cow's thyroids; some, however, gets into the milk and is then consumed by human beings, who concentrate it further. (The existence of this process was not suspected at first.) One of the organisms in which radio-activity can be concentrated is seaweed, and in Wales people eat a food known as 'laver bread' made from it. The levels for the discharge of radio-active effluent in Britain had to be set so that an enthusiastic laver-bread eater would not receive more than the amount of radiation regarded as acceptable. Oysters and shellfish likewise concentrate radiation. The situation is worst when there is little of the non-radio-active variant about to dilute the active one. Algae concentrate phosphorus from water 100,000 times. It also concentrates in the bones and scales of fish. The process is selective, however: fish in the Columbia River, for instance, were found to have taken up sodium–24, concentrating it 130-fold, but little else. Fish in a river in which the concentration of phosphorus–32 is below the level permitted in drinking water may eventually become too radio-active for human consumption.

Other well-known examples of this process are the concentration of fallout in moss, eaten by caribou, in turn eaten by Eskimos, who thus receive considerable doses.

Some of what we know about biological concentration comes from a large-scale experiment by the AEC at Oak Ridge; here the creek was dammed to form a 55-acre lake, known as White Oak Lake, into which wastes were dumped and allowed to trickle into White Oak creek. Another such lake was Par Pond.

Though the concentration of cesium in the lake water was only three hundredths of a millionth of a millionth of a curie (or 0.000,033 microcuries) the flesh of bass caught in the pond contained thirty-five times this amount. Strontium in the bones of bluegill was 2,000 times and radio-active zinc

8,720 times the level in the water. Caddis-fly larvae, in the Columbia river, into which the Hanford plant discharges, achieved concentrations 350,000 times that of the water!

Birds also concentrate radio-activity: swallows may carry 75,000 times the ambient level, because they feed on insects which have in turn concentrated it from algae, which in turn have concentrated it 2,000 times above the level in the water. Moreover these birds are often migratory. As Novick drily puts it: 'What was happening in White Oak Lake was that the highly dilute wastes dumped into the water were being reconcentrated and then neatly packaged and dispatched all over the continent.' And not only the continent, since some doubtless went to the Arctic or Antarctic or crossed the Atlantic. On a smaller scale, insects perform the same trick, and one Russian team of investigators noted that the area round their lake was getting as much 'fallout' in the form of dead insects as would have come to the same area from two hydrogen bombs. However, 80 per cent of the insects, they reckoned, were being eaten by birds, so that much of the activity was being carried further afield.

With these facts in mind, let us proceed to the question of what danger radio-activity affords, and what is a reasonable degree of risk to take.

ACCEPTABLE DOSES

Since there is no known safe dose of radiation, the authorities, being determined to introduce fission processes, have to find some kind of standard: they do so by taking the background non-man-made radiation as a norm. Some rocks, notably granite, are slightly radio-active. Radium is present in small amounts in some sources of water. Cosmic radiation from outer space, though mostly filtered out by the atmosphere, arrives in small quantities. Like all radiation, this 'natural' radiation is potentially damaging. Thus a survey in New York state showed that families living on igneous rock or consuming water with a relatively high radium content were more likely to produce malformed children. On igneous rock the malformation rate rose to 17.5 per 1,000 live births, compared with an average of 13.2 for the whole area. The rates were 20 or higher in 186 out of 942 townships examined. (Errors due to differences in reporting practices were carefully eliminated.) Similarly, differences can be shown for leukemia rates and so on. This background level is reckoned at 150–200 millirems a year. So the authorities set the permissible exposure to man-made radiation at the same amount as background—specifically 0.17 rads.

But for many people the word 'natural' implies 'harmless' and even 'desirable'—as in the case of those people who advocate using 'natural' methods of cure, or 'natural' fertilizers instead of 'artificial' ones. So it becomes possible for the authorities to dismiss a given radiation risk as 'similar to the natural background'. What such a statement really says is: the existing risk will be doubled by what we propose. If any public authority proposed to double, say, the number of road accidents he would be condemned as a monster or a madman, yet radiation authorities make such statements all the time. And since they can't use the term 'safe dose' they have coined the term 'acceptable dose'—but in fact this dose has never been accepted in any democratic sense at all. The only people who have accepted it are experts who proposed it. The question of just how much it is worth paying in disease and mutation, in human suffering and social cost, for the benefits of nuclear electricity is, on the contrary, one which urgently requires to be publicly debated. In a moment, I shall discuss what the price in disease and mutation is likely to be.

I have spoken in general terms of 'authorities' for the position is remarkably similar in the USA and western Europe. Most countries have followed the recommendations of the International Commission on Radiological Protection. In the US 'guidelines' are set by the Federal Radiation Council, with a watching brief by the National Council on Radiation Protection. In Britain, the Ministry of Health relies on the recommendations of the Medical Research Council, and sets RPGs or Radiological Protection Guides. Within these guidelines the respective atomic energy authorities set their own limits for their working personnel, but there is no need to go into all the details for the purposes of the present discussion. (Incidentally the Department of Defense is not bound to observe the FRC guidelines.)

In both countries, the acceptable dose to the whole body is set at 0.17 rads (170 millirads) per year. As I shall show in a moment, this is almost certainly far too high on any reckoning.

The Acceptable Dose, however, is far too low to be practical if people are to work in the atomic energy industry, where 'it is impossible to avoid all radiation'. Picking a figure out of the air, the authorities say that 'occupationally exposed' persons can receive a dose *one hundred* times the Acceptable Dose. And, presumably for the sake of symmetry, invent a third group—people living near an atomic centre —who can receive ten times the Acceptable Dose. So, even if we regard the Acceptable Dose as acceptable, it is clear that the authorities are quite unambiguously authorizing Unacceptable Doses for a proportion of the population—a proportion that will steadily increase as atomic centres are built. The industrial dose must be spread evenly over the year to reduce the impact, and there are various regulations governing this.

The authorities also lay down acceptable doses to particular organs of the body, such as the eyes, marrow, and gonads (ovary and testes). In the last case, the risk is genetic, so another fiction is introduced, the Mean Reproductive Age, which is said to be 30. Industrial workers are allowed to accumulate 50 rems by this age. The fact that some men may have children at 40, 50 or later and that these children will have an unduly high risk of leukemia, malformation and genetic defect is considered to be offset by the fact that those who have children at some age younger than 30 will have a lower-than-average rate. That must be a great satisfaction to the defective children concerned. The whole calculation is typical of the bureaucratic approach, in which the individual becomes a mere statistic.

Indeed, this extraordinary piece of casuistry is carried further. It is argued that persons with defective ova or spermatozoa will marry into the general population, spreading the defect broadly; and that therefore it is all right for a small proportion of the population (e.g. workers in atomic centres) to be exposed to high risks, provided the risk to the rest of the population is kept low, as this will lead to an acceptable amount of genetic defect over the whole population. Again, a third, intermediate, group is allowed for, those working near an atomic centre, who have a middling risk. The sort of calculation which satisfies the authorities is:

0.2 per cent of the population receive 5 millirems/yr. from age 18 to 30

2.0 per cent of the population receive 0.5 millirem/yr.
  up to age 30
whole population receives genetic dose of 2 millirems/yr.

Thus the average genetic dose is reckoned to be 2·6 milli-rems/yr. or about half the recommended rate of 5 milli-rems/yr., so all is well. In reality, 200,000 people, in the US, are receiving an overdose, in such a case. Or in the UK, 110,000.

Apart from the ethics of this, we do not *know* how far workers who are occupationally exposed marry into the general population or how long it would take to disperse the damaged genes among them. No studies have ever been done.

Having agreed on Acceptable Doses, the next step is to agree on Acceptable Releases of radio-activity and Acceptable Levels in atomic centres. These are calculated so as to produce not more than the Acceptable Dose in the Standard Man. This imaginary man drinks so much water, breathes so much air, and has internal organs of a certain size. For some purposes he also eats certain quantities of food of certain kinds, and has a certain number of medical or dental X-rays. Thus in calculating the amount of radio-activity permissible in water, we assume it will be drunk by a standard man, who will be getting standard doses from air, food, etc. Conversely, in reckoning what the populace got in the way of radiation after an accident, it is 'least-unsatisfactory' to assume it consists of Standard Men.

Unfortunately there are a lot of non-standard men about and even more non-standard women. There are people who have had long courses of radiotherapy or numerous X-rays. There are people who wear watches made luminous with radium paint, who fly in aircraft a great deal, who look at television, and eat oysters. Worse than this, there are pregnant women, carrying foetuses which are especially sensitive to ionizing radiation, which has been shown to pass from the mother through the placenta to the offspring. Careful studies by Dr Alice Stewart of Oxford University have established that diagnostic X-raying of pregnant mothers raises by as much as 50 per cent the risk of the child subsequently developing leukemia. MacMahon's studies in the US give similar results. It follows that the notion of an Acceptable Dose to the whole population is a lot of tosh, not to use a ruder word. Naturally, the authorities have considered the case of pregnant women, and made some recommendations, but such cases are forgotten in making general pronouncements about the risk associated with a particular form of radio-active waste-disposal or a reactor mishap.

The extremely chancy nature of the whole conception is obvious. When radio-active gas is released from a tall smokestack, or in an accident for that matter, it may rise high in the air or be blown down to ground level almost immediately, before it has become diluted. It may be blown out to sea, or hang around in still air under a temperature inversion. It may be biologically concentrated or even get into some Non-Standard women bearing foetuses which will promptly become Sub-Standard. One of the things which saved the Atomic Energy Authority's bacon in the great disaster at Windscale was the fact that the wind was offshore, so that most of the radiation descended in the Irish Sea or in Eire, where it was unlikely to be noticed. If there had been an onshore wind, the history of atomic energy in this country would have been changed. As it was, all milk had to be condemned and cows removed from pasture over an area of 200 square miles. Increased activity was recorded over a large part of Northern Europe.

Let us now turn to the question of what an Acceptable Dose of 0.17 rads means to those who received it. According to Dr John W. Gofman and Arthur R. Tamplin of the Lawrence Radiation Laboratory in Livermore, California, it will mean, if everyone receives this amount, an additional 16,000 cases of cancer plus leukemia each year in the United States, some 4,400 cases in the United Kingdom and so on proportionately to population in other countries.

The fact is, as Gofman and Tamplin remark, that a valid scientific justification of this dose has never been presented. We do not, as a matter of fact, have the information on which we can make an informed judgment of the maximum advisable limits.

CANCER AND THE ACCEPTABLE DOSE

Gofman and Tamplin have now attempted such a calculation, on the basis of data which have come in since the guidelines for radiation were first established. These figures show that a dose of 100 rads will double the rate at which most cancers occur in a large population, usually taken as a million. Lung cancer may require rather more: Japanese figures suggest 100, but American figures range between 125 and 250. Gofman and Tamplin, therefore, take 175 rads as the doubling dose in this case. If a hundred rads doubles, then one rad causes an increase of 1 per cent. For various less common types of cancer, the doubling rates are not far different, with increases ranging between 0.4 and 2.5 per cent per rad.

Younger people seem to be more sensitive, the doubling dose being only 5–10 rads (10–20 per cent increase per rad). For thyroid cancers, the rate is probably even higher.

All these figures may turn out to understate the position since, owing to the time-lag (latency) in the appearance of cancer, more cases may yet appear in the series which have been studied.

Infants in the womb appear to be more sensitive still. Alice Stewart's work suggests the doubling rate is 4–6 rads, and this is confirmed by American work. However, as this was based on one-shot doses of two or three rads, and we are concerned with 0.17 rads over 9 months, Tamplin and Gofman leave the question of unborn children out of their calculations.

By age 30, if exposed to 0.17 rads/year, each person would have accumulated 5 rads, implying a 5 per cent increase in the incidence of cancer. As there are about 2,800 cancers per million, normally, and as there are about 100 million people over 30 in the US, this would mean 14,000 additional cases a year, in this over-30 group.

There will be some cases, particularly leukemias, in the under 30's, and Gofman and Tamplin put the figure conservatively at 2,000, making 16,000 additional cases a year in all. This figure is almost as large as the casualties in Vietnam in 1969. In England, Scotland and Wales, with some 30 million over-30's, the comparable figure would seem to be 4,400 additional cases. This is quite without reference to possible foetal and neonatal deaths, genetic effects or life shortening.

Two main counter arguments are often brought forward. First, that the authorities do not actually intend that everyone shall get the legal maximum. To which one may reply, why have a limit if you don't really mean it? This way, *some* people are going to get hurt, even if not as many as here calculated. The second is more profound: it asserts that there is a threshold below which radiation is harmless. It is true that our earlier knowledge was derived from large doses, but small doses have been used on animals, while Alice Stewart's work concerned doses as low as 2 or 3 rads. The principal exponent of the threshold argument has been Dr Robley D. Evans of MIT, but in 1967 Dr Walter showed that Evans's figures did not support his conclusions. Gofman and Tamplin, in their evidence to the US Senate in 1969, included an appendix carrying this refutation further on the basis of a much larger number of cases. The fact is, we still have no decisive evidence either for or against the existence of a threshold at very low doses, still less do we know at what level such a threshold might be located. Until we do, it is rash to build on it, since the price of being wrong is irreversible damage to many human beings. Discussing the questions raised by their paper, Robert W. Holcomb in *Science* ended with the comment: 'In short, the term "acceptable risk", as used in radiation standards, could mean a risk that is actually present but that cannot be demonstrated to exist by scientific studies.'

A third argument frequently comes from official sources. In America, it takes the form: if you move from the mid-West to Denver, you expose yourself to doubled background radiation. So what we're doing is no worse than moving to Denver. In Britain, Aberdeen is substituted for Denver in this argument, since the granite of which the houses are largely built is more radio-active than brick and stone, while the underlying rock is granitic. But another way of putting this would be: we propose to expose people who already have twice their share of exposure to three times their share. And at least those people who dislike the idea of leukemia are free to move from Denver or Aberdeen as the case may be, to less perilous surroundings—but no one is free to reject the environmental exposures created by man, such as I have described.

Gofman and Tamplin propose that the permitted level be immediately reduced to one-tenth, a suggestion which caused screams of agony from officialdom.

Mr Paul C. Tompkins, executive director of the Federal Radiation Council, said this proposal 'might well price society out of business. To reduce radiation exposure tenfold would cost billions; it might even cost more than the Vietnam war.' Dr Gofman said he doubted this, but it might mean abandoning the projects for digging harbours and canals with atomic explosions, and the underground nuclear natural gas exploration programme.

Gofman and Tamplin sum the matter up thus: These guidelines 'represent a set of numbers having as great an impact on the future of the human race as any set of numbers ever could. Therefore society must demand, as an item of the very highest priority, that such guidelines be absolutely above reproach and question, for the consequences of error can even mean the deterioration of the human race on earth.'

Conceivably Gofman and Tamplin have overstated their case; even so one is left with the conviction that the given limits are based on optimism rather than reason, and that the costs in human suffering need re-evaluating.

THE ACCIDENT RISK

Finally, let us not underrate the possibility of accidents occurring in nuclear reactors, for, while the initial blast of radiation and heat can hardly be described as 'pollution', much of the radiation will remain in the environment—all the long-lived nuclides—and this will constitute pollution.

The history of nuclear fission to date is studded with accidents, each due either to mechanical failure of safety devices or human error, or a combination of both. The most recent is that near Denver; the fact leaked out that the AEC asked the government for $45m. to repair the damage. Minor escapes of radiation are quite common. Statistically, it is certain that the power stations of the future will suffer a proportion of accidents. Unlike ordinary industrial accidents, minor ones cannot be speedily forgotten, for a thousand releases of 1 curie put just as much radiation into the environment as one release of 1,000 curies, whenever the half-life is long in relation to the period over which the releases occur. Metals become brittle, under the influence of radiation, in ways which are not fully understood, and our experience with the highly corrosive fluids now being used as coolants is still very limited, especially at high temperatures —typically about 1,000°F.

As Edward Teller, the 'father of the H-bomb', pointed out in 1967, 'if you put two tons of plutonium together in a reactor, one-tenth of one per cent of this material could become critical. . . . A small fraction of the original charge can become a great hazard.' Teller, who is well known as an advocate of atomic energy, has nevertheless observed: 'In principle, nuclear reactors are dangerous. . . . In my mind, nuclear reactors do not belong on the surface of the earth.' It is already the case that reactors planned for California, to be located near the San Andreas fault, where earthquakes are to be anticipated, have been prohibited. If a reactor were severely affected by an earthquake, it is probable that the safety devices would prove useless, and the containment structure would be ruptured. A single 1,000-MW reactor after a year of operation contains more radio-active cesium, strontium and iodine than all the nuclear weapons tests ever conducted. A calculation made for a reactor half the size of the proposed reactor at Bodega Bay, 50 miles from San Francisco, which assumed only half the radiation would be spilt, suggested the death-roll might be as high as 3,400 killed and 43,000 injured, with property damage up to $7m. A calculation for a 300-MW reactor at Lagoona Beach, Michigan, which assumed total release in stagnant air conditions, estimates 133,000 killed, 181,000 injured immediately, delayed injury (e.g. cancer, life-shortening) to 245,000 and did not even attempt to estimate property damage. Moreover, large reactors cannot just be left to cool off: they explode.

In addition to the reactors themselves, spent fuel will be transported to processing plants in growing quantities. At present they travel in 70-ton containers which have been described as 'the most hazardous objects, short of an atom bomb, known to man'. They contain enough radio-activity to poison whole cities. Radio-active materials are also shipped by air, and leaks have occurred, some of them exposing hundreds of people to radiation. It is reckoned there will be one serious accident in every 100 million miles of transit. Two million miles had been clocked up by 1962. We can anticipate several by the end of the century.

Lastly, there is the problem of the growing wastes and

'tailings' of uranium mines. In America there are 12 million tons of radio-active sand lying in uncovered heaps, in the Colorado River Basin. They have lain there for 20 years, 'being washed by the rain into the tributaries of the Colorado River and eventually into Lake Mead: a water system which provides water for drinking and irrigation to parts of California, Nevada, Utah, Wyoming, Colorado, New Mexico and Arizona.' The danger was not realized until the late 1950s, when it was found that water in the San Miguel River contained thirty times the permissible levels of radio-activity, while algae and alfalfa were heavily loaded. When the AEC cut back its demand for uranium in the sixties, many mines closed, simply abandoning some 3 million tons of tailings, containing 2 kg. of radium–226 (half-life 1,620 years), to say nothing of radio-active thorium and lead, some of it directly on river banks. Attempts to cover them with gravel and establish vegetation are being made, at the instance of the Water Pollution Control Administration, but nothing will grow on them. Altogether there are now 30 million tons of this stuff in the US and the amount increases daily.

GULLY-GULLY

What the ordinary man finds almost incredible about this whole business is the degree of deviousness, amounting to deceit, displayed not merely by the business interests involved (to which one is resigned) but by public authorities and particularly the AEC. For instance, what were originally known as 'hazard analyses' were rechristened 'safety analyses' because the latter sounds more comforting. Similarly, the 'Radiological Protection Guides' are not *protection* guides at all—they are statements of how much additional risk the authorities are willing to expose people to. It is the fact that it is an *additional* risk, which people never had to run before and which they could, given the chance, choose not to run now, which makes the use of the word 'protection' unjustifiable. Such tricks have left in many people's minds the idea that these standards, like those for pure food, say—assure absolute *safety*.

A similar piece of gully-gully consists in the argument that all industrial work entails a certain risk, so that there can be no objection to workers in atomic energy and nuclear weapons establishments being exposed to certain hazards. There are three main twists in this argument, as well as several minor ones. First, it is a different kind of risk. Industrial risks do not affect the genetic potential of the race. Where they are found to entail a risk of cancer or other fatal disease, protection is expected to be absolute, only a breakdown or failure to observe the rules causing exposure. If this cannot be achieved, the process is abandoned. Second, exposures to the public are calculated at one-hundredth of the exposures laid down as all right for industrial workers. It is not the case that, for every hundred coal-miners killed, a member of the public has to die. If it were, the standards would be considerably more severe in the coal industry!

Finally, there is the argument that the risks are justified by the advantages. Who is to say what price in human suffering justifies a possible reduction of a few cents in the cost of electricity? Here the argument is often used that the increase in deaths is only a small percentage of what is caused by other factors. On this argument, almost anything could be justified. Only a small percentage of the population takes drugs, so why not allow drugs? Why forbid traces of carcinogens in food: only a few people would die if margarine were still coloured by butter-yellow, as it once used to be. DDT does not produce consequences fractionally as serious as does radiation, yet we limit that. The attitude we take to radiation is, in its ruthlessness, quite unlike our attitude to any other threat. I can only suppose that this is a consequence of public ignorance, and a touching faith in the goodwill of experts.

The AEC's bland desire to pull wool over the public's eyes is also revealed in the turgid phraseology adopted in their reports and statements. Thus if you wish to refer to a reactor running away and the whole plant exploding, you do not use any such crude, unlettered expression: you say that there is a prospect of the core going 'prompt critical' following which the plant 'will disassemble'.

But the most outrageous of all the casuistries is the setting of background level as a standard for permissible radiation exposure. Let us be clear that this means that we propose to *double* our existing risk, by deliberately creating another man-made risk as large as the existing non-man-made one. The reason for choosing this standard is that, owing to the chance manner in which radiation hits, as I have explained, it is impossible, in any given case of cancer or other damage, to know whether it was due to man-made or to natural causes. The chances are exactly 50 : 50 in every case. In short, the level is set simply on the basis which best enables the atomic energy authorities to avoid blame. This strikes me as a degree of ruthlessness which is obscene.

Furthermore, as Sheldon Novick points out in his book *The Careless Atom*, the AEC policy has been to give a small dose of radiation to everyone, rather than a large dose to a few. The standards have not been set in terms of how much radiation may be released, as such, but in terms of how much any one individual would be likely to get. Thus the AEC does not seek to limit *pollution*: it is apparently, willing to pollute the entire ecosystem up to the gills, worldwide, provided only that no individual, capable of sueing it, can stand up and say: 'Look what you did to me!' Thus the pattern set by DDT has been repeated: every living person on the globe, not to mention animals and plants, now carries some burden of radiation, as a result of these activities. Nothing can now remedy this. The only option remaining open is: shall we continue to make the situation worse and worse?

To quote Sheldon Novick: 'It is long past time that we realized that in radiation "no measurable damage" eventually means "just not quite fatal" for everyone.' And he adds: 'The haste with which the commercial reactor program is being pursued at present simply does not allow reasonable consideration of this problem.'

The irresponsibility of the AEC's attitude has even been commented on by members of the US Supreme Court, though without much noticeable effect. Justice Douglas, with Justice Black concurring, in connection with the AEC's decision to go ahead, despite an unenthusiastic report from its own Advisory Committee on Reactor Safeguards, with the construction of a new type of reactor at Lagoona Beach, Michigan, called its interpretation of the law 'a light-hearted approach to the most awesome, the most deadly, the most dangerous process that man has ever conceived.'

The AEC has a long history of light-heartedness. Thus it asserted that fallout from weapons tests in the desert would stay where it fell and afford no risk to surrounding populations. Despite this, a team led by Professor Robert C. Pendleton of Utah observed a steady build-up of cesium–137 and strontium–90 in soil and in living organisms. He also found that soil from the high valleys washed down into lower valleys, where it concentrated in 'hot spots' on which it was undesirable to graze cattle or even walk. In regions of heavy rainfall, soils had from five to twenty times the activity of the high valleys. Nodules also began to appear on the thyroid glands of children living in the area. In 1969, the AEC suddenly decided to make a gigantic grant—$250,000, to be spent in only three years—to Pendleton to study the effects of fallout in the inter-mountain west. Air-monitoring stations are to be set up all across Utah, and Pendleton will study drainage in three river valleys, as well as making uptake studies in animals, plants and soil.

The history of atomic energy is one of repeated over-optimism. Thus the AEC at first assumed that strontium presented no problem. In 1953 the AEC stated that the only possible hazard to humans from strontium–90 would arise from 'the ingestion of bone-splinters which might be inter-mingled with muscle tissue during butchering and cutting of the meat'. No mention was made of the fact that the milk from such animals would also contain strontium–90. By 1956 the AEC had acknowledged that milk represented the 'most important source of strontium–90 in human food'. They also assumed that iodine, being short-lived, was no real problem. It has been widely assumed that the iodine risk came only from nuclear tests, and that following the banning of all but underground tests, this risk had vanished. But Professor Pendleton showed in 1962 that cattle thyroids in Utah continued to display radio-active iodine; in the absence of testing, it can only come from reactors and fuel reprocessing plants. In 1968 the US Public Health service released figures which showed a much more serious situation: radio-activity in cattle thyroids in Georgia, Iowa, Kansas, Louisiana, N. Carolina, S. Carolina, Oklahoma, S. Dakota, Tennessee and Texas. And if it is in the thyroids of cattle, you can be sure it is in the thyroids of human beings too.

Professor Barry Commoner has calculated that, if this situation continues for fifty years, it will deposit more than the permitted dose for human thyroids. But the AEC plans a thousand-fold increase in atomic power by the year 2000, so the probability is that the limit will be exceeded very much sooner and the thyroid cancer rate in these states should begin to rise quite soon.

The guideline set for thyroid-dose by the Federal Radiation Council is 10 rads: one calculation suggests that such a dose would cause the thyroid cancer rate to rise 50 per cent; another that it might rise twenty-fold.

As late as 1957, the official AEC–Department of Defense handbook, *The Effects of Nuclear Weapons*, claimed that fallout would descend so slowly that half of it would not reach the earth for seven years: the 1962 edition of the same handbook admitted this was false. Similarly, the 1953 AEC report declared: 'Fall-out activity is far below the level which could cause a detectable increase in mutations, or in inheritable variations.' Apart from the double think in the word 'detectable', by 1957 the AEC's Biological and Medical Advisory Committee had concluded 'that fall-out from tests completed to that date would probably result in 2,500 to 13,000 cases of serious genetic defects per year throughout the world population.'

Barry Commoner from whose *Science and Survival* I take these last facts, comments: 'It is now clear that the government agencies responsible for the development of nuclear weapons embarked on this massive program before they understood the full biological effects of what they proposed to do.' As one of the 3.5 billion people now at risk in consequence of this irresponsibility, I ask: why are the individuals who sanctioned these actions allowed to stay in business?

CONCLUSION

In the foregoing, I have discussed only the danger posed by radiation to human health. But of course it will affect plants and animals as well. Much of the radio-activity produced on land will seep into the oceans, and the krypton and tritium will tend to be absorbed there. Some of the routes may prove roundabout and unexpected. Nuclear submarines and ships will add their quota. A Russian worker, G. G. Polykarpov, has shown that, when the eggs of various species of Black Sea fishes are cultivated in water containing as little as 0.2 millicuries, significant spinal defects occur in the fish which develop from them. So far, very little work of this kind has been done. The plankton which form the basis of sea-life—the so-called 'grass of the sea'—is also affected by radiation, and the possible consequences of this I have discussed in a previous chapter.

The moral of this chapter, let it be clear, is not that radiation is bad for you, but that an informed public opinion should assess how much hazard it is willing to accept, against a background of information about the alternative sources of energy (and there are many) and their risks if any.

The International Commission on Radiological Protection in its main report, says that the recommended maximum genetic dose, coupled with medical exposure, 'would impose a considerable burden on society due to genetic damage, but that this burden may be regarded as tolerable and justifiable in view of the benefits that may be expected to accrue from the expansion of the practical applications of "atomic energy".' When I read this, I ask, with E. B. White: '*Who* regards it as justified? How many people have they asked? Certainly not me.'

For a closing thought, I offer an explanation put forward by Dr Alvin Weinberg, the director of the Oak Ridge National Laboratory, for the ruthlessness with which the development of nuclear energy has been pressed forward. He said: 'There is an understandable drive on the part of men of good will to build up the positive aspects of nuclear energy simply because the negative results are so distressing.'

I've drawn the picture of growing environmental contamination mainly in terms of its effect on human health because that is how the facts mostly emerge: we seldom begin to take notice until we ourselves are directly affected. But I want to stress again that the significance of this trend is that it represents a growing strain on the ecosphere. The natural balances are liable to give way at some point. We do not know what point or when, just as we do not know where or when the next earthquake will hit the west coast of America. But we can be sure it will.

Of the imbalances developing around us, certainly the greatest and most obvious is the human population explosion. It is *man* who is out of balance with the environment.

All the dangers we have been looking at derive their

importance from the sheer mass of the world population. How big could it become? At what point will famine put a stop to further growth? Let us now turn to these larger questions.

9 The Population Limit

FROM A BIOLOGICAL point of view, the earth is already overpopulated or nearly so. Nevertheless, many economists maintain that the earth could support a population far larger than the present one. It seems extraordinary that experts should be divided on a point of such basic importance.

There are eminent authorities who speak glibly of a world population of 30 billion, of 120 billion and even higher figures, for which they reckon food could be supplied. It is worth looking at such arguments, since they are, I believe, totally unrealistic and morally reprehensible, inasmuch as they mislead people into underestimating the problem with which the world is faced.

If you are willing to assume that no sacrifice of comfort or wellbeing is too great to make, and that technology can achieve anything it wants, then the figure can be put as high as you like. You can assume that everyone will live beneath the ground, in order that the entire land surface shall be free for agriculture, and that the sea can be cultivated like a fish-pond. You can assume that all living creatures not actually wanted for food are killed off. You can assume that everyone is prepared to eat just enough synthetic food, made from petroleum, yeast or algae, to keep alive. You must also assume that unlimited energy has become available, that the pollution problems can be completely solved, and the psychological problems likewise. Professor J. H. Fremlin of Birmingham University, in a spirit of ridicule, has pushed this argument to the logical limit, where the earth is entirely covered with buildings ten miles high, the farming being conducted on the roofs, and half the interior being services, transport and cooling. The limiting condition becomes the point at which the heat produced becomes too great to radiate into space. He calculates that this point would be reached when the earth's population was 60 trillion, which should be reached in 895 years' time, though he concedes it would be awkward when the oceans begin to boil.

But if we confine ourselves to more realistic assumptions, of the kind which are meaningful over the next hundred years, such as that people will continue to live on the land surface, wish to eat complex diets, and devote much of their energy to other things beside food production, the limits are naturally lower.

Essentially the argument used by the optimists is as follows. You double the cultivated area of land; you increase yields by perhaps three times, by using better strains and more fertilizer, and so you can support six times as many people as now—say, 20 billion. If you are even more optimistic, you visualize trebling the cultivated area, and increasing yields by a factor of 4, giving you eight times the present population. If you are completely euphoric, like Professor Colin Clark, the director of the Institute for Research in Agricultural Economics at Oxford, you talk of increasing the cultivated area by six times, the yields by a similar amount, and also declare that everyone could be made to live on 1,600 calories a day, the present average in India, where people are dying of hunger, instead of the 2,400 calories which the FAO thinks the minimum for adequate nourishment.

In their discussions, the economists—it is only economists who argue in these unrealistic theoretical terms—completely ignore the sociological problems of bringing such changes about: in reality there would be revolutions before anything of the kind occurred. They completely ignore psychological factors, such as stress. They even ignore problems of energy supply and pollution. Even more incredibly, they ignore questions of water supply, fertilizer and so on; for instance, they do not allow for any land disappearing under water, as irrigation and power schemes are created. They do not allow for the effects of the vast mining and extractive industries which would have to be developed to provide raw materials for a population ten, twenty or thirty times the present. Obviously these would sterilize more land. Ditto, cities, roads and airports. Finally, most of them ignore the need to grow non-food crops, such as rubber, fibres and wool and the nonessential foods, such as sugar, coffee, tea and fruit. Some of them even ignore the question of protein. All of them ignore questions of ecological imbalance, caused by these programmes, and climatic consequences.

The error which bedevils all such calculations is expressed in the phrase 'other things being equal', a phrase which always means an unrealistic argument is to follow. But the lesson of ecology is that other things never *are* equal—that is, undisturbed. The agronomist calculates what the acres will yield, given that the hydrologists can find the water and the engineer can produce the fertilizer. The hydrologist declares that he can find the water, provided the agronomist does not require any more land. The engineer says he can provide the power, provided no one objects to the radio-activity he will produce.

To give a pertinent instance, it is believed by many food experts that the quickest and most practical way to raise the protein-intake of undernourished peoples is to add fish-concentrates to their cereal diet. But a recent study has shown that concentrating the fish concentrates the radio-activity—due chiefly to polonium—to the point where such concentrates are becoming unacceptable.

And in all this, general amenity and quality of life is considered least. A recent article on whether Britain could be provided with the water which will be needed by the end of the century, concluded that it could certainly be arranged. It would mean throwing a dam across the Wash estuary at a cost of £800m., and another across the Solway Firth. It would probably mean damming the River Severn and pumping the water over the Cotswolds into the Thames, to supply south-east England, where many new reservoirs would also have to be created. (Where?) And of course, the Lake District, where Wordsworth walked, would have to be sacrificed, all the lakes being dammed and filled to the maximum and emptied during the summer to provide water for the industrial north. To anyone but an engineer, the price seems a little high.

But even on these artificial terms these arguments are remote from reality. Can the cropped area be doubled? Can yields be multiplied by four times? To arrive at a realistic conception, let us briefly explore these points.

Large areas of the world are uninhabited, to be sure, and from an aircraft it is easy to suppose they might be developed. But the harsh fact is rather more than half the land surface of the world is either too cold, too dry, too rough or too steep, or too inaccessible to farm by any methods available at present.

As one writer puts it: 'Only about 3.3 billion of the world's acres are really cultivable: this represents about 10 per cent of the total land surface. Another 10 per cent is marginal land which would give, at the best, only poor yields of progressively more expensive food. . . . Thus for the foreseeable future we can take it that we have to eat off a little more than 3 billion acres.'

This is perhaps over-pessimistic. Conceivably, some of the land which is too cold could be made available for pasture by climate control before the end of the century, though the shortness of daylight would prevent it being used for crops, and a climate change might well reduce yields in other areas. Of the 15 billion acres (6,199 million hectares) which the UN reckons is open to use, about one-fifth is agricultural land, the rest is pasture or reasonably accessible forest. To increase the crop acreage, you would have to plough up pasture, and to replace the pasture you would have to fell forests.

Dr Ozbekhan of the RAND Corporation maintains that the cultivated area could be increased to 9 billion acres by ploughing up one-third of the pasture and felling one-quarter of the forest, which would cost about $2,000 billion to do, he reckons. But forests are needed for wood and wood-pulp and also play a vital role in water conservation, so there is a limit to how far one can sacrifice them. (A synthetic substitute for newsprint and paper would help, of course.) Felling them would also cut the oxygen supply. Furthermore, it is common delusion that because tropical jungles are lush, the soil must be good. In fact much of it is laterite, good for making building blocks or road-surfacing but scarcely for agriculture, though it will support bananas, rubber, coffee, sugar cane, etc., if carefully tilled and drained. Very permeable soils, notably sand, become too dry in summer to support crops. Some clays bake solid, and when wet are too gluey for roots to penetrate. All soil must contain humus—broken down organic matter—both to provide food and to preserve the crumby structure which plants like. The townsman's belief that plants will grow anywhere, if watered, is just a joke to the farmer. It was sublime unawareness of these limitations which caused the disastrous failure of the British Labour government's plan to grow 3 million acres of peanuts in Kenya, N. Rhodesia and Tanganyika. 'Scarcely anything was overlooked,' says Osborn, 'except the vital factors of soils and climate, as well as the working habits of the Africans.'

At a guess, we might double the crop area, no more, without causing disaster, but with some loss of amenity and a high price for newsprint. In practice, while theorists talk glibly of reducing the area under forests, many countries are making great efforts to increase their forests. Zambia, for instance, recently received $5.2m. from the World Development Bank for just this purpose, and the FAO has some thirty afforestation schemes in hand.

A more serious limiting factor than land is probably water. There is plenty around, of course—sometimes too much—but most of it is either in the wrong place or comes at the wrong time. Hence the world's interest in vast irrigation schemes, but these too have their limitations. Very inconveniently, water prefers to flow downhill, and it is costly to pump it uphill. Already some crops are worth less than the water it takes to grow them, were the water charged at its true economic cost. This is also the difficulty with desalination, which produces water at around 60 cents or 5s. a thousand gallons. This is an acceptable price for drinking water, since people drink little, just possibly acceptable for some intensive crops, e.g. tomatoes, but quite out of the question for ordinary agriculture, let alone industry. It takes 4,000 tons of water to grow a ton of maize. To grow 320 tons of food on one square mile in the temperate zone requires 1.3 million tons of water. The Thames entire would not irrigate Kent, if there were no other water supplies there. Industrial demands are also much larger than you might think: it takes 15,000 gallons of water to make a car, to say nothing of cooling water for power stations, 600 tons of water for every ton of coal burned.

So, even if some semi-arid lands could be developed for agriculture, they could never be the site of large-scale industrial development. The scarred terrain of southern Utah, like that of the Arabian desert, will never become populous in any future which we can foresee.

Lastly, the question of yields. In India, it takes an acre to support one person. In Holland, with fertilizer applied at 360 lb. per acre, four people can live off one acre. Ergo, says the economists, yields can be quadrupled. But India isn't within a thousand miles of being able to apply fertilizer in these quantities or anywhere near, still less so Africa and South America. To apply fertilizer at this rate to the whole 3.3 billion acres of cultivated land would call for 600 million tons of fertilizer, about twenty times current world consumption. On a doubled crop-area obviously 1.2 billion tons would have to be reckoned. Contrast this with the FAO's hope that we shall be using 100 million tons by the year 2000. And bear in mind that pasture land also needs fertilizer when grazed intensively.

To obtain these vast quantities would be far from easy, the phosphates being already in short supply. Low-grade rock would have to be worked, and the cost of fertilizer, already too high for many farmers in have-not countries, would become much higher. Thus food would also become more costly.

Even more difficult than manufacturing these vast quantities of fertilizer would be to ensure that it is applied correctly. Over-fertilization can stunt crops, as can an unsuitable proportion between the three main constituents—and the proportion varies for different soils.

I have said enough to make it clear that those who cheerfully talk about the earth supporting populations of 30 billion or so are talking about a period so remote that existing political, economic and technological limitations can be ignored. But at its present rate of expansion, a world population of 30 billion would be reached by 2070. It seems highly unlikely that such changes will have been brought about by then.

However, where economists really slip up is in not knowing enough biology: there is a biological consideration which makes it unlikely the world will attempt to support such large populations even at some distant date. This is the energy budget of life. Indeed, it calls for eventual population levels *smaller* than we have at present.

ENERGY DEBIT

Biologists argue thus: the amount of plant life which the earth can sustain depends, in the last resort, upon the amount of sunshine falling upon the earth, because solar energy alone drives the photosynthetic reactions which enable plants to construct themselves out of simpler materials, chiefly water, nitrates and carbon dioxide. This solar energy is equivalent to 2.5 billion h.p., but one-third is immediately reflected and much of the rest is reradiated before it can do any photosynthetic work. Only 0.04 per cent actually goes to operate the metabolic processes of plant growth. This amount of energy would create, every year, about 410 billion tons of plant matter—much of it inedible, such as trees, reeds, lichen and so on. According to Professor LaMont Cole, who is the deviser of this calculation, about 120 billion tons of 'consumers'—such as animals and men—could live on the vegetable matter produced.

The exact quantity of vegetable-consumers which can be supported depends on food habits—the length of the food-chain. For instance, for every 1,000 calories of energy embodied in algae, the small aquatic animals which live on algae will incorporate about 150 calories. The fish which eat them will extract about 30 from the 150, since some of the energy will go to maintain the fishes' life processes, and another part of what is eaten will be excreted. A man eating the fish may synthesize about 6 calories' worth of fat or muscle. But if he eats a trout, which lived off the smaller fish, the yield will shrink to 1.2 calories. The moral is, if you want to support the maximum human population, keep the food chains short, for every link wastes energy. Some food chains have six or seven links. The most efficient course would be for man to eat 'planktonburgers'. (The full picture is more complicated, since we have to allow for parasites, faeces-eaters and other variations in the normal pattern of the food-chains.)

When all is said and done, Professor Cole considers, man —even if he shortened the food-chain by eating only plants —would require about one per cent of the total plant-growth of the planet, including the plankton and the timber. 'I suspect that the human population is already so large that no conceivable technical advance could make it possible for all mankind to live on a meat diet,' he says. On this basis therefore, the planet is already overpopulated—and the population has grown by nearly a billion since Professor Cole made this calculation in 1958. He adds: 'I can't see very much to be optimistic about for the future.'

More recent work suggests that the efficiency of plants may be three or four times higher than Cole assumed, making a population slightly larger than the present one possible, without running into energy debt, on normal assumptions—and a hundred billion or so if we are prepared to go to extremes, such as putting everyone underground, killing all unnecessary animals and living largely on algae.

A calculation of this kind is necessarily rough, in the present state of our knowledge, and must be read in the light of existing technological limitations. The day may well come when we can increase the efficiency with which solar energy is trapped. Cloud dispersal might open up areas at present unsuited for rapid plant growth; we might be able to establish artificially warmed greenhouses on polar snow and ice, or even disperse it. And so on. But these are minor factors.

How then is it possible that the world manages to support the population it does, and that economists can argue that a vastly larger one can be contemplated?

The joker in the deal is the fact that we do not confine ourselves to incoming solar energy, but 'cheat' by adding to it the energy from fossil fuels—the stored sunlight of the past —to which we now add nuclear fuel also. Few people realize the extent to which agriculture depends on the input of energy.

Intensive farming calls for tractors and other implements (and fuels to run them), transport systems (and fuels to run them), fertilizers (made by chemical processes which consume large amounts of energy) and much else, pesticides, milking machines, even fencing. There is probably more steel embodied in agricultural fencing than in the entire railway system in a small country like Britain. All this steel, like the other metals used, not to mention concrete and asbestos, is made by using fuel. The truth is that, in energy terms, most of our food is bought at the price of *more energy expenditure than the food itself contains*. We are running down our account in the energy bank.

Taking a very long-term view, this is a process which can

only be continued as long as the fuel lasts out; sooner or later the population will necessarily drop to a level much lower than now. It is a matter of policy how far it is wise to use up irreplaceable resources. Do we really want to maintain the population at a biologically unnatural level by using up capital?

The discovery of nuclear fuels may enable us to postpone the evil day by a great many years—by which time, say the optimists, still further discoveries which we cannot foresee will save the situation. No need for us to worry.

There have been many forecasts that the world would run out of fuel, all of which have proved wrong so far, since new sources of fuel have repeatedly been found. I don't doubt that the world could continue for thousands of years at least before becoming bankrupt of energy. Long before it did so we should upset the earth's heat balance. It is certainly dubious, however, whether we can tap the new sources as fast as the demands of a mushrooming population require. It is widely imagined that the invention of atomic energy has solved all foreseeable problems, and it has constantly been said that a teacupful of uranium would propel the *Queen Elizabeth* across the Atlantic. The facts are very different, in practice. Only 2½ per cent of the fuel is utilizable. The fuel-charge for a 600 MW reactor of the kind now being built is about 320 tons of uranium, costing $6,400,000 with a further 60 tons a year, on average, for topping up. Supplies of uranium at current prices—about $5 to $10 a lb. —are expected to run out in the mid-1970's. Lower-grade sources can then be developed, however, provided people are willing to pay double the price, but this would make uranium uneconomic compared with coal and natural gas.

Tremendous sums are therefore being spent—the AEC has already spent $400m.—to develop 'breeder' reactors which can make the needed uranium–235 from the more plentiful uranium–238, a process which also makes the deadly plutonium–239. But the engineering problems are fantastic. Liquid sodium is highly corrosive and bursts into flame spontaneously if it touches water. For safety's sake magnetic pumps have been used in pilot plants to pump the sodium—but these have proved inadequate for scaled-up installations. It may cost another $1 billion to produce a successful 'breeder' and the risk of major accident in such plants will always be severe. I shall be profoundly surprised if there are any of these infernal machines producing commercially significant amounts of electricity as soon as 1980.

But in the long view, the growth of radio-active contamination and thermal pollution sets limits which entirely rule out maintaining the kind of populations and levels of industrialization currently foreseen for the opening decades of the twenty-first century, unless we are prepared to tolerate much higher leukemia rates etc. Only a technological miracle method of disposing of radio-active wastes could make the even larger populations foreseen for 2070 possible.

In the meantime, it seems folly to run down our energy resources banking on the performance of a technological miracle to save us from eventual bankruptcy. If this is true of energy, it is even truer of other resources. Nickel, tungsten and some other metals are already in short supply. But of all the raw materials we need, none is more critical than phosphorus, an essential constituent of DNA, the information-carrying molecule which programmes cell-growth and division. About 1 per cent of the dry weight of the human body is due to phosphorus. At present we discard enormous quantities of phosphorus in the form of sewage. The rivers wash down to the sea 3.5 tons of phosphorus a year, not to mention 10 million tons of fixed nitrogen and 100 million tons of potassium, the three main components of fertilizer. Ironically, we then collect the excreta of birds, under the name guano, and expensively convey it to farmers to replace the loss, but this meets only 3 per cent of it.

A corn crop at 60 bushels to the acre removes 10 per cent of the phosphorus in the top 6 inches of soil, and this the farmer must replace. This is why Cole observes that 'phosphorus is the critical limiting resource for the functioning of the ecosphere.' The earth contains plenty of phosphorus in the form of phosphate-bearing rock, but the concentrations are low, which makes it costly to extract, while much of the rock is buried deep until volcanic upheaval exposes it.

Another limiting factor is sulphur, required to make proteins, and usually applied to crops as ammonium sulphate.

Looking to the far future, some physicists contemplate the day when we can construct every kind of molecule we want from the basic atoms. Professor Harrison Brown declares: 'It can be shown that man could, if need be, live comfortably off ordinary rocks. A ton of granite contains easily extractable uranium and thorium equivalent to about 15 tons of coal, plus all the elements necessary to perpetuate a highly technological situation. Indeed, it would appear that we are heading for a new stone age!'

I take leave to doubt whether the energy in 15 tons of coal would be anything like enough to make the molecular syntheses of which he speaks so glibly. I suspect it would be too small by several thousand times, and that it would not even serve to process the granite, from which it is not really easy to extract uranium, which is why we don't do it. In any case, energy expenditure on this scale would upset the earth's heat balance.

And if we are really to trade on such remote possibilities, we must reckon that there will be a constant loss of material in the form of gas, much harder to recover from the atmosphere. Thus we shall have to nibble away at the earth, which will slowly get smaller! According to one calculation, by 1½ million tons a year.

Professor Harrison Brown points out that there is in use in the US, for every person, some 160 kilograms of copper, 140 kilograms of lead, 100 kilograms of zinc, 18 kilograms of tin and 110 kilograms of aluminium. To synthesize material on this scale for everyone in the world when the population is ten billions (Professor Harrison Brown's figure) is a project at which I am afraid my imagination boggles.

When population explosions occur in animal species, they are often limited by exhaustion or actual destruction of the food supply. There is an Australian leaf-eating psyllid—a bug —which so damages the leaves when it becomes too numerous that they drop off, leaving the psyllid with nothing to eat. Man may be headed the same way.

All these are long-term considerations. What are the chances of famine (possibly followed by plague or war, or both) cutting down the population within a much shorter period?

FAMINE OR GLUT?

Various eminent authorities have forecast something of the sort for man, and quite soon. The most serious of these warnings was perhaps that of the Director of the Food and

Agriculture Organization (FAO) of the United Nations, Dr B. R. Sen, who in 1965 felt impelled to write to Ministers and Secretaries of Agriculture throughout the world: 'The outlook is alarming. In some of the most heavily populated areas the outbreak of serious famines within the next five or ten years cannot be excluded.' Others, from the Swedish economist, Gunnar Myrdal, to former US ambassador Chester Bowles, agreed, using words like 'catastrophe' and 'calamity.'

Curiously enough, other eminent men were quite optimistic. In the same year as Sen's warning, the US Secretary of State for Agriculture, Mr Orville Freeman, rejoiced: 'It now seems possible to win the war against hunger within the next ten or twenty years'—though three years later, in his book *World Without Hunger*, he was more hesitant: 'At this hour, we are in danger of losing the war on hunger.' Two distinct schools of thought still exist as I write.

The optimists point to the doubled yields afforded by new strains of rice and wheat; they stress the achievement of Mexico, which, with massive US help, has raised agricultural output per head. The pessimists point to the difficulties in introducing the new strains in countries where water, fertilizer, capital and skill are in short supply; and point to the case of Peru, which with massive American help has *not* succeeded in raising agricultural output per head.

A plant is simply a machine for making more plants, and must be given more raw material when its output goes up. Hence the high-yield strains only give high yields when provided with greater quantities of water and fertilizer. The vast increases in output which the optimists hope for, on the grounds that tenfold increases are obtained in ideal conditions, are all predicated on enormous increases in fertilizer. At present most have-not countries do not put on as much fertilizer as the traditional strains could use, if they put on any. The entire continent of South America uses about as much fertilizer as Holland.

Some scientists have great confidence in the power of nuclear energy to solve food problems. Thus, according to one calculation, if the state of Uttar Pradesh installed five reactors between now and 1988, this would close the food gap. For 1 million KWh would suffice to pump water and make fertilizer for 4.7 million acres, one-quarter of the sown area of this state. An estimated yield of 3,000 lb. of grain per acre would feed the state's 92 million population, whereas at present a shortfall of 72 million tons is foreseen for 1990. (One may doubt whether a fertilizer application at a modest 100 lb. per acre would really bring about such huge yields and whether 1.5 million tons of fertilizer could really be extracted from the low-grade rocks and sources available.)

Obviously it is highly important to decide which party is right. Three things are immediately clear. First, there is no inherent reason why the world should not grow enough food for seven billion people or even more, eventually. *Technically,* there is no obstacle.

The problem is entirely one of *time.* Taking into account political, economic and social difficulties, is it likely that the world will expand output as fast as, or preferably faster than, population expands? That is the issue. If the world population reaches seven billion by 2000, but we do not produce food for this number until 2010, that means famine. Consequently, we first have to take a view on how fast we really think the population *is* going to grow.

ARE POPULATION FORECASTS CREDIBLE?

How seriously are we to take the prediction that world population will rise to about seven billion by the end of the century?

People often think that these projections are made simply by drawing a graph of past data and extending the curve by eye. Such a method can be justified for short-term forecasts, when the curve is mathematically regular, the commonest instances being when it is a straight line or a curve of the compound-interest type, known as an exponential curve. If you invest money at 5 per cent compound interest, it will double in 14 years; at 2 per cent it would take 35 years. But the population curve up to now has been more than exponential: the rate of interest, so to say, keeps increasing. A few years ago, the doubling time was 40 years; now it is down to 35 years, i.e. the growth rate is exactly 2 per cent.

However, demographers can do better than this. Population growth really depends on the number of females born and whether they eventually have families. If, for some strange reason, only boy-babies were born from now on, eventually there would be no women left capable of bearing children and the population would rapidly decline to zero, however high the birth rate this year or next. So the question is really whether fertile women are replacing themselves. Variations in the proportion of the sexes, and the proportion of women who actually have children, and when they have them, must be taken into account. A figure known as the net reproduction rate can be calculated in this way. It is still better to look at each country separately, calculating its probable population growth in the light of all the relevant facts, and then to add all the countries in the world together. Demographers do all these things. They also make alternative predictions, based on varying assumptions. Thus the United Nations produces a low, median and high forecast, based on different assumptions about how much effort will be put into birth-control and population planning. The low assumes some progress in introducing birth control by 2000 and foresees a world population of 5.3 billion; the median is 5.8 billion, but if the trend continues as it is going, the figure is 7.4 billion.

These predictions, published in 1964, have already proved too modest. World population today stands well above the 'high' curve on the UN chart. The fact is that all population forecasts, without exception, have proved to be too low, even when made by people anxious to prove the existence of a population explosion. Fairfield Osborn, of the Conservation Foundation, in his book *Our Crowded Planet,* published in 1963, described how one widely accepted projection of the US population, made in 1938, concluded that America would reach a peak of 140 million in 1969 and then decline; another thought the peak would be 154 million, but would not be reached until 1980. By 1947, the peak was being put at 165 million. Osborn himself then hesitates about a recent estimate that the figure would be 200 million to 300 million by the end of the century, commenting 'This seems an extreme view. . . . It is sufficient to take the now generally-accepted opinion that our population will reach a figure of at least 190 million by the year 1975.' In reality, of course, the 200 million mark was passed in 1969, and the current forecast for the year 2000 is 350 million at current rates of fertility, or 290 million at reduced rates.

Many people seem to have a built-in fear that the population will decline unless strenuous efforts are made to prevent this: this may be the remnant of a deeply-ingrained instinct. One eminent British demographer, writing in the 1920's, prophesied a population of 4 million for Britain by the 1970's! Indeed, in 1945, Mass Observation published a book declaring that 'a declining population in this country is inevitable, and will start almost immediately.' Britain's Royal Commission on Population, just after the war, after reviewing the evidence that an increase might cause difficulties, recommended that nothing be done to limit population, as one could not be absolutely certain that the difficulties would actually arise! Twenty years ago, the UK population was not expected to reach 55 million until the year 2000; in the event it has already reached it. Now 68 million is forecast for 2000.

World population forecasts are equally liable to underestimation. One of the most far-sighted prognosticators was Sir George Knibbs, who, as long ago as 1928, perceived that the world could not sustain its growth rate of 1 per cent per annum. He declared: ' . . . in the course of the present century mankind will be involved in very great difficulties, for which unquestionably it is unprepared.' His calculations suggested a population of 3.9 billion by 2008, which he felt was 'barely possible' while his projection of 7.8 billion by 2089 seemed to him so incredible that he added that AD 2138 seemed a more likely date. He would, one may suppose, have dismissed as ridiculous the suggestion that his figure for 2008 would be reached by 1975 or sooner. Knibbs's squib was, needless to say, treated as an old man's maundering by his contemporaries.

Naturally, such forecasts do not pretend to consider wholly unpredictable catastrophes, such as famines, plagues or wars on an unprecedented scale. Up to this time, such events have been too local to make much impact on the world trends, and population figures for the past naturally include the effect of these factors.

Nevertheless, people often argue that the population explosion will correct itself, on the grounds that people, as they become wealthier, reduce the size of their families. As far as the next 30 or 50 years are concerned, this is a vain hope. In the first place, the western countries have not *stabilized* their populations, but continue to expand at about 1 per cent per

annum (the rate which alarmed Sir George Knibbs). Even
Japan, so often quoted as an example of successful population limitation, still has a 1.1 per cent growth rate. In the
second place, the countries which now are expanding most
rapidly, notably Latin America where growth rates are
nearer 4 per cent than 3 per cent—are not wealthy, but
desperately poor. Their growth is not, as was the case in
nineteenth-century Europe and North America, associated
with rapid industrialization.

This comment does, however, pinpoint the crucial factor:
family size. It seems that people aim to replace themselves,
with perhaps a small safety margin, by producing two to
three children who reach adult status. Large families are a
response to high death-rates in infancy and childhood. In
many oriental countries the figure is 10 or 12 children born,
of whom formerly only 2 or 3 would survive. Now that death
rates have been cut dramatically, people begin to attempt to
limit their families, but not by the full amount required.
Custom is important, and a family of two seems ridiculous in
a culture geared to twelve. Experience shows that it takes
several generations for people to make a full response. The
first generation cuts back from 10 to 7 or 8; the next to 5 or
6 and so on. But the period we are looking at is little more
than one generation.

Indeed all the people who will be over 30 in the year 2000
have already been born.

If you think carefully about the mechanism of the population explosion you will see that it contains a built-in threshold
effect. As the health position improves, females survive to
childbearing age who would formerly have died before
reaching it. As soon as this happens, the effect on population
growth is sudden and dramatic. Thus if the death rate in
Guatemala should fall to that of the US in 1950—a realistic
possibility—the number of new-born females who would
survive to the beginning of the childbearing period would
increase by 36 per cent, and the number surviving to the end
would increase by 85 per cent. In other words, there would
have to be a decrease of more than 40 per cent in the birth
rate to have maintained the status quo.

Currently, many people are putting their faith in the
spread of contraceptive practices to limit population, both in
Europe and the world at large. All the evidence is that

contraception will only exert a small effect—perhaps a 5 per cent reduction in the over-all growth rate. In the United States, for instance, the size of family which people, on average, prefer to have is found to be either three or four children. Thus even if contraception is universally available in the US the population growth rate will be at least 2 per cent per annum. In Great Britain, the figure is a little better: 2.4 children per family. In oriental countries, where preferred family size is double or treble this, contraception will have even less effect. (For many countries, there are little or no data on preferred family size, and it is urgent that it should be gathered.) Unfortunately, it is not the case that, when people are poor, they try to restrict the family to a size they can afford. Sometimes they hope their position will improve; sometimes they see children as an asset, able to work in the fields or support them when they are old. There is thus little hope that the provision of contraception will, of itself, make much impact. The prime need is to convince people that *two* is the best family size.

There therefore seems no escape from the fact that, short of plague or nuclear war, we shall have to feed a population of about 7 billion by the year 2000.

The observation that all the people who will be over 30 in the year 2000 have already been born draws attention to the abnormal and highly inconvenient age-distribution which results from rapid expansion. It is already the case that in the under-developed world, about half the population is under 15 years of age. At the same time, improved medical care increases the numbers of elderly people. Hence in the year 2000, less than half the population, those in the 15–65 age-group, will be carrying the majority on their backs. The problems of providing schools and teachers become immense. In some African countries, already, despite unprecedented programmes of school-building, the percentage of children receiving education is falling: children are born faster than schools can be put up to receive them.

This is why during the past decade, although the illiteracy *rate* has declined, the actual number of illiterates has actually increased by 70 million. In 1970, out of 2,335 million adults in the world, 810 million (34.5 per cent) will not meet the minimum standards of education. Since some education is needed to employ modern farming methods, or to work in industry, this state of affairs must affect food prospects. Earlier estimates of illiteracy were, it is now thought, unduly low because it was not appreciated that the drop-out rate after enrolment is high: as much as 68 per cent in mid-African primary schools. The battle for literacy 'is still not won and could still very easily be lost', says UNESCO.

The problems created by the youth-bulge are only a special instance of the problems created by high population growth rates generally. Capital investment, which in a stable population could be devoted to industrialization, which would improve the standard of living, has to be devoted to providing more of the basic necessities—schools, hospitals, houses, transport and so on. The advocates of unlimited population growth frequently assert that population growth is stimulating to economic advance, and point to the nineteenth century as a supposed case in point. But it is not the case that the Industrial Revolution occurred *because* the population was growing: if anything, it was the other way about. And while a small rate of growth may, perhaps, be stimulating, the present explosive rate is certainly an economic drag, and tough on existing populations. As can be shown mathematically, expenditure on population control can do more to raise living standards, by releasing capital for industrial expansion, than any other type of expenditure.

To sum up, a rapid *rate* of population growth, quite apart from creating more mouths to fill, actually makes it harder to fill the mouths there are, by distorting the social and economic structure. This fact, though less obvious than simple shortages of equipment and the like, may in reality be the biggest obstacle to the solving of immediate food problems.

PROTEIN SHOCK

When one speaks of feeding the world population it is necessary to be clear what one means. If 'feed' means ensure everyone the minimum necessary for health, then we do not feed the existing world population now. Every day some 15,000 people die of hunger. Many others are undernourished to the point where their vitality is impaired and their liability to disease increased. Those who play down the talk of famine fail to realize that famine is here, now. In the year

2000, with a doubled world population, a doubled output of food will merely mean that 30,000 people a day will be dying of starvation instead of fifteen, unless some drastic redistribution between rich and poor has occurred. To ensure that all are adequately fed by then calls for something like a tripling of food output in thirty years. This means an agricultural growth rate approaching 4 per cent per year. But let us look into the problem more closely.

In the first place it is necessary, broadly speaking, that the food be produced in the country which is to consume it. If it has to be transported long distances, this will make it unreasonably expensive, especially as transport systems are ill-suited to the new, and shifting, patterns of surplus and shortage which are developing. Thus in 1968 India had a surplus, but Russia a shortage of wheat. Needless to say, there are no easy links between these countries, which are separated by the Himalayan range of mountains. Furthermore, the needy country may lack the foreign currency with which to purchase surpluses, as is generally the case in South America, for instance. Nor do developing countries have the vast storage facilities which have been built up in places like Canada and the US.

The coming years will inevitably see 'surpluses' of certain products in some countries, with shortage of the same products elsewhere. This kind of imbalance can also exist within a country. As agriculture becomes more mechanized, labour is displaced and must be found work in industry, if the individuals concerned are to have the wherewithal to buy food. It follows that, unless industry expands *pari passu* with agriculture, starvation and surpluses will both increase, unless the surplus is given away. Industrial products will also be needed to provide exports in a world of food surpluses. Unfortunately, there is nothing equivalent to the new strains of wheat and rice which will double the yield of industrial concerns in a single year. The new strains, therefore, may create as many problems as they solve, and prove a very mixed blessing. Industry *must* be expanded in the developing countries.

A further difficulty arises because, as incomes rise, people do not simply buy more of the same basic foods, but begin to branch out, first probably asking for meat and a variety of fruit and vegetables, later for preserves and so forth. At the same time, they cut back their demand for basic grains. As a country advances industrially, therefore, the demand is for specific foods, not for just 'food'. It becomes necessary to build up market-gardening and stocks of sheep, cattle, hens and pigs. As Europe discovered after World War II, this is a slow process. Again, town-dwellers tend to be worse nourished than country-dwellers for lack of effective distribution arrangements; country-dwellers can also supplement what they buy by home-grown produce from gardens or 'allotments'.

Grain surpluses will co-exist with shortages of meat and vegetables. Apart from the question of food preferences, protein is a necessary component of an adequate diet. It is the primary material of which muscle is made. Lack of protein causes the wasting disease known as kwashiorkor— meaning 'first-second disease', a name given it in Africa where the first child commonly developed the disease when displaced from the mother's breast by a second child. Kwashiorkor leads to permanent stunting, lassitude, mental retardation and eventually death. It also renders the victim liable to infections, as blood globulin falls. What this means is shown by the fact that 20 children per 1,000 in the 1–4 age group die in 'have-not' countries as compared with one in 'have' countries.* Though the importance of protein is widely known, calculations based simply on calorie-values are still frequently made by economists.

Furthermore, there is protein and protein. The word used should be 'proteins' for there are thousands of different proteins. All are made from the chemical units known as amino-acids, of which there are about twenty kinds, arranged in varying sequences. Plants contain some protein, but it is for the most part low in certain amino-acids (e.g. lysine) which human beings need. Meat, fish and eggs contain more suitable proportions of these amino-acids, and are known as high-quality protein. Some plants—beans, peas, nuts and other pulses—also contain high-quality protein. Those who advocate a vegetarian diet for whole nations must therefore allow for the fact that these high-quality-protein plants would have to be grown in large quantities. A gleam of

*In India, where anemia is common, due to malnutrition, attempts to limit population with IUDs (intra-uterine contraceptive devices) have often failed because of the bleeding they induced.

hope dawned recently when it was suggested that missing amino-acids might be added to cereals. Experiments are being made in enriching grain with the amino-acid lysine, but it is not yet established how far enriched grain can act as a substitute for meat protein.

Dr P. V. Sukhatme, the director of Statistics of the Food and Agriculture Organization, has produced a paper based on figures from one state in India which argues that the protein problem has been greatly over-stated, since, if really adequate amounts of cereals are produced, their protein content will be sufficient to meet most basic needs. This may be true of India, where starchy roots are not much eaten; it is unlikely to be true of Africa, however.

Those who pin their faith on the normal practice, meeting protein needs with meat, fish and eggs, must allow for the fact that cows, sheep and hens consume vegetable matter and require grassland to live on. Again, some economists are guilty, when they calculate how many people could be supported on a given land-area, of overlooking the fact that a proportion of the land must be devoted to these secondary purposes. They also overlook the need to devote some land to growing sugar, coffee, tea and even grapes and hops, if a reasonably agreeable diet is to be available. And to this may be added the need for wool, rubber, sisal, timber and wood-pulp and other non-food items.

Animal protein, too, is relatively expensive. To bring diets in have-not countries up to the basic minimum of 20 grams (¾ oz.) a day would raise the cost of the poor man's diet by two-thirds, small as the amount is.

The task of providing adequate protein will, I believe, emerge increasingly as the important issue in the years ahead.

There are other difficulties which optimists leave out of their calculations. Thus, it has recently been found that when people are receiving a good protein diet, they consume their stocks of vitamin A much more rapidly, so when protein is made available to under-nourished peoples, vitamin A deficiencies may suddenly appear. The health of the respiratory tract, the stomach and intestinal linings, and the surfaces of the eye depend on vitamin A. Obviously this vitamin must be given along with the protein.

There is no need to describe all the other vitamin and

trace element requirements of the human body, which a nutritional programme must aim to satisfy. I wish only to drive in the point that feeding the world adequately is a highly complicated task. Those who are optimistic base their optimism either on rather crude calculations about the quantities of cereal which could be produced, or on the assumption that if people are not actually dying in the streets from simple hunger, their diet is satisfactory, or on both.

EROSION

In all this, I have said nothing about erosion. So much is heard of the reclamation of deserts by irrigation and the need to plough up grassland, that it is seldom realized that, thanks to bad agricultural practices and the felling of forests, the world is losing agricultural land at a fantastic rate.

In the US the dust-bowls, which deprived the country of an area equal to two French departments in 10 years, have been almost forgotten. In Brazil, rapid erosion has followed the development of coffee growing. In Madagascar nine-tenths of the land has been rendered unusable. In France, André Guerrin reports, nearly 6 million acres have been ruined in the south-east, where erosion is active and landslides and torrents are common; in the Dordogne–Jura area, another million acres are badly damaged; while in the rest of France about 2.4 million acres are being actively eroded. In all, about 11 million acres or one-thirteenth of the land area of France.

Another way of measuring erosion is by the amount of soil carried down to the sea by rivers. For the Seine the figure, in millions of cubic yards, is 5.2—but for the Mississippi it is 392.4, for the Yangtse Kiang 457.8 and for the Yellow River an incredible 654.0 every year.

An FAO paper summarizes the position thus: 'Erosion is threatening the continued productivity of more than half the world's irrigated land, some of which is losing an inch of topsoil every 3 years.' The position is particularly serious in Africa, where over-grazing is common and excessive numbers of cattle, kept for prestige reasons, crowd round the villages, destroying the grass which binds the topsoil. The rainfall is terrific—the Congo has over 70 inches. In North Somaliland, where there are no rivers, three or four million tons of water may pour down the wadis in a single day. In many areas, such as Tanganyika and Kenya, water-erosion is interspersed with water-shortages, so that wind-erosion occurs while the land is dry. In some places, the Sahara desert is advancing at 30 miles a year. The productive capacity of South African agricultural soils has been reduced by 30 per cent within the last 100 years.

Cultivating land can accelerate erosion. An area of forest on the Ivory Coast, which had been cleared, lost 93 tons of soil per hectare in the first year, compared with 2.4 tons lost by neighbouring uncleared forest. In the following year, the proportions were 28.7 and 0.03 tons. Overall, Africa is losing 300 million tons of soil a year and may be unable to feed its population in only 15 years' time.

Other areas where erosion is serious include the Punjab and Bengal (with rainfall over 90 inches per year), the foothills of the Andes in Venezuela and Colombia, and parts of Brazil and the Argentine. The very climate has altered from humid to semi-arid in SE Asia and the Amazon basin, thanks to soil erosion in headwater areas. China is probably another instance.

All this is due to man. Before man came the rivers moved 9.3 billion tons of solids to the sea annually; now the figure is 24 billions, 2½ times as much. It is only in the last decade that world-wide soil-erosion surveys have even been made. The scale of the problem is still not generally appreciated.

With erosion and all these other difficulties in mind, let us try to assess realistically the prospects of averting malnutrition and undernourishment during the next thirty years or so, starting as we do with 80 per cent of the world's population undernourished (i.e. short of cereal) and one quarter of these also malnourished (short of protein).

THE PROBLEMS AHEAD

Towards the close of 1969 there was a spurt of optimism when it became known that, in 1968, while world population increased by 2 per cent, the output of food, over the world as a whole, rose by 3 per cent. It was the first time for several years that the figure of food per head of population had shown an improvement.

But a closer look at the figures shows that optimism is

premature: most of the improvement was in the industrially-developed countries. And, though India was much better off, in many under-developed countries, notably in South America, food-per-head continued to decline. The truth is, it is only those countries which are fortunate enough to have an efficient government, determined to tackle the problem of increasing food output, where advances are made. In all the have-not countries there are problems of land ownership, of supply of capital to farmers, of agricultural price policy, of lack of expert knowledge, and so on, which block the path of agricultural growth. Some governments prefer to strengthen their currency position by fostering the tourist trade, pouring into hotels and highways money which might, in a long view, be better spent on re-equipping agriculture and providing it with power, water and transport. In some South American countries, land ownership is still on a quasi-feudal basis; landowners may prefer to grow a crop, like coffee, for export, rather than food for local consumption. And, in some, government measures are nullified by corruption.

My judgment is that, while cereal needs will largely be met protein needs will not; the situation will be worst in the quasi-feudal countries, where even cereal needs will not be met, unless massive aid is organized. In some of these countries revolutions will occur, as a result of which the food-picture will begin to change. In addition to the tensions within such countries, there will be growing tension between have and have-not countries, as the former grow richer both in food and goods, and the gap widens. There are already signs of the trouble I predict: late in 1969 widespread unrest was reported from India, where mechanized farming has displaced hundreds of thousands of agricultural workers, and the disparities between the wealthier farmers and the landless or sharecropping tenants is growing steadily more blatant.

It is a cliché in some quarters (and not always true) that well fed people do not revolt. It would be nearer the truth to say that undernourished people do not revolt: it is when they become a little less undernourished that they find the energy to do so. There are unquestionably many things mankind could do to alleviate immediate food shortages. The sea could be more intensively farmed, though not as intensively as is often suggested—many areas are over-fished already. Russian trawlers exhausted the St George Bank of haddock in a single visit recently. Halibut fishing between Norway and Greenland has vanished. Fish congregate mostly over the continental shelves, where the plankton are numerous, thanks to nutrients washed from the land. In the last decade no over-all increase in the yield of fish has occurred, and in the worst cases it has actually fallen—chiefly as a result of man's overstressing the environment. The idea that the deep oceans are crammed with fish waiting to be caught is a landlubber's delusion. Enormous wastages of stored food due to moulds, rats, etc., could be reduced. Wild animals from the hippo ('a large hunk of edible pork', according to Lord Ritchie-Calder) to the saiga antelope of Russia, which tastes like mutton, could be hunted for protein: even the giant African snail, twelve inches across its base, has been proposed as a source of protein. All this could, and should, be done. But will it? Eventually, no doubt—but the pace at which things are now moving does not suggest that it will be done in the limited time available. People are reluctant to change food habits and will even starve rather than do so. Some American prisoners of war in the Far East died because they would not eat rice. The same thing occurred two centuries ago, when the potato was first widely introduced in Britain. The peoples of the developing countries are no different from Britons and Americans in this respect. 'It is my opinion,' says H. F. Robinson, Vice Chancellor of the University System of Georgia, 'that these most difficult decisions . . . will not be made in time.'

It is a natural and sensible course, for any country trying to expand food production, to attack first those areas which will give the most rapid return—to plough good soil before starting on the poor; to bring water short distances for irrigation before bringing it longer distances; and to concentrate on those crops where yields can be raised fastest. So, as time passes, the situation gets tougher and tougher. The improvements in output which were seen in 1968, and which may continue to be seen for several years, reflect this policy. It is later on that output will increase ever more slowly, while population increases ever faster. The high-yield strains only exaggerate this contrast. In my view, therefore, the crisis will not come in 1975 but will become more and more imminent as we approach the end of the century. If, on top of this, we have a steady worsening of the climate, and if radiation dangers limit the output of nuclear power, the situation will obviously deteriorate still faster. Finally, if disturbances of the ecosystems affect plants and animals used for food, the position could well become catastrophic, not merely for the have-nots, but for the haves as well.

The food problem arises because man, like a plague of locusts, has outrun the capacity of the environment to support him. If he tries to meet the situation by modifying the environment still further, he merely ensures eventual disaster. Postponing the evil day only makes the crash worse. It is man who must be brought under control.

But the food supply is not, as so many economists seem to think, the usual limiting factor in population explosions. Much more often the cause of collapse, which comes long before food supplies are exhausted, is stress.

10 Population Crash: When?

IN 1916 FOUR OR FIVE Sika deer were released on James Island, in Chesapeake Bay, half a square mile of uninhabited territory less than a mile from the shore. By 1956 the herd had built up to nearly 300, when John Christian, an ethologist who believed that animal populations are regulated by mechanisms which respond to density, moved in. He did not have too long to wait. In the first three months of 1958, over half the deer died. The next year, deaths continued until the population levelled off at about 80.

This is about normal for a population crash: it falls to around one-third the original level and it does it fast. The first interesting point is that the deer, though crowded, were not as crowded as all that: the density of population was about one to the acre and the food supply was perfectly adequate. Twelve dead deer were collected for close examination and seemed to be in good shape, with shining coats and fat deposits between well-developed muscles. Why, then, had 190 deer died?

Christian had shot five deer when he arrived and made a very thorough examination of them; in addition to weighing them, recording the presence or absence of fat, and noting the contents of their stomachs, he made miscroscopic examinations of the adrenal and other glands, and the main organs. He also examined deer taken in 1960, after the die-off. He soon found that the adrenals were much enlarged in the deer which died during the crash: 46 per cent heavier than in those which died in 1960. In immature deer the difference was strikingly greater: 81 per cent heavier. Abnormal cell structure in the adrenals of these deer confirmed the idea that they had died from stress. For adrenal glands enlarge in response to continued stress conditions. The fact that 1958 was a cold winter in this area no doubt increased the stress, but would not in itself account for such a massive die-off.

The idea that stress might be a factor in regulating population had first surfaced in World War II. As early as 1939 it had been observed that snow-shoe hares were dying in convulsive seizures; there were curious contractions of the head and neck, extensions of the legs, and the animals made sudden leaps and went into spasms on alighting. Others, however, were lethargic or comatose. When dissected, they were found to have haemorrhages of the adrenals, thyroid, brain and kidneys, with fatty degeneration of the liver. During the mass migrations of lemmings, which follow a population explosion among these animals, so tense are they that the sight of a female will sometimes cause a male to drop dead, the additional stress on his adrenals proving the last straw. A loud noise can have the same effect.

Nevertheless, until Christian, who was head of the Animal Laboratories of the Naval Research Institute at Bethesda, wrote his classic paper in 1950 on 'The Adreno-Pituitary System and Population Cycle in Mammals' the significance of these observations was overlooked. Christian argued that animals which have gone through a severe winter, involving additional effort on insufficient food, undergo adrenal stress in the spring and burn all their sugar. In this condition, any additional stress causes sugar-loss leading to brain starvation.

Strikingly enough, American prisoners in Korea also sometimes became lethargic or died from convulsive seizures; the disease was dubbed 'give-up-itis'.

The Rev. Thomas Malthus had propounded the idea that populations tended to expand until they outran their food supply. His fears that population growth might lead to starvation in the near future proved wrong because—so economists are fond of saying—the output of food was enormously increased by the development of fertile lands in the New World and Australia, coupled with the growth of industrialization and improved farming techniques.

But there are many observations which suggest that, in animals at least, starvation is not necessarily the limiting factor. Another factor is predation, as we saw from Conway's account of the pests which attacked the Malayan cocoa-trees. But it has been noted that jack-rabbits die off even where there is plenty of food and the number of predators is no larger than usual. (They show stress symptoms, however.) Similarly, mice kept in cages at the University of Wisconsin fluctuated in numbers although there were no predators, they had plenty of food, and seasonal rigours were excluded.

As biologists have studied how animal populations are regulated it has emerged that animals have evolved many mechanisms for avoiding increase to the point at which starvation takes a hand. For instance, flour beetles, when crowded, produce a gas which is lethal to their larvae and which is also anti-aphrodisiac. Many species of animals, from fish and crabs to rodents and lions, kill or even eat their young when conditions become crowded: infanticide was also practised by primitive man. Dr Hudson Hoagland of the Worcester Foundation declares: 'In all species experimentally investigated, the mortality is found to be dependent on population density and to cease below a certain critical population density.'

The current view is that population explosions occur when these various methods of regulation break down, and then the population may expand to the point at which starvation becomes the regulator, except when the pressure can be relieved by migration. If, however, the rapid growth of population leads to serious crowding, stress may prove to be the limiting constraint. It is when no space is available to spread out that starvation becomes significant. The panicking lemmings are seeking more space, as they desperately try to swim the ice-jammed rivers and drown. The locust, having eaten all the food, moves on and only meets his doom when no more food can be found. The Sika deer could not spread out.

Man is in no way exempted from the laws of population growth. He has rejected the practice of infanticide, but he has, up till now, been able to expand into new territory, thus avoiding the build-up of stress. But now expansion is becoming very difficult, while his preference for living in ever-larger cities introduces a new element into the situation. Is it now likely that he will be constrained by stress more than by starvation? In either case, biology suggests that the population will not merely press against the limits, as Malthus supposed, but will decline catastrophically. Unless something quite unforeseen happens, we must assume that mankind is heading for a population crash. Is it possible then to deduce when it may come and how near to such a crash we are?

The point is so fascinating that you might suppose that someone had attempted such an analysis. But I know of none and am forced to offer my own prognostications.

CROWDED HABITATIONS

If mankind were seized with claustrophobia and spread itself out as thinly as possible over the habitable land surface of the world, how much privacy and isolation could each person obtain? Each man, woman or child would find him or herself about 150 yards from his nearest neighbour. By the year 2000, the distance will have shrunk to 120 yards and by 2070 to 60 yards. Imagine the plains of the Middle West with dwellings 120 yards apart in every direction and you have the picture. When the deer on James Island began to die of brain haemorrhages they were about 80 yards apart.

It is therefore fortunate, no doubt, that man does not spread out thus, but crowds into cities, which complicates the question of stress. He is, in addition, unevenly distributed as between different countries or areas. I propose accordingly to examine both these factors.

It is unfortunate that we have to make use of political units in order to discuss densities, but that is how the figures are gathered. Recalculation according to more sociologically-interesting areas is urgently needed. Thus the United Kingdom, at 570 persons to the square mile, appears more densely populated than India, at 385 persons to the square mile, and very much more than the US at 58 persons to the square mile. But the United Kingdom includes mountainous Scotland and Wales, where only the valleys are habitable, and underpopulated Ireland. If we take England alone, the figure rises to 910 persons to the square mile, which handsomely exceeds Madras State (about the same area) and is probably the highest for any administrative unit of comparable size in the world. In India, only the small state of Kerala (15,000 square miles) tops it at a terrific 1,260 to the square mile. Is it only coincidence that Kerala is the most Communist-disposed area in India?

The significance of such figures will become clearer when

we have considered the other element in the situation: the growth of cities. Professor Kingsley Davis, head of the International Population and Urban Research Center at Berkeley, calculates that by 1990 more than half the world's population will be living in cities of over 100,000 inhabitants. In the forty years between 1920 and 1960, the world's urban population (defined as living in towns of 20,000 people or more) trebled, but its non-urban population rose only by one-third.

Country-dwellers outnumbered town-dwellers by 6.4 to 1 in 1920, by 3 to 1 in 1960. By 2000, town-dwellers will outnumber country-dwellers. 'Neither the speed nor the recency of this evolutionary development is widely appreciated,' he says. In developing countries cities are growing at a terrifying rate, far outstripping the city boom of the nineteenth century. The biggest spurts have been in South America, where 21 million now live in cities of 1 million or over—in 1920 none did so. The doubling time is often around 15 years, sometimes even faster. Thus Caracas, which held 359,000 people in 1941, had 1,507,000 in 1963. São Paulo, which held 879,000 in 1930, is 6.9 million now and will be 19.2 million, it is estimated, by the year 2000. Russia now has 204 cities of over 100,000 population, including 8 over 1 million. Seemingly overnight, unfamiliar names have joined the roster of great cities—Kazan (837,000), Tbilisi (866,000), Chelyabinsk (851,000), Donetsk (855,000), Perim (811,000) and so on. The USSR claims that already 55 per cent of the Russian population lives in cities and towns, and the figure will reach 70 per cent by 1980. An average of twenty new towns are erected every year.

Calculations of the rate of urbanization are usually based on towns of 20,000 and upwards, but it is the cities which count (as we shall see) and they are growing faster than the towns. In the past 40 years, big cities quadrupled where urban areas as a whole tripled in population. At a guess, there are 300 cities of over half-a-million population in the world today.

The main (but not the only) reason for the phenomenal growth of cities is the mechanization of agriculture. As a rule of thumb, one may say that an under-developed country will have 80 per cent of its population in agriculture, 20 per cent in industry, and a developed country will have the proportions reversed. Most of the 60 per cent who are displaced from agriculture will head for the towns and probably for one of the biggest cities, in the hope of finding work. Let us see what this means when it is combined with a rapid population expansion. Take the case of Turkey, where at present 27 million people work on the land, and 7 million people live in cities, a ratio of about 80 : 20. Now Turkey's population is increasing at about a million a year, doubling every 25 years. The birth rate at 55 per 1,000 is near the theoretical maximum (60 per 1,000). The death rate is 21 per 1,000. By 2010, it is calculated, the population will be pushing 110 million, with 20 million or so on the land, and 90 million in the cities. Let me repeat that: the city population will have grown from 7 million to 90 million. How are the houses, schools and other services to be provided, in a country which is still in the early stages of industrialization? To pick out a single item, the increase calls for the provision of 30,000 *additional* teachers a year, leaving aside that the existing teaching force is inadequate.

However, the question of interest here is: what will the conditions be like in such cities? Are they likely to be such as to impose intolerable stress on the occupants? Afterwards, we can consider the quite different problems of cities in industrially-advanced communities.

The extreme instance of city growth is expected to be Calcutta, which is currently expanding by 300,000 a year; Kingsley Davis estimates that it is headed for a population of between 36 and 66 million by the end of the century, when population growth and agricultural modernization are allowed for, though its growth is due more to its central role in the area than to these factors. Already it is in a state of social disorganization. The Metropolitan Planning Commission says that it sees 'no prospect' of housing the population over the next 25 years. At the moment, open-sided sheds are being built to provide some sort of shelter. Twenty or thirty people share a single cold tap. Sewage runs in open gutters in the streets, and at times of river-flood may be washed anywhere. People wash their clothes and themselves in the polluted water. Other parts of the city, of course, are highly civilized—but the disorganized sector is growing. Traffic problems are already acute, especially at the main bridge across the river, crossed by half a million pedestrians every day, in addition to animals and motorized traffic. It is inconceivable that the city can continue to operate at a level of 30 million inhabitants or more.

New York, with a much longer experience, finds it hard enough to function at 12 million. Cities like Calcutta can hardly avoid becoming jungles, in which crime cannot be controlled, in which health standards cannot be maintained, and in which people die on the pavement without the fact even being remarked.

Many of the burgeoning cities in 'have-not' countries consist of a developed core, surrounded by a shanty-town of squatters on a colossal scale. In Mexico City, one-third of the population of 1.5 million lives in the *colonias proletarias*—the proletarian colonies, as they are called. In Ankara, one half lives in the *geçekondu* districts; in Kinshasa (former Leopoldville) the squatter town is larger than the city itself. Lima adjoins two settlement areas, each with over 100,000 population—one is in effect the third largest city in the country. These areas, though thrown together from petrol-cans and whatever else can be found, are not necessarily slums. Often the inhabitants are artisans with a steady income and struggle to improve their surroundings, often in the face of government opposition, since the government has long-term redevelopment plans for the area. The inhabitants are understandably more anxious to get a school, however ramshackle, *now* than to have a beautiful one in twenty years' time. Other areas, however, are going steadily downhill, their inhabitants defeated by the struggle for existence.

The situation is likely to deteriorate, since the populations are expanding faster than the authorities can cope. For example, Lima, which had 600,000 inhabitants 25 years ago, will have 6 million in 25 years' time, and while one-quarter of the population now lives in the *barriadas,* by 1990 three-quarters will be doing so. I fancy the world will see explosive unrest in such cities well before that date.

CONDITIONS IN CITIES

The physical conditions in cities are, in general, inferior to those in towns. Studies in Britain and America show that cities receive 15 per cent less sunshine on horizontal surfaces (and 30 per cent less ultra-violet in winter) and 10 per cent more rain, hail or snow. There are 10 per cent more cloudy days, and 30 per cent more fog in summer, and 100 per cent more fog in winter. Visibility is 1 mile or less for ten times as many hours. However, they are 5° to 15°C. warmer, and wind-speeds are lower. Small towns which lie downwind from great cities also show similar effects.

The incidence of many diseases is markedly higher in cities, and not simply infectious diseases. Thus, in cities of a million population or over, bronchocarcinoma (lung cancer) is just about double the rural rate. Bronchitis is also much higher.

More significant are crime and mental sickness rates. A classic study was carried out in Chicago in the thirties by Faris and Dunham. The city was divided into 11 types of area comprising 120 sub-communities, and rates established for each. In every case, the rates were high at the centre and declined steadily as one moved further away from it. Thus there were 362 cases per 1,000 of schizophrenia in the centre, grading down to 55.4 on the periphery. There were 240 cases of alcoholic psychosis per thousand in the centre, grading down to 60 at the periphery. Crime, suicide, drug-taking all showed a similar pattern.

Even at the periphery rates were higher than in small towns. Check-studies made in Providence, Rhode Island, showed schizophrenia ranging from 45 to 0 against Chicago's 362 down to 55.

The question was at once raised whether city-existence caused these high rates, or were the insane, suicidal and alcoholic drawn to the centre of cities just because they were round the bend? The smooth grading from the centre outward made this look unlikely, and closer study showed that the rates were linked with the level of social organization. Thus first-generation Polish communities, with a well-knit family life, exhibited relatively good rates; second-generation Poles, torn between the two cultures, were frequently unstable. Again, blacks living in all-black areas had low psychosis rates, but high ones when they lived in mixed areas. Even normal adults, when totally isolated, undergo a deterioration of personality. More recent studies in other cities confirm this impression, though much more work on the nature of social organization in cities is badly needed. Honolulu, for instance, includes a central area known as Hell's Half Acre, where social pathology is high. Cities evolve social structure, given time. It is rapid growth which creates the problem, especially where there is movement in and out or between different areas in the city. Exactly similar signs of disorientation are found on new housing estates in Britain. A tendency to believe in magic or irrational forces, and to act on whim is a common response to living in a world which seems arbitrary and unintelligible.

In short, it seems certain that the mushrooming cities of the immediate future will be plagued by crime and mental disturbance of various kinds. These are certainly evidence of severe stress. Persons affected are less likely to reproduce. But cities exert stresses over and above social disorganization and greater risks of disease. It used to be said that three generations in a big city would bring a family to its end. The city is fed from the country's healthy stock, and many of its inhabitants retire again to the country before they die. These beliefs also require detailed investigation.

Among the stresses imposed by the city is noise: one which we are ill-equipped to regulate because its effects are hard to quantify. As is often pointed out, a noise which is acceptable in one context—the roar of a football crowd, perhaps—is unacceptable in another. Late at night, even quite low-intensity sounds can be disturbing. Furthermore, we interpret sounds in terms of their possible meaning and those which suggest danger cause alerting reactions, with adrenal discharges; and adrenal reactions are precisely what we are on the watch for. Man, like many other animals, has instinctive reaction-patterns to noise: a loud noise is one of the three things which alarm a newborn baby, still innocent of experience. Noises which have a high 'attack-rate', i.e. the intensity builds up to a peak in microseconds—are particularly disturbing, probably because in nature they occur only when large stresses are being released, as when a tree starts to fall.

Professor Joseph P. Buckley, at the University of Pittsburgh, conducted experiments in which rats were subjected for several weeks to the sounds, on tape, of compressed air-blasts, bells, buzzers, etc., at high intensity (100 decibels) for half a minute every five minutes. Flashing lights and oscillation of the cage were also introduced, and the stress periods continued for four hours a day. All rats developed hypertension within three months, and many had enlarged adrenals. Some died. Incidentally, tranquillizers not only failed to block the effects of stress, but actually increased the death-rates. In Australia, Mary Lockett discovered the curious additional fact that noises too high for man to hear stressed rats, while very low notes caused a quite different glandular reaction. Other experimental work, this time due to Dr Lester Sontag at Yellow Springs, Ohio, showed that the foetus within a pregnant woman can perceive sounds and its heart-rate changes, while it is also affected by changes produced by noise in the mother. If a mother is apprehensive or emotionally disturbed, during the later stages of pregnancy, the offspring will show effects, such as undue apprehension and over-activity at the age of two or three. Sontag concludes that we need to be concerned about the possibility of foetal damage from such violent sounds as sonic booms. 'It seems not unlikely that adults are not alone in their objection to such noxious stresses. The foetus, while he cannot speak for himself, may have equal or greater reason to object to them.' Other experiments show that maternal anxiety of this kind can actually be inherited.

These recently uncovered facts demonstrate, once again, how calm we remain about the possible danger of insults to our system, until the consequences can no longer by shrugged off.

I suspect that an even more important stressor than noise is the mere presence of strangers. In many languages the word for stranger and the word for enemy are identical. For countless generations man has been conditioned to regard the stranger as a potential threat. In urban life, we encounter strangers continually every day, some few of whom may indeed offer a threat, whether from malice or from carelessness. There is some psychiatric work which confirms the idea that every stranger arouses a degree of unconscious alarm, which we conceal, even from ourselves, by various social formulae. Every traveller knows how exhausting it is to meet strangers socially, day after day, however friendly they may be. I suspect that research will show that people prefer to limit the number of such contacts, and that cities impose stresses by obliging their inhabitants to exceed these limits.

Failing research in these areas, we are obliged to study the pathology of overcrowding in animals.

CROWDING IN ANIMALS

Crowded animals exhibit signs of adrenal stress accompanied by a failure of maternal behaviour. Litter-size falls and embryos are sometimes resorbed. As maternal care diminishes, infantile mortality rises. The newborn are underweight and growth is stunted. Meanwhile the males are more aggressive, sexually and otherwise. At 50, or even 100, to the acre rabbits show few signs of stress. But at 200 to the acre, death rates rise dramatically.

John B. Calhoun, a Scot with a long family history of emigration because of land shortage, took up Christian's proposition and carried out some experiments with mice and rats which have become famous. In his first enquiries, he found that rats placed in a quarter-acre enclosure increased in number until there were 150 of them, after 27 months. The population then levelled off, due to the high infant mortality.

Subsequently, he ran experiments in which the numbers of animals were kept constant, by removing the young as they were born, at very high densities—80 rats in a cage 14 ft. by 10 ft. They displayed the usual male aggressiveness and inadequate maternal care, which characterize overcrowded animals, but with some strange additional features. Bands of young males roved about assaulting the females. Much homosexual behaviour was observed among both males and females. Dominant males engaged in tail-biting of other males: normally males fight when challenged but do not engage in sly aggression. Many people thought they saw similarities between such behaviour and that of modern city-dwellers of the human kind.

Calhoun also observed what he calls 'pathological togetherness'. Rats would get so used to feeding when other rats were present that finally they would refuse to feed unless other rats were also feeding. When he provided four inter-communicating pens, the rats crowded together in two of them, leaving the other two largely unoccupied. This further disrupted maternal behaviour, and infantile mortality, which had been around 80 per cent before, now rose to 96 per cent.

Soon after Calhoun reported these observations, Dr Alexander Kessler, then at the Rockefeller Institute, began what Calhoun has called 'one of the most important experimental studies of population of recent years'. He developed two enormously dense populations of mice which did *not* show stress symptoms. These mice were in standing-room-only conditions at about 100 to the square foot. Calhoun did similar experiments, which suggested that it all depends what you are used to. Mice accustomed to moving about a large area were more distressed by crowding than those which had always known cramped conditions; the males fought more and the females made worse mothers.

But the situation cannot be understood unless we take into consideration the social structure which prevails in any group of animals, even caged mice and rats. Much has been heard of the 'pecking order', first observed in hens, in which a hierarchy is established, Hen A pecking B, but not being pecked; B pecking C and so on. More recently it has been found that such hierarchies develop only where animals are to some degree crowded. The more normal pattern is for animals to claim territories, which they defend. Battles are fought to determine these territorial ownerships, the losers being driven to the margins of the desired areas, where they often perish as these areas are less suitable for existence. When territory is established, it is protected: but with the passage of time, neighbours grow more friendly, and tolerate a certain amount of trespass, though they at once attack strangers. They may even greet their neighbours at the margin of their territory in a friendly manner. To these territories they can retire to heal their wounds or regain their confidence, knowing they will be unchallenged.

Human beings behave in a closely similar manner. While there is always some risk in arguing from animals to man, Dr Paul Leyhausen, a leading German ethologist and a student of these processes, believes that a true homology exists between man and animal in this area. Certainly human beings have strong territorial instincts.

When animals in which no hierarchic structure or 'pecking order' is normally observed—such as the brown rat or night heron—are crowded together a rigid hierarchy begins to develop and finally becomes so tyrannical that even the dominant animal at the top of the social tree is stressed by the repeated challenges received from subordinate males. Calhoun's rats likewise exhibited dominance and territoriality, and it was the rats accustomed to the occupancy of large territories which felt the pressure of crowding most. At the bottom of the social scale were rats which withdrew from the struggle, and avoided stress by never challenging superiors, going out to eat at times when the latter were asleep, in order to avoid trouble. (Human 'night owls' are also known.) In the middle rank were males who constantly challenged the dominant males, in an attempt to obtain territory and females; these were the ones most likely to show physiological signs of stress. It may be that the survival of the standing-room-only animals was due to the disappearance of all territory and social structure in these conditions.

So we may imagine that the class resentments of modern urban society present a parallel to the challenges of the pecking order in animals, and are most likely to develop where pressure on space leads to the development of a hierarchic structure.

Human beings certainly have a strong need to keep the number of social stimuli they receive within bounds, and often retire to their nests or to uncrowded territory for this purpose. Where this is impossible, the stress is reduced by forming small groups, whose members get to know each other and work out techniques for coping with the problems which arise. It has been found in mental hospitals, for instance, that formation of small groups helps patients; conversely in World War II, the Nazis shifted concentration camp inmates from one camp to another, so as to break up such groups and increase the stress on the individual. Correspondingly, a society which compels people frequently to move their job or residence imposes stresses on its members.

The modern urban society therefore may reasonably be suspected of imposing stresses similar to those which stress Calhoun's rats, and the parallels in behaviour are probably not coincidental: René Spitz has shown, for instance, that human mothers in crowded conditions exhibit poor maternal care: the 'battered babies' which constitute a current social problem may be one consequence of living in crowded conditions. Paul Leyhausen says: 'I have no doubt whatever that a great number of neuroses and social maladjustments are, partially or totally, directly or indirectly, caused by overcrowding.'

'What every normal man wants for himself and his family is a detached house in an adequate garden, with neighbours close enough to be found if needed, or if one feels like a social call, yet far enough away to be avoided at other times,' he considers. Psychologists often talk of people adjusting, or failing to adjust, to modern life—as if man's power of adjustment were unlimited. But man's psychological requirements represent the result of millions of years of evolution, and adjustment can only occur within narrow limits thus set. It is true, to be sure, that children can be habituated to living in crowds, just as they can be habituated to particular foods, amusements, or sexual patterns. But a price is paid for addiction to crowds, just as it is paid for addiction to chocolate creams. Leyhausen thinks there is a real danger that man may 'exceed the limits of human tolerance towards the presence of other humans'.

The test is not whether people feel safe in crowds, but whether bodily, mental and social health are preserved in such conditions. Leyhausen believes that people can only participate effectively in a democracy when they can withdraw to their own territory for relaxation and consideration. Calhoun makes a similar point when he says, 'the process of identifying with values and goals beyond the bodily self requires periods of solitude and reflection.' In the absence of this he becomes 'a hollow, sterile shell'. In the quite different context of industrial psychology, it has been noted that employees take radical decisions, such as leaving their job, after vacations during which they have had time to reflect. Crowded conditions thus favour a loss of social cohesion and responsibility.

Calhoun also makes the interesting suggestion that the attraction of psychedelic drugs is that they restore a sense of personal space to people who feel 'hemmed in'.

The weight of this evidence, then, supports the idea that urban society already shows signs of the effects of overcrowding; but this does not reach the point at which infant mortality rises so sharply as to limit the population. Partly, this is due, no doubt, to modern medicine and to the state stepping in where a mother ceases to care for her children. But partly it may be due to the fact that the densities still fall short of those at which such behaviour becomes general. And there is one additional factor present: unlike rats, man can get out of the city from time to time. (It may be significant that the deer on James Island had their population crash during a winter in which ice floes prevented their swimming to the mainland.) At least, western man can. In the crowded mushrooming cities of South America, the Middle East and elsewhere, cars are few and public transport inadequate, while densities are often double those of western cities. If these forces ever become paramount it will be in these cities rather than in the developed countries. And social disruption may bring about a social collapse before physiological reactions do so. In my view, this is the form doomsday will take.

WILDERNESS AND SUBURB

The fact that so many people endure up to an hour of crowded travel twice a day in order to live out of the city while working in it provides some indication of how reluctant they are to live in the centre. The man with a family, especially, feels that his wife and children benefit from the more spacious and natural surroundings at the periphery. Those who do not commute maintain, if they can afford it, a week-end cottage or perhaps a boat, or make some similar arrangement.

Annual vacations, too, are usually taken 'away from it all'. This is now so usual that it is worth recalling that the whole concept of a vacation is historically a novel one. Holidays were 'holy days'—a single day of respite from work. Not till the nineteenth century did the week-long holiday become usual. Because of this reluctance to live in the city, round every city there grows up a ring of lower-density housing we call suburbia, and outside this a ring of what is technically country, inhabited predominantly by week-enders and wealthier commuters, for which the name exurbia has been coined. Suburbia has the advantage of providing access to the city on one hand, to country on the other. The trouble starts when the exurbia of one city coalesces with the exurbia of another. This is what is happening in the New York–Washington strip, with Baltimore fringing on Washington to the south and on Wilmington which adjoins Philadelphia to the north, while Trenton and other suburbs fill the space between Philadelphia and New York. It is calculated that by the year 2000, the entire 500-mile strip between Boston and Washington will be suburbanized. The New York metropolitan area will comprise 30 million people at a density of 24,000 to the square mile by 2010, though the urban core will comprise only 8 million of these. Similar fusions are occurring in California, where the San Francisco–San Diego strip is already partly exurbanized, and south of the Great Lakes. Thanks partly to poorer communications, partly to planning controls, London's growth beyond the suburban ring has been slower, but by the end of the century it will fuse with the south coast resorts and with Reading and Oxford, unless strong measures are taken.

At the same time, as the central built-up area grows, it becomes harder to escape from: the routes become more congested and the distance to be driven before countryside is reached grow longer.

As a result of the disagreeable features of urban life, there is an increasing tendency for the countryside to be regarded primarily as a resource area for the refreshment of city-dwellers. A recent British government announcement warned farmers that they must be prepared to allow people to walk across their fields and must provide parking and other facilities. Only a townee could have made such a pronouncement. The farmer knows that the land is as highly organized as a factory. The grass field which the townsman imagines nature has provided, free, has been ploughed and sown, fertilized and sprayed, and will be systematically grazed or hayed. One can imagine how industrialists would react to a proposal that visitors should be allowed to wander through their factories at will.

The policy of treating the country as a resource area for the towns will destroy its rural character, as has already happened in exurbia. Apart from the physical impact, local social groupings are broken up and the countryman begins to look to the town as the source of his inspiration.

But it is not the fate of the countryside which here concerns us, so much as the question of how long it will remain adequate to provide the townsman with the relief which preserves his fertility and his sanity. Already in the United States the National Park system is hopelessly overburdened. It is already necessary to book months ahead to get into Yosemite and other national parks. There were more than 141 million park visitors in 1968 compared with 3 million in 1948. More and more trails have to be covered with blacktop because they cannot stand up to the pedestrian traffic. (For identical reasons, the French have had to fence off the ancient oaks of Fontainebleau: the pressure of feet is impacting the soil to the point where the trees cannot survive. Thus each man kills the thing he loves.) In the US, parkland is in any case maldistributed: only 4 per cent is in the north-east, where a quarter of the population lives. Three-quarters is in the west where 15 per cent of the people live. One-sixth is in Alaska.

As work-weeks get shorter, vacations longer, and car-ownership even more general, the wilderness will come under ever greater pressure. This will be especially severe in the San Francisco region, where population is expected to grow by a factor of nine by 2000. This means nine times as much litter on the trails of Yosemite and nine times as long a wait to get in.

The wilderness is further threatened by new vehicles, such as the snowmobile, of which there are now 600,000 in the US. Some of these are capable of 70 m.p.h. and already much damage is done to young plantations of conifers, just covered with snow; to game, which is run down for sport; and to property. Theft from remote cabins has become a problem and in some areas snowmobiles are now forbidden to leave marked trails. They are also noisy. Before the end of the century hovercraft will cross lakes and invade the previously isolated territory beyond, and disturb quiet marshes and estuaries. Trail-running machines are being devised, capable of carrying considerable loads over mountainous territory. Soon there will be wider, heavier vehicles. By 2000, there will be few corners of the US where nature can be enjoyed undisturbed.

Though America leads the way, other countries are following as best they can. Mountain roads 20 miles inland from the Côte d'Azur are littered with abandoned cars, kitchen cookers, oil drums and assorted junks; and broken glass and orange-skins adorn the look-out points on remote Scottish islands.

Land often looks deserted to the passing motorist (still more from an aeroplane) which is actually frequently disturbed. Professor Kenneth S. Norris complained not long ago, in a scientific journal, that he had placed lizard traps on the margin of an uninhabited crater, 35 miles from Barstow,

Texas, itself way out in the desert. In the course of two years, 20 per cent of these traps were wrecked or removed and his enquiry had to be abandoned. In the same manner, a rock in a Californian tide-pool, apparently as nature left it, may be turned over several times a year by human hands.

All over the world the wilderness is vanishing. In Alaska, the North Shore oil strike, next to a nature reserve, is attracting a stream of engineers, and a port capable of receiving quarter-million-ton tankers is being built. Tractors cannot operate over permanently frozen tundra without causing permanent damage to the environment. As the permafrost melts under the pressure, the track of the vehicle turns into a deep ditch, impassable to animals, which alters the drainage system. When the Navy explored the territory adjacent to the new strike, which is a naval oil reserve, they left discarded drilling equipment, oil drums and general trash which will remain indefinitely and is visible for miles. The new exploiters will doubtless do the same. There are indications that oil exists on the far side of the nature reserve, and pressure is already developing to open the reserve itself to exploration. The interests of the local Eskimos have been disregarded in a disgraceful manner. Fairbanks has become a boom-town, with topless entertainment in the bars and saloons, in the pattern of the gold-rush of 70 years ago, but more so.

Further east, in Labrador, the Grand Falls of the Hamilton River, renamed the Churchill Falls, are about to be poured into a tunnel, to operate the largest hydro-electric scheme in the western world, and feed New York with electricity. Some 50,000 cubic feet of water are discharged every second, and fall 312 feet. Described as 'an ecologist's dream', the vast spray from the several falls, which rises like smoke above the river and descends on sub-arctic wilderness, creates an ecological niche such as has never been studied. Now it never will be. The Trans-Labrador Highway is creeping up to Goose Bay, and Labrador is 'facing the greatest change in its history'. In 1963, Paava Kallio, the head of the Sub-arctic Research Station of the University of Turku, Finland, saw osprey nesting near the falls, and otters running across the path. When he returned in 1968, neither were to be seen and the ground was littered with film-cartons.

Serious as is the threat to the colder regions of the world, it is minimal to what is happening and will happen in the Pacific. As more and more jet-ports are built, it will become the world's resort area, and above all the resort of the Japanese, inveterate travellers, who will by the year 2000 have a national income per head far larger than any other country in the world. The median estimate for 2020 is $33,000 a head—nearly ten times the present US figure—and twice what the US figure will be by 2020.

I have already described the damage which is being done to lagoons by US military forces and the signs of ecological disaster. To this must be added the effects of intensive phosphate mining: the world will need more and more phosphate for agriculture and there are few places where it is found. Already one small island has had to be abandoned by its inhabitants, as the phosphate mining company has destroyed the vegetation and upset the drainage and water-supply system. Small islands, as I have already described, are especially vulnerable to ecological assault, and are also unlikely to be visited by well-wishers, so that gross commercial exploitation goes unchecked.

The islands of the West Indies are already far advanced down the same path.

But it is the wilderness which is at hand to centres of population which matters most—the highlands of Scotland, the woods of the Adirondacks, and the Black Forest or the Causse; but whenever water or power supplies are needed, amenity is promptly sacrificed to economics, as we all know. To cite instances is unnecessary.

Do people need the wilderness, as distinct merely from a low density of population? It is often asserted that they do. Wallace Stegman writes: 'Something will have gone out of us as a people if we ever let the remaining wilderness be destroyed; if we permit the last virgin forests to be turned into comic books and plastic cigarette cases; if we drive the few remaining wild species into zoos or extinction; if we pollute the last clean air or dirty the last clean streams and push our paved roads through the last of the silences.' What is it that the wilderness gives to people who feel this way?

We must recognize here, I think, two distinct processes. First, people prefer certain levels of stimulus, and this varies from time to time, as well as from person to person. In choosing a place for a vacation, one person will say 'I want

a bit of peace and quiet,' where another will say I want
to go where there's a bit of life. I want to see some action.'
Probably extroverts prefer more stimulus than introverts.
Equally, people who have been over-stimulated want to com-
pensate by a period of under-stimulation, and conversely.
Perhaps also people become conditioned to prefer a high
level of stimulus; and some may need external stimuli to
distract them from nagging unconscious problems, doubts or
fears. Yet others may never have developed the internal
resources which enable some people to sustain and enjoy a
measure of solitude. More research on these preferences and
their distribution among the population is badly needed.

Important as this is in understanding the pressures of the
city, it is not, I think, the explanation of the demand for
wilderness. If reduced stimulation were all that were required, a dark room would suffice; and the man who enjoys
the wilderness is not under-stimulated—his senses are alert to
colours, sounds, shapes, odours, textures and other impressions. The appeal of nature has been succinctly expressed by
poets, who stress its moral and religious character:

> One impulse from a vernal wood
> May teach you more of man,
> Of moral evil and of good,
> Than all the sages can.

Thus Wordsworth, but it is an idea also put forward by
Christian mystics, such as St. Bernard. Wordsworth goes further, and speaks of a kind of trance, in which one has deep
insight into the life of things:

> We are laid asleep
> In body and become a living soul:
> While with an eye made quiet by the power
> Of harmony, and the deep power of joy,
> We see into the life of things.

Indeed there is an actual sense of the presence of the divine:

> O'er the wide earth, on mountain and on plain
> Dwells in the affections and the soul of man
> A Godhead, like the universal PAN;
> But more exalted.

In *Lines written above Tintern Abbey* he explores this idea in detail, recognizing in nature 'the anchor of my purest thoughts, the nurse, the guide, the guardian of my heart and soul, of all my moral being'. Other poets, from Shaftesbury to Rousseau, from Cowper to Tennyson, from Thoreau to Huysmans, have expressed similar feelings. More recently, Freud has discussed the topic under the title 'the oceanic feeling'. There is no need to delve here into the origins of this feeling, which I have analysed at some length in earlier books, particularly *The Angel Makers*: it is enough that the experience is a religious one and of central importance to those who experience it. In the last chapter, I shall argue that it is of central importance to us all, those who fail to experience it being the victims of a psychological disability, akin to hysterical blindness.

A country which professes freedom of religion should not therefore destroy the conditions of a quasi-religious experience; and those who do so inflict irreparable loss on those who benefit from such experience.

In his tongue-in-cheek book *The Environment Game*, Nigel Calder has proposed that men live on artificial islands in the oceans, in order that land can be left free for human beings to explore, enjoy, fish and hunt in. Being cooped in cramped ship-like cabins in order to have access (by air?) to unspoiled country at week-ends seems a second-best solution; a reduction in the population which enabled you to live in the country all the time, if you wished, would suit me much better. The human population crash will come, I suspect, when a majority of men are deprived of the opportunity for this kind of refreshment.

Fred Hoyle, the mathematician and science-fiction writer, calculates that the crash is due in 2250, when, he thinks, world population will have reached 25 billion—but demographers expect this figure to be reached before 2070 at present rates. The population will collapse to a mere 2 billion, and the cycle will repeat itself every 300 years. Personally, I doubt if we shall make it to 2070.

OPTIMUM POPULATIONS

When the British Institute for Biology called a conference on the Optimum Population for Great Britain in September

1969, there was much talk of how the country could manage to support the higher population forecast for the end of the century, but none about where the optimum might lie. On the last day, however, the chairman called a straw vote: almost everyone agreed that the country was already over-populated.

Demographers are embarrassed when the question of optimum population is raised, for it is notoriously difficult to avoid generalities; and when I ventured to raise it at the first Conference on Population called by the Interdisciplinary Communications Program, the New York Academy of Sciences and the Smithsonian Institution at Princeton in 1968, there was a shocked silence; after which the chairman ruled that that subject be postponed to the end of the meeting. It was never, in the end, discussed. Yet the fact that one cannot decide on a figure does not make the question an unreal one; and the fact that almost every member of a well-informed audience of over a hundred felt that Britain was not at the optimum, but decidedly over it, suggests that it is possible to evolve a social policy. After all, it is possible to advise the driver of a car that he is going too fast for safety even if one cannot name the exact speed at which he should be going.

To be sure, the optimum population of a country cannot be expressed merely as a figure expressing the total number of inhabitants. How they are distributed is vitally important. Parts of the US today are certainly under-populated, just as parts are certainly over-populated. Redistribution is the immediate problem; when this has been done (if it ever is) it will be easier to see whether there are too many or too few. What each of us is interested in is the area we normally move about in, say a radius of 50–100 miles from our home, or something of that order. If that area is dense, the presence of wilderness fifty miles off is of limited value; if it is too lonely, the existence of a town two hours away will only make it slightly less so.

With this caveat, I believe we can detect three main kinds of criterion for defining an optimum. The commonest criterion is the economic, which tends to favour a relatively high density. A bigger population provides a bigger market, supports a richer social and cultural life, and so on. Thus Professor Victor R. Fuchs points out that the economies of scale make hospitals of at least 200 beds desirable, and may even operate up to 500 beds. This implies the existence of a population of 100,000 to 200,000 within driving distance. It has even been suggested that larger populations mean better local government but I suspect this is chiefly a matter of setting reasonable sizes for administrative units.

The economist only recognizes a limit when pollution, traffic congestion and other economically measurable factors begin to undermine the economic benefits. Motor-accident mortality is inversely correlated with population density across the United States. In point of fact the car, by bringing people into contact more often, has the same effect as an increase in population. The pressure in a gas rises, and the molecules collide more often, when it is heated, or when more gas is introduced into the vessel; if both are done at once, the pressure rises proportionately to the product of both factors. Analogously, mankind has both added more units and more energy to the situation. The proper course, when the car became generally available, was a reduction in population. Instead we increased it.

At the opposite pole from the economic, is the biological set of criteria, according to which the land should not carry more people than it can support without the consumption of irreplaceable resources, such as fossil fuel.

No one appears to have calculated just what this would mean in practice. This, too, is an economic criterion, but based on a much longer view than that of the dry-as-dust economist.

Between the economic and the biological criteria lie the psycho-social criteria which I have attempted to discuss: the need to avoid loneliness on the one hand, and lack of neighbourly support, feeling 'hemmed in' on the other. These I think call for levels of population intermediate between the economic and the biological.

On an even longer view, the rate at which all irreplaceable resources are being consumed—not merely fuel—is a limiting factor. In this context, a special committee of the National Research Council has concluded, after a three-year study, that there are already too many people on earth. Irreplaceable natural resources are simply not sufficient to meet future demands. Says the Resources Committee, headed by Professor Preston E. Cloud, Jr., of Santa Barbara, 'A population less than the present one could offer the best hope for comfortable living for our descendants, long duration for the species and the preservation of environmental quality.'

Professor J. H. Fremlin, a physicist at Birmingham University, has discussed the extreme cases of a population for Britain of 1,000 million (20 times the present figure) and of 30 million. At 30 million, he points out, everyone could own a car without undue congestion, food could be grown without battery methods, housing standards would rise and change of abode would be easier, while more people could enjoy country recreations. At 1,000 million in contrast there would be a better chance for far-out writers and artists to find an audience, more cultural facilities and 'several Newtons and Shakespeares'. But everyone 'would have to want to stay under cover nearly all the time.' There would be space to roam outside the cities 'provided only one in a thousand wanted to spend more than a few hours in it a year.' He is not disturbed by this prospect and says: 'I doubt very much whether this would be a difficult state to achieve in a generation or two. Many animals become dangerously disturbed when heavily overcrowded, but we can learn to accept enormous numbers of social contacts if we don't have to take any notice of most of them and if we each have our own in-group with whom we feel secure.'

Frankly, this is the sort of outlandish nonsense you get when physicists move out of their sphere and start laying down the law in social fields where their knowledge is quite superficial. Ethologists, like Leyhausen, know better.

Professor Joseph Hutchinson has proposed as a realistic long-term aim to reduce the population of Britain to 40 million, a process which he thinks might have to be spread over 200 years. For the US Professor Kinglsey Davis would like to aim even lower: 20 million.

With so many kinds of criterion there are naturally many definitions of an optimum population. For the agriculturalist it is the level at which the land can be farmed without deterioration. Characteristically, Professor Fuchs, as an economist, offers this definition: 'We can define the optimum as that size where the amount that people in the society would be willing to pay to have the population reduced by (say) 10 per cent is exactly equal to the amount other people in the society would be willing to pay to have it increased by that amount.' But this would depend on the way incomes were distributed, and assumes that people are wholly rational in such judgments, which everyone knows is not the case. I prefer the definition of a biologist, Professor Southwood: 'The optimum population of man is the maximum that can be maintained indefinitely without detriment to the health of the individuals from pollution or from social or nutritional stress.'

Over and above all this, there are in addition some political implications of large populations. Montesquieu said that democracy was only possible in a country appropriately small in size, a thought expressed two thousand years earlier by Plato. It is possible that expansion of population leads to greater centralization of control; the demand for decentralization may be only a form of protest against the inevitable. Paul Leyhausen is one who has pointed out that the sacrifices which the individual must make for the common good grow greater as population density rises—a point I also made twenty years ago in *Conditions of Happiness*. If you live in a forest, you can keep pigs or even let your house burn down without offending your neighbours, for you have none. In a city, you are forbidden to do either, and cannot even play the radio loudly at night! As populations rise, you cannot leave your car where you will, or build a house without approval. Eventually the whole ownership of real-estate may have to be abandoned. Such restrictions become increasingly onerous, and must be weighed against the advantages to which the economists draw attention.

Finally be it noted that, even if we decide that the world, or any large part of it, has not yet reached an optimum population density, there is still the question of how rapidly it is sensible to move towards that level. Too rapid growth creates strains, as we have seen, and I conclude, with Professor Athelstan Spilhaus: 'When we can treat all existing persons as human, it will be time enough to think about having more.'

11 Hurt Not the Earth!

THE WARNINGS of scientists, it seems, are justified. The world is faced with a problem of a kind never known before. Failure to solve it would be, at best, uncomfortable; at worst, catastrophic. What can we do?

It would be nice, of course, if there were some simple answer to such a question—some one thing which would solve all the problems. But life is not like that, and action at many points is required.

Certainly the top priority is to stabilize world population growth, and this undoubtedly means, in the present state of world disorganization, that each country must attack its own problem. That it can be done is shown by the case of Japan. America, Britain and western European countries, though their growth rates are relatively low, must follow Japan's example, and we must hope that the countries which are really exploding, like the Middle East and South America, will catch on. In the United States, there is already an active organization named Zero Population Growth campaigning to this end, which should be supported.*

If a density of 60 to the square mile is desirable for the US, Britain would have to reduce her population to less than one-tenth the present figure to put herself in a comparable position, i.e. to 4.7 million in England and Wales. But so low a figure would create great economic problems and the process of contraction itself would be painful and wasteful.

A realistic target for Britain to halve its population—or, let us say, to aim at 30 million by 50 years from now. This would represent about 320 to the square mile, even with

*A list of names and addresses of organizations concerned with popula-
tion and environmental problems will be found at the end of the book.

Scotland, Ireland and Wales included, and is still really far too high, so that the process should continue thereafter, unless the overall position has changed in some way. West Germany, with an identical land area—perhaps rather less of it inhospitable—and a slightly larger population, should set a similar aim. France, to achieve densities similar to these, could afford to increase her population by about 40 per cent, but would be better advised to level off as fast as she can. Italy, at 458 to the square mile, lies midway between Britain and France, but South Italy is parched and inhospitable, so that a considerable reduction in her population—say to 30 million—would make sense. These, obviously, are rough figures: each country should examine its resources and settle on the most appropriate targets.

The difficulty will be to prevent the economic interests which, as I have indicated, prefer large populations, combining with governments, which also prefer large and indeed rising populations, to play down the social, psychological and even moral elements to which it is so hard to attach figures. The only hope I see is to make sure that the debate is conducted publicly. The formation by the British government of a secret committee (news of which only leaked out by chance) to settle the matter is a sign, hardly surprising, of the efforts which will be made to stultify the democratic process. The only way to smoke out the nest is to demand the establishment of an open committee, and to make sure its membership is representative. Citizens of other countries might be well advised to discover whether there is anything similar in their backyard.

As I have already argued, it is a false hope to imagine that the availability of contraceptives or even abortion will of themselves significantly reduce the population. The only things which reduce population are decisions to have fewer children, to start having them later, and to space them more widely. Especially the first two.

In Japan, a situation has been reached in which it is positively embarrassing to have a large family. Such attitudes are created by education, both at school and in the larger sense of what the news media carry. At the same time, the government must provide incentives, rather than disincentives, as at present. An obvious possibility is a tax bonus for every year of married life prior to the birth of the first child:

variations on this idea can easily be imagined. It is arguable that there should be an actual increase in tax on having children; at present many countries offer some reduction in tax, usually in the form of child allowances. Such allowances are intended to ensure that the children are adequately nourished and cared for, but do not necessarily have this effect, since parents are at liberty to spend the money as they please. This device should obviously be abolished, and more direct methods substituted. It will then be possible to tax children and to step up the tax sharply after the second child. How far such measures would influence people is, of course, uncertain. But unless such fiscal measures as these are applied resolutely and prove effective, we shall eventually be forced to issue licences to have children, a course so likely to be unpopular that few governments will feel able to take it until the situation has grown very much worse than it is. My guess is that governments will shilly-shally even about taxing children, and that the situation will get worse. Naturally, the difficulties will be greatest in Catholic (and some Middle Eastern) countries. But the most awkward situations will be in countries like Canada, where there is a distinct split between Protestant and Catholic elements, and where the latter are deliberately expanding population to increase their influence. I have little hope that nationalist or sectarian groups will subordinate their ambitions to the over-all need for population limitation and no doubt bitter strife on this issue will be the result.

WEW AND GEO?

Since population stabilization will, even if attempted, be slow to take effect, it is clear that we must make a major assault on the problem of super-pollution. This assault involves at least six main areas. First, it must be recognized as a world problem. Not just a world-wide problem, in the sense that every country should tackle its own pollution, but an international problem in the sense that the wastes of each country affect, or may affect, the climate and the health of other countries or even the whole world. Though I have no starry-eyed faith in international organizations, many of which I suspect could do with help of top-flight management consultants, yet it is certain that an international organization is needed. Its first function should be that of monitoring the state of pollution. This will involve collating figures from different countries, and helping to establish local monitoring groups where none exist though they are needed. Its second function should be the exchange of know-how in meeting pollution problems. Its third function should be to work towards effective international control, by agreeing upon suitable standards and policies—perhaps also by giving financial help and expert advice to countries which need it.

In all this, I use the word 'pollution' in the widest possible sense, to include heat, noise, particulates, pesticides, radioactivity, etc. More than this, I also mean to include climatic effects and ecological imbalances. Close co-operation with meteorological and wildlife organizations is therefore called for, as with agricultural organizations which already concern themselves with erosion, forest-felling, and the like. Harm to birds and other organisms is often a useful 'early warning' of a threat to man. Finally, it is essential to bring in what I have termed 'planetary engineering'. Perhaps World Environment Watch (WEW) would serve as a descriptive title for the monitoring aspect of the operation, while for the wider function I suggest Global Environment Organization (GEO).

Second, it is essential to increase by many orders of magnitude the scale and scope of research into these problems. The repeated conclusion of reports on these topics is: 'But really we know very little about it.' In particular we need research into (a) ecological processes, especially population explosions, (b) means of cleaning up pollution or preventing it happening, (c) the consequences to health of pollutants and of new substances generally, (d) psychological effects of crowding and nature of stress, including effects of noise, (e) social effects of crowding, including crime and social pathology generally, (f) climate and weather, (g) economic aspects, especially the quantification of social, psychological and other factors which tend to be ignored or under-rated, (h) psychosocial aspects, especially the distribution in society of attitudes. Each of these is a large research area, with many subdivisions. The scale we should think on is certainly not less than the scale of the moon-race. That took 5 per cent of the US national budget, and involved setting up immense research organizations and testing facilities. We should also think in terms of similar urgency: a clean and safe environment *by the year 2000*. Similarly in every other country.

Thirdly, we need a decisive educational effort. When Poland, soon after the war, passed strong legislation protecting the environment, she included a provision that every schoolchild must be taught about man's relation to his environment. Other nations should belatedly follow this admirable quarter-century-old example. This does not mean just a few vague lessons on ecology, but a planned attempt to give the student a sense of man's place in the scheme of things. To take but one instance, he should certainly understand the dangers of the situation I describe in the next chapter under the tag 'the commons'. The whole question of how people manage to live together should be part of every education, and from this grows the question of how they should live with the rest of nature. Of its real function—that of helping people to live the life they are going to live—education is currently less aware than it was 500 years ago.

Fourthly, there is the actual attack on polluting activities as they now exist. Here the dangers are of a partial and ineffective attack, sufficient to damp down public criticism, without really tackling the issue, or even of a completely ineffective response. Even a superficial acquaintance with the situation in Britain and America shows that far too many bodies are concerned with different aspects of the problem: a much tauter structure for pollution control is needed. I suspect most other countries are in a similar position. In the US the problem is made more difficult by the relative weakness of the central government, and the sensitivity of the various states to supposed infringement of their rights. Whatever the difficulties here, there can surely be no justification for continuing the obsolete practice of leaving the rivers under the control of the Corps of Engineers, a body which may build fine dams, but is certainly not so constituted as to take a balanced view of the environment. Nor should rivers be placed under a water-supply authority as in Britain, though the idea of treating entire catchment areas as units is a good one. The rational solution is the establishment of regional Environment Authorities, with water-supply authorities subordinated to them, and dam-building specialists called in as required. Again, atomic energy authorities should not be left to police themselves: independent inspectors are required.

Whole books, I know, can be written about structure and organization, but I am not the man to write them. I simply want to make the point that pollution cannot be successfully controlled simply by passing laws, as is often assumed. The creation of an effective organization, with a clearly defined mandate and adequate powers and resources, is the indispensable first step.

Fifthly and finally, though one could lengthen the list, I put the need to reconsider far more thoroughly the setting of acceptable standards of purity, including freedom from radioactivity, for water, air and soil. As I have shown in some detail, it is not enough to look for obvious and immediate signs of disease. The effect on life-span and the incidence of diseases not yet known to be associated with the pollutant must be studied, and the time-lags (latencies) of up to 25 years must be taken into consideration. This calls for re-education of local health officers, the setting up of new and far more thorough reporting procedures, and closer co-operation between health authorities and the authorities monitoring the environment.

All these endeavours require to be carried out on an international and world-wide scale. A glimpse of what might be possible was afforded when in July 1968 the *New York Times* published a paper by Andrei D. Sakharov, the father of the Russian H-bomb, entitled: 'Progress, Co-existence and Intellectual Freedom'. Departing entirely from the conventional attitude expected, he argued that civilization is imperilled by the threat of nuclear war, famine, degenerating mass culture and 'bureaucratic dogmatism'. (I know just what he means.) In such circumstances, he said 'Only universal co-operation . . . will preserve civilization.' He pinpointed the problem of hunger and over-population, proposing a fifteen-year tax equal to twenty per cent of national income on developed nations to help in stabilizing the situation. The silence which greeted this suggestion could be heard round the world.

PERSONAL EFFORT

The most hopeful sign is the increasing number of instances of individual involvement. For instance a Swiss pharmacist, Karl Stehle, has personally promoted a three-nation effort to clean up Lake Constance, which lies between Switzerland, Austria and Germany. Thousands of tons of junk have been removed from lake-shores and neighbouring territory; a special dredger was built to clear the shallower waters. The French army even sent in a contingent of soldiers to help, making it a four-nation effort.

In Germany, the Assistant Chief of Police in Dortmund has waged an anti-noise campaign which has made that city one of the quietest in the world, for its size. In Sweden, eleven lakes are being revitalized, under the guidance of the Limnological Department of Lund University. In Britain, a remarkable salvage operation is under way in South Wales, where ruined industrial landscapes are being made green again. After the Aberfan disaster, in 1966, a Derelict Land Unit was set up in Cardiff, which has approved sixty-one clearance schemes costing £3.1 million in Wales. John Price, head of the unit and born near Aberfan, estimates that there are 13,000 acres worth treating, which may take another 20 years. 'But well over 1,400 acres have been completed, which, from a standing start in 1966, isn't bad going,' says Price enthusiastically.

For some £10,000 a colliery ridge tip covering ten acres can be reduced in height and turned into grazing land with clumps of trees. Leeds University, which recently held a symposium on derelict land, has developed a quick method of aerial identification and has spotted 31 kinds of dereliction in 80 square miles of the West Riding.

Also indicative of individual effort is the growing interest of university students in the ecological problem. Two hundred students from forty campuses met recently at Stanford University and formed the Student Environmental Confederation, to co-ordinate existing student bodies, such as Students for a Better Environment, and to act as a clearing house for information. Hopefully students in other countries will follow this lead. Nor need such activity be confined to petition and protest. At the University of Indiana, where the condition of the Jordan river has been a matter of controversy, 210 microbiology students tested the water for waste products in a week-long study, and proved that it was indeed contaminated by human or animal wastes, despite assertions to the contrary.

The signing by President Nixon of the Environmental

Policy Act, and his State of the Union message calling for 'the most comprehensive and costly program' ever mounted in America to fight pollution is an encouraging sign, even if the appointment of an oil industry executive as Special Assistant for Environmental Control may arouse some doubts—especially in view of the ecological risks associated with the North Shore oil-strike. Nevertheless, Congress is being asked for 10 billion dollars to fight water pollution alone—twice as much as was spent on the space effort in its most active year. This certainly makes the efforts of Britain and other European countries pale, even if Congress pares the figure down some.

In Japan where pollution is even more a problem than in the US, various organizations formed to protect victims of 'public hazards' have formed themselves into a national body, so as to be able to put more pressure on the government and conduct legal actions more effectively. In each prefecture a Public Hazards Countermeasures Council will be set up: some have such a body already. In 1969 the Tokyo Metropolitan Government issued a Public Prevention Ordinance, which was the first comprehensive treatment of the problem; hitherto noise, smoke and factory hazards were covered by separate ordinances. The preamble stresses the right of everyone to a minimum standard of healthy and civilized living—a new departure for such documents. All citizens have an actual obligation to avoid 'destructive activity' likely to cause public hazards. Thus anyone building a factory must prove that it is equipped with devices which will prevent it emitting smell, noise, smoke, vibration or noxious gases, or polluting water. Public-address systems are to be strictly controlled, and an inspection committee is to be established. Such measures go further than any foreseen in the US or Britain, though Dr Nicholas Golovin of Harvard has proposed Golovin's Law, which says that the obligation of proof shall lie with the manufacturer (in the case of drugs, pesticides and similar products) rather than with the government or regulatory authority.

Tokyo's problem is that it cannot protect its citizens from nuisances originating in Kawasaki City which lies just across the river. In any case the Ministry of International Trade is likely to oppose the measure, on the grounds that it will handicap exports. In general the Japanese government has shown itself reluctant to act, except in the matter of reducing sulphur dioxide levels. However, it has reduced the permitted level of carbon monoxide in automobile exhausts from 3 per cent to 2½ per cent.

YOU PAY ALREADY

Sooner or later someone inevitably raises the question: who is going to pay the cost of cleaning up pollution? Industrialists commonly assert they will be unable to compete if they have to carry the additional costs of preventing pollution and will go out of business. Therefore, they claim, the government must, by means of subsidies, cover the cost of so doing.

Some of this protest is based on simple technological defeatism. For instance, it is said that it costs money to extract the sulphur from coal or oil, in order to prevent the emission of sulphur dioxide from the chimney stacks of power stations. However, the Japanese Kiyoura process recovers all but $600 of the $4,600 cost per megawatt of extracting sulphur from the flue gases, when the oil carries 3.6 per cent sulphur. The sulphur is sold, in the form of ammonium sulphate as fertilizer, at $32.20 a ton. Rather a small rise in the price of sulphur would turn this into a profit. In the US the Penelec-Monsanto process, based on a similar principle, also recovers marketable quantities of sulphur. More recently, Lockheed's Palo Alto laboratory has announced the development of an electrochemical process for making sulphuric acid from sulphur dioxide effluents at a price which is fully covered by the sale of the acid.

The truth is, industry does not really know what it can do with the assorted chemicals it so wastefully discharges until it tries. Still, we cannot assume that all effluents could be profitably cleaned up. The real answer to the question of costs is more fundamental: we need to take a close look at out system of accounting.

It has been estimated that every US family pays an invisible $80 a year, over and above its electricity bill, to undo the effects of the air pollution caused in manufacturing the current; that is, in washing drapes and curtains, in medical costs resulting from increased bronchitis rates, and so on. Obviously, if the cost of cleaning up the smoke before it left the stack came to less than $80 extra on each bill, the switch would be worth while in simple financial terms—to say nothing of the decline in pain, suffering and sheer human effort at the washtub. The figure $80 naturally has no great scientific validity—probably it is too low—but it makes the point that we *already* pay the costs of air pollution. The question is whether we would rather pay to prevent the pollution or pay to clean up the mess. According to another calculation, the cost of air pollution generally comes to $200 for every person in the US annually. In Britain the figure is £64.

It can be shown scientifically that it is always more economic to prevent a mess than to clean it up, and sometimes you cannot clean it up. You can package an egg to prevent it smashing but you cannot put it together again once it is smashed. And while you can pay the medical bills of a person dying from bronchitis, you cannot restore them to life. The principle of entropy, known to all physicists, guarantees that it is more costly to restore organization than to destroy it—just as it is easier to dirty a garment than to clean it.

But human beings are far from rational, and pay more heed to a rise in the cost of electricity, which they cannot help noticing, than to a fall in the bronchitis rate. You don't notice the bronchitis you don't get, or the soap that you don't use.

The rational principle to go on is that any industry should pay *all* the costs of manufacturing whatever it manufactures and should cover them in the price it charges for the product. Up to now, many industries have profited from a 'free' waste disposal service, which, though free to them, was a cost to the community. They have no right to this unfair commercial advantage. Economists have reinforced this misconception by referring to such avoidable costs as 'externalities' as if they were somehow outside the system. But costs are costs, whoever pays them. If the principle of paying all costs is introduced, the price of some items (e.g. electricity) may rise very slightly, but the cost of others (e.g. medical care) will fall by more than the rise.

Logically, there is therefore no case for the government subsidizing manufacturers who are affected, and so prolonging indefinitely the unfair advantage they have already profited from. There is, however, a genuine difficulty where exporters are concerned: if the country to which they export does not have a similar policy with regard to 'externalities', they will be at some disadvantage. The same could occur if some states within a country adopt this principle and some do not. There might then be a case for subsidies until such time as the principle could be made universal.

My own guess is that in the United States, where the public tends to feel that it is of primary importance not to handicap industry, and where industry can exert strong pressures on government, the tendency will be for the Federal government to carry at least a part of the costs of preventing pollution, by the making of capital grants toward the installation of equipment, if not by subsidies. The same may be true in Japan. In Europe, however, the tendency will be to make industry bear the costs. Rumour has it that many large and responsible firms would be quite willing to undertake such steps to reduce pollution if they could be sure that their rivals, whether at home or abroad, were going to do likewise. If so, united government action is what is needed.

Nevertheless, the principle that people should accept responsibility for their own actions is sound, and as a general policy I go along with Dr Ray Dasmann, of the Conservation Foundation in Washington when he says: 'I do not believe that in the long run we will solve the problems of pollution until the polluter is faced with the consequences of his own actions.' To take a different kind of instance, one could tax people or concerns which allow their land to deteriorate.

Fred Singer, at the AAAS meeting in 1969, made the important point that the cost of coping with pollution rises exponentially—twice the pollution means four times the cost, and so on. For every country, therefore, there is a pollution point beyond which the effort of controlling pollution becomes intolerable. A greater and greater part of the national effort has to be put into undoing the harm caused by the remainder. Or trying to. It seems probable that the US, Britain, Japan and perhaps W. Germany are already at or near the poison-point. It has been estimated that the US will spend $275 billion trying to control pollution between now and the end of the century. The other countries named might be well advised to attempt a similar projection. Frederick Gorschboth estimates that by AD 2000 the world will spend $50 billion on air pollution control alone.

And to the costs of controlling pollution, we might add the costs of traffic congestion, the medical costs of poor physical and mental health in an urban environment, and the increased costs of prisons, police and legal action in consequence of higher crime rates. A great part of such costs, needless to say, are met by raising taxes. But eventually, high tax rates discourage enterprise and capital accumulation, slowing the economy and lowering the standard of living. Thus pollution leads to an economic bind or deadlock. The only way out is to stop polluting.

PROGRESS TO DATE

Since I began to write this book there has been a dramatic increase in public interest in questions of pollution, in Britain and the US, and even some signs of awareness that the problem goes beyond pollution and raises doubts about our whole way of life. In Japan, the world's most heavily polluted country, there have been signs of intensified activity also. But apart from Sweden, which has been a leader in the field for some time, and Poland, the rest of Europe, is only stirring in its sleep.

The United States was late in the field. Numerous attempts to pass legislation were defeated in the thirties and the Water Pollution Act of 1948 was its first specific piece of anti-pollution legislation. In the past five years there has been a spate of new acts: the Water Quality Act of 1965, which set up the Federal Water Pollution Control Administration; the Clean Waters Restoration Act of 1967, which made increased funds available; the Solid Waste Disposal Act of 1965 which followed Congress's condemnation of 'the appalling state' of this function; and the Air Quality Act of 1967, which put teeth into the Clean Air Act of 1963—to name only the most important. Under the Air Quality Act a fine of $1,000 a day can be imposed on any firm failing to comply with the regulations, after it has been given 60 days' notice. The Bishop Processing Co. of Selbyville, Delaware, had the dubious honour of being the first company to be so ordered by the Department of Health, Education and Welfare, following public hearings in November 1967.

In New York, sulphur oxides fell 25 per cent in two years,

following Consolidated Edison's reluctant switch to low-sulphur fuels.

Unfortunately, the money to carry out these admirable projects is not being made available. The sums authorized by Congress, themselves inadequate to the need, greatly exceed the amounts actually appropriated. What public pressure can do, however, is shown by the history of the Administration's request for $214m. for waste-treatment facility grants, where the figure authorized by Congress was $700m. in 1969 and $1,000m. in 1970. As a result of Congressional pressure and the Citizens' Crusade for Clean Water, the sum was raised, first to $450m. and then by the full Appropriations Committee to $600m. When the bill came to the floor of the House, a move to increase the sum to the full $1 billion was defeated by only two votes. Finally, after the Senate had proposed $1 billion, the sum of $800m. was granted.

As this instance demonstrates, it is essential for the concerned citizen to maintain pressure on government and industry if anything is to be achieved. In the US at least, the situation has been reached where politicians believe there are votes to be gathered by climbing on the anti-pollution bandwagon. It is essential that they be held to their promises. Everyone should therefore lend support to organizations concerned with conservation, and these organizations should pool their efforts and avoid rivalries.

Other countries might well follow the pattern set by the US Air Quality Act, which requires public hearings before air quality standards are adopted. Thus when the Pennsylvania Air Pollution Commission proposed as a standard an annual average level of 100 micrograms of particulates per cubic metre of air, public pressure forced them to make the figure 65. Similarly in Chicago, the figure for sulphur oxides was forced down from the 0.05 ppm proposed to 0.02 ppm, and particulates from 80 to 60 micrograms.

Great Britain tends to be complacent about pollution problems, largely on the strength of two facts: the air in London is now much cleaner and more transparent than ten years ago, while the once-familiar fogs have all but vanished; and fish have been seen again in the Lower Thames. Salmon, which formerly could face the conditions no higher than the Pool of London, now sometimes reach the waters above Richmond, where they are stopped by the locks.

Pleasing as these improvements are, there is little room for complacency. The Clean Air Act of 1956, which encouraged local authorities to declare 'smokeless zones' in which only smokeless fuel might be burnt, confined its attention entirely to 'dark smoke', saying nothing whatever about gases, except in relation to chimney heights. The sad fact is that, although the smoke pollution has declined considerably from its 1956 figure of 2½ million tons, the amounts of sulphur dioxide have risen sharply from their 1956 figure of 5½ million tons.

Moreover, the example of London has not been universally followed. There are still many local authorities which have no plans for smoke control, while others have used only part of the powers given them by the Act. And in 1969 the number of areas operating smoke control schemes actually declined from 355 to 308. One may also wonder why eight years passed before Northern Ireland was provided with the same legislation thought necessary for the mainland.

With the one exception of the prohibition of 'dark smoke' it is legally necessary to prove the existence of a 'nuisance' and even to show that the area affected is inhabited. Thus severe damage can be done (and often is) to plants and animals, while there is no recognition of the conception of a total atmospheric deterioration. It is still assumed that it has unlimited powers to dilute and disperse pollutants. The regulations call for the erection of tall chimneys, so that gases will be discharged too high up to affect people. (Not that this always works: downdrafts sometimes sweep gases to the ground, while in still conditions, pollution may build up to levels which affect health.) But even if it did protect the local population, it would still be a wholly unsatisfactory solution. Any gases which are too dangerous to release lower than 650 or 850 feet above the ground are too dangerous to release at all.

Peter Gregory studied what was once ā 'garden city', Haverton Hill, near the great Imperial Chemical Industries plant at Billingham, one of the largest industrial units in the country. Every month one hundred tons of grit and ash fall on Haverton Hill, while the rain contains sulphuric acid. The area is treeless and dust-covered, the soil impoverished. Maintenance of houses on one of the estates was found to cost 20 to 33 per cent more than on comparable estates elsewhere. Gregory's report says: 'Plant life is stunted and destroyed, metals and fabrics corrode rapidly, and there is usually an unpleasant smell.' The area has 'an atmosphere of dereliction'—tenants move away as soon as their economic circumstances permit.

America, too, has its blasted landscapes, especially near copper smelters, where fluorides often poison vegetation for miles around, and affect livestock: it softens the bones of cows. I mention the case of Haverton only to convince British readers that they have little cause to suppose that British regulations are any more adequate than American ones. Nor is it the case that manufacturing industry alone is at fault. Brick-kilns, lime, scrap-metal and other outdoor industries produce pollution which can be lessened or removed by wet-sprayers, screens and filters, but, as Robert Arvill mildly remarks: 'it is sometimes difficult to get the industrialist to employ them.' It is 'difficult' because legal obligations and sanctions are lacking.

The position is little different as regards river pollution: if the Thames is clean, the Trent certainly is not: much of it is little more than an industrial sewer. Local authorities move at a snail's pace in enforcing regulations, and sometimes the offender is the same individual who, as a local councillor, is expected to enforce compliance.

It was revealed in 1966 that three out of five local authority sewage works in Britain are producing effluent below the required standards. In 1970 the position was unchanged. The scale of fines is so absurdly low that offenders prefer to pay them and continue polluting. In the House of Lords one speaker openly said that the government had shown bias: not only are fines ridiculous, but river authorities have no right of inspection. The reason was given by the Chairman of the Thames Conservancy. There are no votes in sewage, he said. We could alter that.

If there is one area where Great Britain, proverbially a land of animal-lovers, might have been expected to take the lead, it would be in protecting wildlife. Yet though the special committee appointed by the government after the war, when it reported in 1947, recommended the preparation of a comprehensive Protection Act, more than 20 years later none exists or is even under discussion. The enterprise of private groups, for example the Royal Society for the Protection of Birds, has led to the passage of Acts protecting birds and some other species of special interest, such as deer and seals. That is all.

All that has been done about controlling the emissions of cars is to prohibit dark smoke—an ordinance which the police seldom trouble to enforce.

THOSE IN AUTHORITY

Governments are reluctant to tackle pollution problems for many reasons. First is their short life. They are much more concerned with immediate losses than long-term ones. If there is ever an immediate danger of the lights going out in the US, governments will take steps to prevent this, whatever the eventual cost in raised disease rates or sacrifice of amenity. The British government likewise will sacrifice Dartmoor or the Lake District rather than have household taps dry up. Second, governments are anxious to balance their budgets, which they find easier to do in conditions of expansion and even inflation. They are also anxious to balance their overseas trade, and so, if they have to choose between amenity and industry, always favour the latter. Fourthly, they nowadays have more votes in the towns than in the country—particularly in the case of socialist governments—so that they are decreasingly interested in rural problems and attitudes.

The ruthlessness with which authority sacrifices all other considerations, including its honour, when physical needs have to be met is well shown by the unforgivable action of the Army Corps of Engineers, who gutted the reservation of the Seneca Indians, drowning approximately 10,000 acres of their only habitable land to do so. To do this they deliberately broke the Federal Government's oldest active treaty, made in 1794 with the Senecas and five other Indian nations at a time when America needed their friendship, and resting ever since on solemn guarantees given by the President. What hurt the Senecas even more then the flooding of their land was the removal of a monument to their ancient chief, the Cornplanter, with his bones and those of many of his people, from the Seneca burial ground—'our Arlington' as a Seneca woman protested, weeping.

It might be supposed that left-wing governments, since they claim to espouse the interests of the common man, would be in favour of conservation as against governments of the right—Conservative or Republican—which are supposedly on the side of big business. But, then again, Conservatives are presumably supporters of the past, or at least the status quo, whereas Socialists are committed to raise the material standard of living and tend to think that the past was bad but the future will be good. In a word, socialists are optimists, conservatives are pessimists and think that things are going to the dogs.

In Britain, at least, it turns out that socialists have given little attention to pollution problems, as we have seen; and statements made by the Minister recently invited to add environmental problems to his other duties, Mr Anthony Crosland, exactly support the above analysis: he stressed the importance of economic growth, and the claims of the towns at the expense of the country, while dismissing current concern with the situation as 'hysterical'. Soon after, the depth of socialist contempt for conservation was revealed by the announcement that two valleys in Dartmoor, a national park area, already under pressure, would be flooded to make reservoirs, in face of strong local opposition. The announcement was timed to coincide with the Strasbourg meeting of European Conservation Year. The justification was that the needs of the towns come before those of the countryside, and that it is part of government policy to attract industry to the area.

Indeed, the way in which the National Environment Research Council was set up, with no powers—not even that of taking a general over-view—suggests that it specifically wished to prevent conservation activities. Incredible to relate, this council recently revealed that 'we are not at present interesting ourselves in air pollution'.

The establishment of the world's second-largest deep-water oil port in another national park area is just one further instance of how hard the British voter will have to fight if he wants to see any action.

On the other hand, the Conservative party has failed to seize the opportunity thus presented to it, one which its very name might have inclined it to, even though much of the opposition to pollution comes from individual conservatives. To me this reads like a case for a political re-orientation—a case for the formation of an environment party cutting right across existing party lines.

In Russia, too, optimism as regards the future and the stress on production has led to neglect of conservation issues by officialdom, with the protests coming from private individuals, as far as I can determine. It will therefore be interesting to see what path America takes in the immediate future. My guess is that the Republican party will seek to make conservation its business, with considerable support from the large corporations, while opposition will come from the supposedly more 'progressive' groups.

But whether this be so or not, governments are always reluctant to take the kind of decisive action which, if my arguments in this book are correct, is needed. The wholly opportunistic attitude of authority in such matters is shown by the suggestion, made more than once, that if it proves impractical to meet current radiation guidelines as a result of the development of the atomic energy industry, you just raise the 'acceptable level'. This boils down to saying: 'We must have power. If it costs us another 50,000 cases of leukemia a year, too bad.'

But a decision of this kind has already been taken, in setting existing guidelines, and protests have already been made. Other decisions have also been taken, concerning how pure the air or water are to be. Yet others about dumping radio-active materials in the sea. It is high time such decisions were brought into the forum of public debate.

As the Duke of Edinburgh recently said: 'I think one needs to be ruder and more direct to the people in political authority.'

The British are constitutionally so concerned to avoid any appearance of panic that they usually go to the other extreme of complete inaction, to the amazement of other nations. Thus it was that they reached the outbreak of war in 1939 with only four heavy anti-aircraft guns in the entire country. To start arming would have been an indication of panic, not to say hysteria. In the same way, they will probably prefer to die quietly of leukemia, thus demonstrating their ability to keep a stiff upper lip, rather than betray concern about the existence of radio-activity.

This national tendency is strongly supported by the establishment, who feel that to admit the existence of a problem would be to admit error. Lest this seem an unfair reflection, let me give one relevant example. *The Economist,* a respected British organ of opinion, recently observed that there was no reason for concern at carbon monoxide in the city streets, since there was no evidence that any harm was caused. The facts are quite otherwise. Carbon monoxide forms a complex with blood haemoglobin, preventing it from taking up oxygen and also interfering with its power to release any oxygen taken up. At 50 ppm, it has a dramatic effect on the power to judge time-differences, and drivers responsible for accidents have been shown to have high concentrations of complex haemoglobin (COHb) in their blood. Point-duty police are similarly affected. The current US standard of permissible carbon monoxide is 50 ppm for eight hours—reduced from 100 ppm, in 1964. In most US cities it is over this level. The effect increases as you ascend above sea-level, and infants, men in submarines, persons with cerebral vascular incompetence or myocardial infarct (a heart disease) are particularly at risk, as are hyperthyroid patients and anaemics. Animal studies show fatty degeneration and scarring of the heart muscle. Every car emits about ⅙ lb. of carbon monoxide per mile of travel when travelling at 25 m.p.h., and twice as much at 10 m.p.h. In the US 94 million tons of the stuff are poured into the air annually, three-quarters of this from cars. In New York, cars emit about 1,500 tons a day. Yet in the US, as in Britain, it has been asserted that 'there is no hard evidence that atmospheric carbon monoxide is a threat to health.'

Such assertions recall the reassuring statements, later retracted, made about radio-activity. Thus President Eisenhower declared in 1956: 'The continuance of the present rate of H-bomb testing by the most sober and responsible scientific judgment ... does not imperil the health of humanity.' But in 1964 President Johnson conceded that: 'The deadly products of atomic explosions were poisoning our soil and our food and the milk our children drank and the air we all breathe. ... Radio-active poisons were beginning to threaten the safety of people throughout the world.' Similarly in 1953, the AEC said fallout would be evenly distributed over the globe (proved untrue in 1958), that it would come down so slowly the fission products would have decayed (acknowledged false in 1962), and that fall-out was far below the level at which genetic damage could occur (disproved by 1957, when an AEC Advisory Committee reckoned it would cause 2,500 to 13,000 cases of serious genetic defect throughout the world). So much for official reassurances.

We need a minor disaster to shake our rulers out of their case-hardened complacency. Perhaps we shall get it in the Great Lakes. It seems that the bulk of the pollutants are held in the bottom silts by iron molecules in the ferrous state. In anoxic conditions, the iron is liable to convert to the ferric state, releasing all the accumulated muck, which will rise to the surface, turning the whole area into some sort of foul swamp. That would just about put a stop to the cries of 'hysteria'.

Failing a warning of this kind, the only thing which will keep governments up to scratch is intense and sustained pressure and supervision by the public. Private bodies to monitor what is happening and publicize it, though springing into existence in America, are desperately needed in most other countries. And the more so because, in the drive against obvious pollution, there are less obvious kinds which are easily overlooked.

BLIND SPOTS

Leaving aside the problem of radio-activity, already discussed, perhaps the most seriously underrated problem facing us, in this year of grace, is that of thermal pollution; or in English, heat. In many parts of the US the capacity of the environment to absorb heat is going to be the limiting condition for the use of nuclear power, especially in the north-west, and restriction will begin to operate in a year or two unless a solution can be found. The projected 1980 power output will need half the total runoff of US rivers for cooling purposes, except in the four months of the year when rivers are in flood. But that's an average: in some industrial areas, more than 100 per cent of the water passes through the heat exchangers of power-stations, i.e. some of it passes twice.

In the Chesapeake Bay, nuclear power plants now planned will pump 3 million gallons per minute of cooling water—which is more than the flow of all but three rivers in the whole Chesapeake complex. Heat is 'a very important lethal, directive and controlling factor in the aquatic habitat,' says

J. A. Mihursky. When it does not kill, it alters metabolic rates. If the water reaches 90°F. the eggs of many species, including oysters, begin to die. By 34°C. (94.2°F.) 'little or no survival was observed in 1 to 8 hour exposures.' Cooling water has been known to heat rivers to 95°F. five miles downstream from the plant, and 115°F. may be found near it. Many small organisms actually pass through the heat exchangers of the power plant, and here the losses rise to 100 per cent, from the chlorine added to prevent fouling.

Plans to use the warm water to encourage vegetable growth may be nice for the vegetables (except for contamination by tritium) but do nothing to solve the thermal pollution problem, since the heat is only required in winter. It is in summer, when flows are low and ambient temperatures high, that the crunch comes. And there will be unforeseen effects. Thus sharks are now entering Southampton Water, attracted by the warmer temperature. Some US rivers may start to boil by 1980, and by 2010 may evaporate completely, according to two Rutgers University experts. The disposal of heat may be the limiting factor in power supply.

Noise is another problem which is brushed off as a nuisance rather than as a threat. Yet there is evidence that it has cardio-vascular, respiratory, glandular and even neurological effects. German steel workers, exposed to intense noise at work, have abnormal heart rhythms, and the Russians report that workers in noisy ball-bearing factories have a high rate of cardio-vascular irregularities. Many Italian weavers who work in noisy surroundings exhibit hyper-active reflexes and electroencephalograph test results on these same people are similar to those normally associated with personality disorders. Dr K. E. Farr of the University of Texas School of Public Health, Houston, believes that noise can trigger ulcers, allergies and mental illness.

Frequently the noise is quite unnecessary: few factories examine their processes to see whether they could be quietened. In one case steel balls were scooped from metal containers, dropped on a metal-topped table and poured into metal hoppers. When the metal parts were surfaced with wood and leather, and the underside of the tables covered with sound-absorbing material the noise dropped to reasonable levels.

For most people aircraft and motor traffic are the chief

offenders. Mark Abrams, a British sociologist, says that 36 per cent of the population of crowded Britain are affected by noise in their homes. Yet the Noise Abatement Act, 1960, does not cover cars, aircraft, or statutory undertakings, such as British Railways. Furthermore it is a defence that the best practical means to abate the noise have been used. By 1983 British airlines will carry 30 million people, against 12 million in 1967, 'with continuous aircraft noise a permanent part of the urban and suburban environment throughout most of Britain'.

Finally, I suspect that, despite the fuss, the full danger of common-or-city air pollution is still under-estimated. Doctors still know practically nothing about the interactions taking place beween several pollutants present at the same time but expect that the effects multiply together (synergism) rather than merely add. For example, rates of absence from work are related to levels of sulphur dioxide and particulates (dust) in combination. Sulphur dioxide affects lung function in healthy persons at levels as low as 0.5 ppm, as an American study shows, while an Italian investigation shows school absence correlated with pollutant levels. Several studies show that people's ability to take physical exercise is reduced by exposure to oxidants.

Such knowledge as we have is based mostly on short experimental exposures; but long exposures may be dangerous at much lower levels. Nitric oxide may seriously diminish the capacity of the blood to carry oxygen after long exposure. (Blood has 300,000 times greater affinity for nitrogen oxide than for oxygen.) Professor Albert F. Bush of the University of California at Los Angeles says that the body's protective system weakens under prolonged assaults.

Evidence assembled by the Federal government shows that bronchitis and lung cancer rates rise when the concentration of sulphur dioxide reaches 0.04 ppm in air. But Philadelphia, for example had levels of 0.08 in 1968, and Chicago 0.116—nearly three times the danger level.

Of all airborne pollutants, we know least about ozone. We do know that exposure to a minuscule 0.026 ppm for one hour is lethal to humans, and that in Santa Barbara the level has sometimes reached 0.023 ppm for one hour. Also that a little for a long time is as harmful as a lot for a short time. Contrary to popular belief, ozone itself has no smell, so there is no warning of a dangerous concentration. There is some-times a smell from associated nitrogen oxides, but this soon becomes unnoticeable. Apart from the direct threat to health, ozone reacts with other pollutants to form smog, and with the oils given off by evergreen plants to form a haze—the famous haze of the North Carolina Smokies is caused in this way. Ozone is damaging to many plants: in 1959 a $25m. crop of cigar-wrap tobacco was lost in one week-end, thanks to ozone.

Despite these blind spots there is certainly a new atmo-sphere of action in the field of pollution control. But are the kind of measures I've mentioned going to limit pollution to the point at which ecological disaster is no longer a danger? And if so, for how long? For technology is growing all the time, industrialization is spreading, and people, over the next thirty years or more, will be becoming more numerous. There are good reasons to believe that measures of the kind we have described will postpone the problem, not solve it. The steps proposed to limit car emissions, for example, will produce a fall in pollutants at first, but by 2000, thanks to increasing numbers of cars, the US will be back where it was in 1970, as far as levels in the atmosphere are concerned. Above all, are such measures going to protect the landscape and preserve a satisfactory way of life? In an over-all view, there are underlying difficulties, both technological and ad-ministrative, of a radical kind to be considered.

12 The Technological Nightmare

THE PROBLEMS we have surveyed are, when all is said and done, two in number, but they interact: the sheer weight of numbers and the destructive potential of modern technology. Technology is what makes the numbers possible; the numbers are what makes technology so dangerous. The solution is to limit the numbers or to limit technology; or maybe you have to do both.

But it is widely believed that we can escape this dilemma. Or, at least, though we may have to limit population we need not limit technology; at most, we may have to tame it a little. It is assumed that we can solve the problems created by man's impact on the environment if we make up our minds to it—that the technical means are there, and it only remains for the government to insist on their being employed. But is this so?

In the US at this moment there is an impasse: the people responsible for ensuring the supply of electric power to all who want it declare that they cannot carry on effectively because of the opposition which has been raised, on grounds of environmental protection, to plants which they wish to construct. Coal- and oil-fired stations are being opposed on grounds of air pollution. Nuclear power stations are being resisted on grounds of thermal pollution and the risk of radio-active releases. And hydroelectric schemes are being opposed from concern for the landscape. They say that, because of these hold-ups, many major power grids are without adequate reserves and that actual power shortages may soon develop. In short, there is a deadlock. It seems that Americans cannot have all the power they want *and* the kind of environment they want.

Is this a typical situation? Taking a general view, how far is it really possible to take the sting out of the technological devices we now employ? I shall argue that there are many problems which cannot be effectively fixed, in the time available, and others where the difficulties are economic, administrative or political. Some of these problems are pollution problems, others are problems of amenity and space.

TECHNICAL FIXES

The purification of industrial effluents discharged into air or into water is the easiest of the tasks we expect technology to handle. This does not mean that we have all the answers now. We have reasonably efficient means of removing grit and particles from smokestack fumes, and marginally efficient means of extracting some other gases, such as sulphur dioxide. But to take out fluorides from smelter fumes is harder. Again, when it comes to liquid wastes, we can remove solids and organic matter, but phosphates are difficult and nitrates all but impossible, while phenols turn to unpleasant-smelling chlorophenols. (Sewage treatment plants dissolve sewage into its components, mostly nitrates and phosphates, which are the cause of eutrophication.) Nevertheless, this kind of extraction is the sort of thing which chemists are accustomed to tackle, and if we were to spend money on research and pilot plants as freely as it was spent on finding out how to get to the moon, no doubt we should before long have acceptable solutions.

The problem is more difficult when it comes to motor-vehicles and aircraft, partly for economic reasons. For instance, we can omit tetra-ethyl lead from gasoline if we are prepared to accept a lower power-output, or find alternatives at a higher price. But in this case the emission of nitrogen oxides will be worse. Eventually, I imagine, we shall accept motors which will 'run lean' and avoid the emission of unwanted oxides.

Or take the increasingly serious question of disposing of solid wastes. In the US people throw away 7 million cars, 30 million tons of paper and 48 billion cans, to say nothing of bottles, plastics, and so on. Some domestic waste can be burnt, and in London, Paris and elsewhere incinerators producing sizeable amounts of electricity are run on solid wastes.

But burning wastes produces more pollution, and, in the case of plastics, dangerous chlorides and fluorides may be released. The gummy substances choke the equipment and explosions sometimes occur. Some experts doubt whether the use of refuse to produce electricity is really practicable, bearing in mind that glass and other incombustibles have to be removed by hand. The Japanese prefer to compress waste into solid lumps and dump it in the oceans. Here again, the problems are quite severe but I would not go so far as to call them insoluble.

The trouble is that all waste-disposal creates other wastes, since matter cannot be destroyed. The final solution is to break all wastes into the component atoms and reassemble the atoms into more useful forms. It has been suggested that the hydrogen bomb could be adapted to make a 'fusion-torch' which would reduce all waste materials to atomic form. But how the atoms are to be reconstituted without using impossibly large amounts of energy is not explained.

Still harder is the reversal of eutrophication in lakes and rivers. Indeed, some scientists believe that the process is irreversible. In Sweden several attempts are being made to cleanse small lakes on an experimental basis. One of these is Lake Trummen, in Småland. Here scientists from Lund University are engaged in an 11-year attempt to bring the lake back to life. They are having to remove a 20-inch layer of sediment from the bottom of the lake: there are 16 feet of sediments, all told, but the top 20 inches contain most of the pollutants.

While this is possible in a lake only 10,000 square feet in surface area, it would scarcely be practical for Lake Erie or Lake Michigan. The cost of the Swedish project is $200,000 (£80,000).

While such problems as these are quite difficult, there are others for which there is no technical solution in prospect at all. The first item in this category is thermal pollution—in a word *heat*. Heat is a form of energy and energy cannot be destroyed. It can only be converted to some other form of energy. We know ways of releasing the energy locked up in fuel, whether fossil or atomic, but we do not know ways of tying it up again, except by the expenditure of even larger amounts of energy.

There is therefore basically no way of getting rid of

unwanted heat, short of radiating it into the rest of the universe. We can deal, at some expense, with local concentrations of heat, such as the hot cooling water from a power station, by pumping it to some distant place where it will do no immediate harm, even perhaps good. Waste heat *is* wasted, and research on ways of utilizing it effectively would not be amiss; but in the long run the combustion of fuels must heat the environment.

We can certainly postpone the heat death by using waste heat to warm the sea or melt the ice-caps in principle, though we are far from having satisfactory techniques for so doing. Sooner or later, however, we shall have to start radiating more heat, so that we may have to accept a controlled turbidity of the atmosphere. We may find ourselves injecting dust particles in known amounts, so as to lower the earth's temperature by an amount which is exactly compensated by the heating effect of combustion. These far-out solutions are not, of course, available at present. The current situation is: we don't know how to cope with the waste heat from power-stations.

Another problem we have no idea how to solve is getting pollution out of food chains. For example, if all releases of mercury were stopped immediately, it is reckoned that fish would still carry mercury for a period between 10 and 100 years. The same is true of DDT. Or again, we cannot as yet prevent masses of impounded water causing earthquakes.

I would also include *radio-activity* in the class of problems for which there is no real technical solution. There are stop-gap solutions: some of them I have already described. We can keep the stuff in a place where it will do little harm, but we cannot detoxify it. The policy of storage is costly, so that there is strong motivation to release the active materials to the environment and rely on dilution to make them effectively harmless. But, as we have seen, this is progressively less satisfactory, the longer we go on doing it. Nor can we prevent a certain amount of activity evading these arrangements. The very cooling water carries some activity, as do the gases emitted—to say nothing of the mathematical certainty of some accidents occurring.

But the really awkward item is the one denoted by that imprecise and unattractive word *amenity*. As David Brower, formerly Sierra Club director, has succinctly said, we know how to take a wilderness apart, but we haven't a clue how to put one together again. Why is a splendid valley less of an 'amenity' if it has a cement works or a coal-mine, or even a big dam, in the middle of it? It is an inescapable fact that people prefer the irregular forms produced by nature to be free of the regular forms produced by man, unless to a very small extent. A dam may be beautiful in itself, a factory well-designed, but the presence of such an artefact destroys that quality which natural landscapes possess. That natural landscapes can be 'improved'—in the sense that people find the aesthetic outcome agreeable—is shown by the great English landscape gardeners. Wilderness is not the only attribute of scenery, though it is important; I am not speaking about that. Our present problem arises from the fact that the amount of territory free from human intrusions is small. World-wide, only one-tenth of the landscape remains essentially uninvaded, according to Brower.

There is no technical solution to this problem. On a small scale, damaged areas can be rehabilitated. Eroded ground can be improved by ground cover. Open-cast mining scars can be filled in and returfed, concrete emplacements can be broken up and buried, and so on. But the costs are high. No one as yet has attempted to remove an unwanted harbour, replace an excavated hillside, or demolish an unneeded dam. On the large scale, the landscape is an irreplaceable resource.

The problem is, if anything, even more acute when it comes to the basic need for space. Space cannot be conjured out of nothing, and more people necessarily means less space for each. And, as I have already argued, more mobile people also means less space for each, where 'space' means freedom from unwanted interaction with other people. There is no technical solution to crowding.

In the long view, the only thing which can be done about problems of over-population is to reduce the population. As we are not prepared to go out and shoot one person in five, the obvious technical solution, population reduction, is evidently going to be a long process, even if we make it a policy —and there are many countries round the world where large families are still encouraged.

While politicians hope for the miraculous appearance of technical solutions, the technologists, aware of their limitations, hope that the problem can be solved by economic or political means. What prospect is there of this?

CRISIS OF THE COMMONS

Professor Garrett Hardin of the University of California, known as the inventor of the principle of competitive exclusion, caused a mild flutter in 1968 with a paper entitled *The Tragedy of the Commons*. In it he drew a parallel between the over-grazing of common land in the eighteenth century and the eroding of amenities, such as clean air, today.

A given piece of land will only support so many grazing animals: put on it more than that number and the grass is destroyed faster than it can grow, so that it dies and finally the piece of land can support no animals. The man who places one additional animal upon the land, however, obtains almost all the advantage of having an extra animal to sell (or to consume) while the disadvantage is spread over all the users of the land, all of whose animals will be slightly under-fed. In the same way, Hardin argued, the man who pollutes a river or the air suffers a trifling loss but gains free disposal of his wastes. Thus exploitation tends to proceed until the common property is ruined for everyone, including the exploiter.

This analogy brought home to scientists a principle already very familiar to economists, about which a good deal more can be said.

The problem of the commons can also take another form, when land is freely available. The users of the land can exploit it and move on, as the American farmers did in the nineteenth century, and as too many forest-consumers still do. In this case, the disadvantages of over-grazing are avoided as long as the supply of land holds out; but since the supply of land is not unlimited, the day comes when the policy must be abandoned. And if the population is growing, such exploitation pushes the costs on to a future generation. The economic system has proved unable to cope with this behaviour too.

How can we tackle the problem of the commons in its modern form? First, as regards land in the eighteenth century, it was met by enclosing the land, giving it to a single owner and trusting he would have the sense to graze it

conservatively. We try to apply this solution when we hand
areas of natural beauty over to a Parks Committee or similar
authority, which is said to hold the land on behalf of the
public. The income of the officials does not depend on
maximizing profitability but on the judgment of the public as
to how well it is discharging its task of preserving the
amenity. More often, we prefer to set up a watch-dog agency
of some kind, charged with the task of regulating the usage
of the resource, by issuing licences, drawing up regulations
and policing them, and so on. But as several studies have
demonstrated in detail, such bodies eventually become sub-
servient to the interest they are supposed to watch, and
eventually are staffed by people drawn from the ranks of
those they are supposed to regulate. 'This has been so well
documented in the social sciences,' says Dr Beryl L. Crowe
of Oregon State Uinversity, 'that the best answer to the
question of who watches over the custodians of the commons
is: the regulated interests that make incursions on the commons.'

The belief that governments can establish agencies which
will effectively preserve the commons is a naïve one for
several reasons. Laws only work when a majority of people
are willing to observe them without coercion: police forces
can only move against the occasional lawbreaker. When the
lawbreakers become numerous, the task is more than they
can manage, and it is made harder by mobility.

The belief that external authorities can be substituted for
internalized controls (once called 'conscience') is one of the
lethal delusions of our age.

In this category we might include such things as preventing
the transfer of species of animal from one area to another in
a slap-happy manner, or limiting the felling of forests and
preventing erosion. I would also place in this category, perhaps, the limiting of noise.

In a perceptive article entitled 'Consumers of the River' an
American poet, Wendell Berry, who lives on the Kentucky
River, a tributary of the Ohio, describes how increasing
numbers of motor-boats invade the river, playing radios at
high volume, littering the banks with junk, and in many ways
destroying the thing they have ostensibly come to enjoy: they
even destroy it physically by the wash which they make,
which undermines the banks. No agency can effectively police

such behaviour, and even if it could, it would not form a complete solution, since the quiet and solitude are part of what one visits the river to find. The pleasures of many people are as destructive as is their work. Moreover the pleasure is, in such a case, an empty one: the river is experienced simply as 'scenery'. Its life is not understood or appreciated. In effect, they consume the river. If visitors are numerous they cannot but destroy the solitude, disturb the wildlife, and trample the grass, however quiet and well-behaved they may be. Rationing access is the only solution—and how is that to be done for rivers and wildernesses, other than enclosed parks?

The attempts of governments to control commons-type situations are also negatived in modern society by the sheer size of the problem. The only technique we have available is to create specialist agencies to deal with specific problems, whether it be water supply, atomic energy or control of the air waves, and to hope that the executive can somehow co-ordinate their efforts. How far this is successful is shown by the fact, which I mentioned earlier, that the milk of American mothers contains so much DDT that it should not be given to babies. In other words, the agricultural specialists have concentrated so hard on their task of food crop-production as to handicap the production of the human crop. But the purity of human milk is not their responsibility. Again, the AEC concentrates on nuclear power production, without caring too deeply what its efforts may do to the fish in the rivers or to the leukemia rate in man. The Corps of Engineers concentrates on providing water supplies, without caring too much about the sacrifice of visual amenity and so on—just as the Water Resources Board does in England. Integrated planning of areas from every point of view is often urged, but no one seems able to arrange it. The problem is created by the density of population and the consequent lack of any margin for error or adjustment.

Not only is it virtually impossible for governments to control many commons-type situations—as a general rule they are very reluctant even to try, as we saw in the preceding chapter.

BANKRUPTCY OF ECONOMICS

Conservatives are fond of saying that everything has its price, and that the price-mechanism should be left to regulate the situation without interference. The pollution situation presents a challenge to this doctrine which is worth outlining, since it is their alternative to regulation. In economic theory, people evoke a supply of goods which they desire in the following manner. More buyers come forward than can be supplied. The seller raises prices until the weaker buyers are eliminated. This gives him large profits, so he expands output and other manufacturers enter the field which they see is profitable. As the supply of goods expands, the price falls, and with it profits, until no further expansion seems worth while. This principle works reasonably well for goods which can be made and offered for sale. But there are areas where it works poorly or not at all. For instance, it does not evoke a supply of things which the whole community wants only one of, such as government. Other arrangements have to be made. It does not evoke things which cannot be packaged and sold for a price, among them clean air. (It attempts to cope with such situations by offering goods—for example, air conditioners—but does not entertain more radical solutions.)

Another thing which cannot be manufactured, when there is a demand, is land, so when there is a demand for land the price rises, but is not subsequently reduced by an increased supply. This is why rising land prices give a socially unjustifiable profit, and why many governments act to prevent this. Economists have tried to bring land into their system, by assuming endless supplies of land of decreasing value to man, which can be brought into use as demand increases. But the point has been reached where these 'endless supplies' are drying up. It was always a thin argument, for unused land in Kamschatka is no use to expanding Los Angeles, and the price of land in California is not limited by the existence of unused land thousands of miles away.

But where it fails most seriously is in preserving unique existing values, which nature provides free. However great the demand for fine scenery, no industry can manufacture it and sell it, just as no industry can manufacture and sell clean rivers or clean air. Moreover, since no price can be assigned to these assets, when they come into competition with something on which a price can be set, they take second place. Thus, the economic advantages of mining or making a dam or using the land for building can be calculated. The economic disadvantages of losing fine scenery cannot. In short, the economic system has built-in biases against all non-priceable values. Hence the resort to regulation.

The fact that people will contribute money to the preservation of something which they may never see, and which they do not 'enjoy' in the legal and economic senses, shows that its mere existence is a value to them. As John Krutilla points out, the total elimination of a 'resource' such as wilderness, or a species, constitutes a loss which cannot be evaluated by simply totalling up the value of small bits. Moreover, in destroying unique resources we have to consider not only whether the present population values them, but whether any future population might. With changing circumstances, people learn to make use of resources, as has happened with camping and water-skiing. A century ago, skiing on snow was unknown outside Scandinavia, and the value of mountain slopes in the Alps or Appalachians was virtually nil.

Thus the overall situation is that the technologists expect the politicians to find economic or administrative solutions, while the politicians hope that the technologists will produce some miraculous 'fix'.

A drastic reduction in population would provide a way out of such an impasse: failing that, we have no alternative but to put limits on our burgeoning technology. Indeed we need to do both. Technology keeps giving people enormously enhanced power to do harm. One man with a loudspeaker can destroy the peace of a thousand. One man with a hand-grenade can wreck a jumbo jet. A single saboteur can put a million people in the dark, or worse. And what is worse, harm can be done without knowing it or intending it. The Utah farmers did not intend to kill the Scottish fish (p. 20). The person who makes use of nuclear power does not intend that someone, somewhere, shall get leukemia as a result. Least of all that the victim shall be himself. We have become too interconnected, physically, too disconnected psychologically. It is our way of life that has to be changed.

THE TECHNOLOGICAL TREADMILL

Futurologists depict a world, less than fifty years ahead, in which we shall all fly around like crazy, though they remain sphinx-quiet on the kind of problems we have been discussing. The forecast sounds like something from a juvenile science-fiction magazine. According to the staff of the *Wall Street Journal*, we shall have 'automated living' in 'multi-family dwellings'. We shall eat mostly 'analog foods' spun from soybean and 'produced to meet almost any conceivable dietary, religious, ethnic or geographic ground rules'. For those of us who obstinately prefer real foods, an automated kitchen will cook everything under punch-card instructions, in microwave ovens. 'A few problems remain to be solved of course. For example, a microwave oven doesn't turn cooked foods their usual colours; a well-done steak still looks raw. But food experts are convinced that such obstacles won't prevent drastic changes in the kitchen.' Says a spokesman of Swift and Company with evident relish: 'By the year 2000, we'll have eliminated the pot and the pan.'

The Foreign Policy Association's forecast for 2018 sees 'more people going more places' though it is hard to see why they will want to, since 'TV will saturate the world with electronic culture'. From the depths of the jungle we shall be able to telephone home, thanks to satellites, while the 1,-000-seater supersonic transports crash past overhead. 'Behavioural technology' will make sure that we enjoy this technological nightmare, and vast computerized files on everyone will ensure that there is no dropping out.

What is crushing is the tone of unbridled optimism in which these forecasts are made. 'You can have a friendly relationship with a computer that a teacher couldn't find time for,' says G. E. Callahan of American Telephone and Telegraph. Brilliant lighting of roads and yards 'will cut the crime rate'. (My bet is the crime rate will be up, not down.) The distant doctor will diagnose your depression from afar. 'By the year 2000 you will be able to do just about everything but shake hands or kiss your wife via electronic communications.' (Surely even that could be arranged?) The only note of doubt is summarized in the observation: 'The rich will be richer, the poor relatively poorer.' Or perhaps that is an advantage too?

How many people seriously believe this is worth the price, or even worth having free? When I was a teenager, I used to read this sort of prediction with the greatest excitement and pleasure. It is the common mechanical fantasy of the schoolboy: speed, tension, power. With increasing maturity, one comes to see that it is not a blissful dream but a nightmare. Unfortunately some people and not only those of low intelligence, continue to hanker after this inhumane fantasy. Precisely because of their strong manipulative urge, they often reach positions, whether in technology or politics, where they can work towards making their fantasy actual. That others, probably a majority, do not want that kind of world they find hard to believe. How valid is the technicist dream taken at its best? André Maurois has warned us: 'An over-populated earth will bring forth unintelligent generations because culture demands leisure and silence, which have become lost qualities.' Is that profound wisdom, or the irritable cry of an old man?

The technicist would probably say the latter, because he is not much interested in leisure and silence—or even in culture as Maurois intends the word. His mistake is to believe that all men are made in his own image. But personality studies show us that there are many types of men—and many life-styles, all equally valid, as far as anyone can judge. Some people like to live the life of contemplation, withdrawn from life. Some like to live a life of service in the world, some a life of quiet enjoyment. The technicist does not really give serious consideration to all these possibilities.

One of the best-established principles in economics is the one which says the more you have of anything, the less satisfaction you get from having some more. Otherwise known as the principle of marginal returns. One car may make a great difference to your life. The fourth car just gives you the choice whether you will go there in the sedan or the convertible. One crust of bread may save a man from starvation; a thousand crusts would simply be a litter problem. While this is well understood for specific items, it is not generally grasped that it also applies to material goods taken as a whole.

In the early stages of industrialization, the benefits in terms of real satisfaction are great. Running water and electric light make life vastly less onerous. A home, sufficient clothes, good food are of basic importance. But industrial civilizations have reached the point where a majority of the population is consuming goods which yield only marginal satisfactions. We consume far more clothing than we need, changing because 'fashion' has changed and discarding clothes which are far from worn out. We know how to make clothes in large quantities, and we do this. But the satisfaction gained is small. It is rather that we avoid the dissatisfaction of being accused of being out of fashion than that we get any positive pleasure. People who live secluded lives seldom bother much about fashion.

How much further, then, would any sensible person press the trend? It is said that the US average income by the year 2020 will be five times the present figure. I, for one, feel little urge to spend five times my present income. (It could be done, of course.)

One more reason why the panic rush of technology cannot continue much longer is the drain on world resources. The inhabitants of North America, about 7½ per cent of humanity, are using about half the world's yield of basic resources. By 2000 they will, if permitted, be using *all* of them. As Professor Preston Cloud has pointed out, the US has virtually no manganese, mercury, chromium or tin and imports most of the bauxite from which its aluminium is derived. Hence it would be impossible to bring the whole world up to the current American standard of consumption. It would mean circulating more than 60 billion tons of iron, a billion tons of lead, 700 million tons of zinc and more than 50 million tons of tin —between 200 and 400 times the present world annual output. No such increase is possible by the end of the century —if ever. Philip M. Hauser, the sociologist, considers that world resources could support a population of about half a billion, only, at the current US standard. Meanwhile America proceeds on the assumption that she can treble or quadruple that standard of consumption.

Many Americans not only aim at an increasingly urbanized, high-consumption society for themselves, but urge a similar course on under-developed countries. It just doesn't make sense.

The high-density, technicist society is not only inhumane, it is also at risk—as the New York power black-out showed. The country-dweller of 50 years ago could ride out a blizzard without help. The modern city-dweller depends on the continuance of power, transport, communication, sewerage, food import and refuse collection for his existence. A two-week interruption of a single public service would constitute a crisis; a four-week break in all of them would be a catastrophe.

I now wish to suggest that such a future is not only so difficult of attainment as to be impossible unless we are prepared to pay enormous prices in ill-health, inconvenience and loss of amenity—and to run enormous risks of actual catastrophe—but that it is actually undesirable on general grounds of human happiness and the conditions which maximize it.

There is considerable and mounting evidence that life in a society devoted to maximizing the supply of goods does not provide, for the majority of its members, the basic sense of satisfaction and peace of mind which we may summarize as 'happiness'. The existence of such unhappiness is evidenced by the extent to which people resort to alcohol, obsessive sexual activity, drugs, and other devices for lowering sensitivity, distracting attention, or inducing euphoria, as also by large numbers of depressives, including suicides: some of these have rational situational causes for their sadness, others however are depressed because their whole life situation strikes them as frustrating or unsatisfying.

Some people seem to find it extraordinarily difficult to admit the reality of man's less obvious psychological demands. Thus today, in wealthier countries, there is a passionate interest in objects made with love and craftsmanship, however useless—from old mill-machinery to model locomotives, together with antiques of a more conventional kind. Yet if anyone suggests that the industrial process could be rearranged so as to readmit craftsmanship, he is regarded as an unrealistic reactionary.

Certainly to plead for a deliberate lowering of the efficiency of industry, in the interest of better social structure or improved job satisfaction, or both, will sound absurd in countries where large numbers of people are short of the necessities of life. It is not my intention to do so: I only propose that in countries which can afford to manufacture huge quantities of evanescent trifles and discard objects from boredom long before their useful life is exhausted, it would pay to seize the opportunity thus offered to restore to life some of its fundamental satisfactions.

The subject is a large one and I have explored it in more detail elsewhere (*Conditions of Happiness*, 1949). Here I want only to make the point that much of this frustration comes from the industrial process itself, now that it has become so largely organized for technical efficiency rather than job satisfaction. A recent study on this topic is that of Professor Harold L. Wilensky of the University of California, Berkeley, who finds that people whose jobs call for little personal psychological investment experience a diffuse malaise in their leisure time, and find it difficult to make productive use of their leisure. Men with demanding jobs, in contrast, make constructive use of their leisure also. Moreover, Wilensky noticed that the first group of people were compulsive television-watchers. They felt guilty about this and wanted to do something else, but 'just cannot tear themselves away from the screen'. They do not even enjoy most of what they see. The second group, in contrast, watch television on a selective basis and enjoy what they see. I am confident that the function of this obsessive television-watching is to distract the mind from contemplating the futility of such an existence. Wilensky puts it differently: alienation from work means alienation from life. Incidentally, this shows how mistaken is the common belief that a greatly increased leisure, due to reduced working hours, will provide everyone with a more satisfying existence. In reality, it will only do so for those who already have managed to make their existence satisfying.

As I have argued in detail elsewhere (in *Hemmende Strukturen in der Heutigen Industriegesellschaft*, 1969) industry could do a great deal to make work more interesting, and perhaps increase productivity thereby, rather than the reverse, since enhanced motivation and reduced incidence of strikes and work-absence might follow. In a British factory, the simple experiment of letting two men switch jobs halfway through the day increased their output 12 per cent; when they were allowed to switch twice a day, output rose to 17 per cent.

But let us not press the point. Let us assume that the whole industrial machine could be reorganized so as to restore social and personal satisfactions only at the cost of lowered efficiency in the narrow economic sense. This is probably the general case, for there is not much satisfaction to be found in producing articles of a trivial character or of poor quality or both. (It is hardly a coincidence that the Rolls-Royce company has far fewer strikes than the mass-production car manufacturers.) Would not such a reorganization be well worth while?

It is intuitive awareness of this possibility, I believe, that underlies the belief of many of today's students that the whole existing system needs to be swept away. This is what they mean by 'the rat-race'—and not simply the intensive nature of the struggle for advancement in many sectors of commercial and industrial life. Thus there is a sort of 'psychological pollution' associated with the industrial society, on top of the physical pollution.

Recently, an ingenious New York toy-maker put miniature tape-recorders playing a short continuous tape of human laughter inside paper bags and sold them at a price of $4.50 (£2). To his joy and astonishment, he received a million and a half orders—doubtless the figure is much higher by now. So we have here a diversion of resources equivalent to some $7m. if not more. To be sure, the gag is a harmless one. But equally society could do without such gags and would be well advised to do without them, if the pay-off were purer air, cleaner water, more unfelled forest, and so on. Still more so, if the pay-off includes peace of mind. Given the society we have, it is a perfectly legitimate choice to have a little fun —even if it would be still better to use the money and resources for some socially urgent purpose. My point is, once again, that there is a choice we *cannot* make as individuals: to prefer a less-spoiled environment and a more satisfying manner of life.

Industrial society is committed to a self-defeating process: the manufacture of ever more goods in the belief they confer satisfaction, by means which create dissatisfaction. No one knows how to escape the process. Advertisement and the deliberate devising of trends and fashions are needed to ensure that what the machine can manufacture is consumed. Advertising agents defend their activities in so many words, saying we must create markets to avoid unemployment developing. Thus we end by consuming in order that we may produce, instead of the reverse. This I call the technological treadmill, since we seem unable to get free of it, but it is more like a 'down' escalator moving faster than we can run up it, so that we shall soon be dumped off it.

I need not pursue the point, which has been made several times before. I wish only to make clear what I am talking about, and to demonstrate that it lies at the basis of the environment problem. The solution of this problem necessitates not only a drastic reduction in population but also a drastic reduction in the intensity of the industrial process. And I mean 'necessitates'.

The reason that governments cannot act effectively on the environment problem is that neither governments themselves nor the people they represent perceive or accept the necessity of such a drastic reorganization. The reason many students wish to sweep existing society away is precisely because they fail in this.

DEFENDERS OF TECHNOLOGY

To say that society needs to be re-organized on a pre-industrial social pattern, so as to restore classic satisfactions, is often seen as an attack on technology, and is arraigned as 'Ludditism'. Actually, it is not. A society organized in a socially more rewarding way could and certainly should make use of technological advances in an intelligent way. In my youth, I lived in Scotland without electric light and for a while without running water: I appreciate sincerely the advantages of not having to pump water on a cold night and the convenience of lamps which do not have to be filled and cleaned. My case is only that technology should be used selectively and in moderation. As David Brower has said: 'From now on it will no longer be enough to ask if man can do something. We must also ask whether he ought to.'

The physicist and Nobel prize-winner Murray Gell-Mann has recently made the same point. Speaking at a symposium sponsored by the John Muir Institute for Environmental Studies in San Francisco, he named the capacity which technology gives man to destroy the environment as one of the three factors which contribute to the problem, and said: 'It used to be true that most things that were technologically possible were done . . . certainly in the future this cannot and must not be so. As our ability to do all kinds of things, and the scale of them, increase—for the scale is planetary for so many things today—we must try to realize a smaller and smaller fraction of all the things that we can do. Therefore an essential element of engineering from now on must be the element of choice. . . . For example, if no supersonic transports fly supersonically over land, that would be an example of something we can do and don't for environmental reasons. If there are no SSTs at all, that's possibly even better.'

Having been laughed at for suggesting this myself, twenty years ago, I am delighted to have such weighty support. We still incline to believe that if the US 'standard of living' is thirty times that of Bengal, Americans are thirty times as happy as Bengalis.

W. H. Ferry, for ten years a vice-president of the Center for the Study of Democratic Institutions at Santa Barbara, has gone so far as to propose a two-year moratorium on technological innovation, as well as the establishment of a national ecological authority.

Even Ludditism is not as bad as it is painted: the term is used as if no justification were needed for the pejorative implications. Ludditism, so those who use the term think, means short-sightedness, lack of imagination, uneducated folly. But to choose a simpler way of life is a choice which every man has the right to make. When Lord Leverhulme undertook to build a fish-curing factory in Stornoway to provide work for local crofters, a town meeting was held, at which the islanders' spokesman courteously rejected the offer, explaining that they preferred the old ways—they preferred freedom and lower incomes to comfort based on servitude. Who can say they were wrong?

It is constantly asserted that it is unrealistic—sometimes the word 'impossible' is used—to turn back to the past. And so it is. No one would wish to do without antibiotics or anaesthetics, for instance. But that does not mean that the good elements of the past cannot be combined with the good elements of technology. The argument is a specious one, in which the word 'past' is first used to mean 'an exact reproduction of the past'; then the meaning is switched to 'any elements of the past'.

The suggestion that any limit be placed on the desire and pursuit of technology always evokes very strong criticism and opposition from a number of people, mostly in the scientific and technical fields themselves. Their comments are usually explosive and indignant, rather than reasoned. We should press on, confident that somehow technology will solve its own problems, they cry.

It is worth asking why the defenders of technology feel themselves to be so emotionally involved. The answer, I think, is this. As has often been said, and as Sir Peter Medawar pointed out once again in his essay "On 'The Effecting of all Things Possible'", the collapse of the medieval belief in the divine order led to a moral vacuum in which nothing had a purpose and man was a cipher. A sense of despair was born. This 'failure of nerve' (the term is Toynbee's) was exorcized by the rise of rationalism; reason was not merely necessary but was sufficient as a justification. Man's inspiring task was to understand the cosmic scheme; his personal dignity was derived from his brilliant successes in doing so. Rationalism in general and science in particular thus took the place of religion—or, if you are willing to define religion as a myth which gives purposes to men's lives, then science *was* a religion. Later, to this notion was appended the idea that rationalism would improve men's earthly lot. Communist belief in man's unlimited power to mould the environment is only the optimism of the eighteenth-century 'improver' writ large.

Today, religious belief has waned still further, not least among scientists, while the sense of man's impotence and futility has become stronger. Man's follies and cruelties are better understood; education and rising living standards have not created a race of kind and rational human beings, as the age of reason expected. The social order has become more unstable. So the need to believe in man's intellectual purpose and in the certainty that it will provide a better life here on earth has become intensified. The optimists cannot give up this belief without abandoning their optimism, and relapsing into despair. Moreover, no one likes to live in a chaotic system. Science provides an intellectual system which promises a stable frame of reference into which all phenomena can be integrated. (This also explains the reductionist tendencies of many scientists and their horror at anything that smacks of superstition.)

This has been called the 'technicist view' by Professor Manfred Stanley, of Syracuse University. It reflects a desire for order for its own sake and is seen as the only basis of agreement possible today. As he points out, the same phenomena are interpreted in opposite senses by the optimists, who believe in technology, and the pessimists, who declare that, under this doctrine, individuals are caught up in a vast organization which has no other end than the maintenance of the system. Thus human beings are reduced to means—the means by which the system is maintained.

This reduction of human beings to means is often quite explicit, as when the advertiser says that markets must be created in order that the output of industry can be consumed. It is common in socialist states, where the people are expected to adopt themselves to the convenience of the 'public service' rather than the other way about.

Stanley points to four phenomena which can be interpreted pessimistically or optimistically. Thus the 'plural society' composed of differing groups means to the optimist that spontaneity is increased and everyone can find the milieu he prefers. To the pessimist it means tribalism and the war of cults. The optimist believes that the human need for some sense of community will be met by the existence of universal humanism, and that the organization of this community will be achieved by information-exchange. The pessimist says that a bogus sense of community will be created by a propaganda of loyalty-evoking symbols and abstractions, and that the organization will be a cybernetic system in which human beings will be helpless units. Finally, the optimist hopes that social problems will be met with clear-cut technical solutions. The pessimist, if he believes that technical solutions are possible at all, fears they will be imposed by a closed technocratic élite on people who cannot understand or take part in the decisions. Which is right, is what Professor Stanley is attempting to discover.

Medawar joins himself unambiguously to the optimists, seeing the present despondency about technology not as resulting from the collapse of the technicist myth, but merely as a temporary 'failure of nerve'. His solution for the miscarriages of technology is more technology. 'The deterioration of the environment produced by technology is a technological problem for which technology has found, is finding, and will continue to find solutions.'

Unfortunately, in addition to finding solutions, it will also create more problems. The crucial question is whether it will find answers as fast as it creates problems, and how big the time-lag will be. By the time technology has found a way of defusing radiation, we may all be dead. Equally crucial is the question whether the solutions will be applied. I have already advanced reasons why the political response may be wholly inadequate. This is the real defect of the 'technology can hoist itself by its own bootstraps' argument—it leaves the ball in the politicians' court. It is one more example of the evasion of responsibility to which I referred at the start of this chapter.

Medawar seems himself to have some underlying doubts, for he offers the alternative hope that there are tens of thousands of years to recover from any mistake. No doubt a Roman citizen, fleeing from the sack of Rome, would have felt faintly cheered to know that in a thousand years or so a comparable civilization would have been erected on the ruins of the old. But he would hardly have regarded it as a reason for not assassinating a Goth or a Hun if opportunity offered.

THE LOVE OF NATURE

The current wave of enthusiasm for pollution-control has united the interests of many disparate groups, from fishermen to hypochondriacs, and among them are conservationists. It is important, however, to realize that conservation is a distinct issue which lies within the pollution issue. I limit the word 'conservation' here to mean the preservation of untouched landscape and ecosystems—though later I shall discuss this definition in more detail. Preservation is a much harder horse to sell than anti-pollution. Many people dislike untidy heaps of junk, simply because they are disorderly; many people object to filthy streams in which you cannot fish or swim, and especially if they stink. Everyone objects to smogs which make the eyes smart, and everyone objects to pollutants which threaten health. But these same people may be quite unmoved to hear of the damming of a remote valley, which they may never visit, the destruction of some species of plant or animal, or even the vanishing of a pre-technical human culture.

As I argued in Chapter 10, the deep sense of unity with

the landscape and with all life described by many poets and writers, and by mystics both Christian and oriental, is rooted in a psychological process in which the ego, the sense of self, is dissolved. Oriental occult teaching, as well as western mysticism derived from it, asserts that each individual is formed from the divine ground, or Atman—bracketed off, so to speak, by the walls of his ego. At death these walls dissolve, the individual loses his individuality and is merged again in the ultimate reality. On this basis, the nature-mystic experience is a supreme religious experience, of the same order as the experiences of Plotinus or St John of the Cross. (There are doctrinal points here, as theological readers will be aware, but they do not affect my argument.) The Puritan, in contrast, is strongly individualistic, and feels cast out and remote from God, or the divine, and seeks, by austerities, to be readmitted.

If it is really the case that nature-love is in some degree a genuine religious experience, of extreme importance to those who experience it, we have no moral right to restrict its availability unduly. And even if we take a rationalist view, and deny the presence of a divine element, it remains an experience of value and importance—which is why people become so deeply involved in attempts to protect it—and one which it would be unjust and unwise to deprive people of. I say 'unwise' as well as 'unjust' because it is evidently an ennobling experience, and we do not have too many of those; and probably it helps people to withstand the stresses of modern life. A world in which people live largely in cities may need nature more, rather than less.

There is no evidence, as far as I am aware, what proportion of the population is capable of this experience. Those who have it rarely talk about it. I imagine that they are, in the modern world, a minority though they may be commoner in less sophisticated societies. The animism of primitive man expresses the feeling that plants and inanimate objects are in some sense to be regarded as equivalent to himself. Modern rationalism erodes this feeling. Thus the technological society is unlikely to turn back on its tracks and give recognition to this experience. Such evidence as we have from unsophisticated countries which begin to become industrialized suggests that they develop appetites for the trivial all too easily.

But it may be that the capacity of such experience is in all men, if it were not obscured by education or rendered impossible by the early experiences which dictate the formation of the ego. In that case, there may at some future date be a general demand for the restitution of a relationship with nature. If by then we have destroyed nature, we shall have committed an unforgivable wrong.

The argument carries a further implication. If all things are the expression of some universal reality or Atman, then all are equally valid and have an equal right to existence and to respect. This, indeed, is the attitude of the animistic 'savage' (as we choose to call him). If he has to cut down a tree, he first apologizes to it, and secondly plants a new one to replace it. Strong taboos exist to prevent wasteful and excessive exploitation of important resources, especially the principal food animal which is normally the totem animal also. The 'savage' sees himself in a continuous relationship with nature.

Modern man feels, in contrast, that nature is there for his convenience. He is entitled to 'master' it, to 'exploit' it, to 'tame' it. He speaks of 'natural resources' as if oil and metal existed only that man should make use of them. As several authorities have recently argued, conservation is only possible if man learns to drop this arrogant attitude and see himself a part of nature. The attitude is a form of anthropocentrism: just as once men believed the earth was the centre of the universe, in a physical sense, so now they feel man is the centre in a sociological sense. Medieval Christianity gave considerable support to this notion. God gave man dominion over 'the fish of the sea, and over the fowl of the air, and over the cattle, and over all the earth, and over every creeping thing that creepeth upon the earth.'

In my view, Christianity did not cause this development; the Bible merely provided convenient arguments to justify behaviour which derived from puritan personality structures. The Bible, as usual, also provided contrary arguments: 'the Earth is the Lord's' and it is man's duty to protect His property, of which he only has stewardship. The puritan chose to ignore this view.

One of the greatest radicals in Christian history was St Francis of Assisi, who rejected the notion of the ant as an example to sluggards, and flames as a symbol of the soul's aspiration for God. For him they were Brother Ant and

Sister Fire, 'praising the Creator in their own way, as Brother Man does in his'. St Bonaventura, the statesman-cleric who took over Franciscanism, tried to suppress his teaching, and later commentators declared that he preached to the birds as a rebuke to men who would not listen. Not so: he 'urged the little birds to praise God, and in spiritual ecstasy they flapped their wings and chirped rejoicing'. Professor Lynn White, Jr., of the University of California, from whom I here quote, has proposed St Francis as the patron saint of ecologists.

Whatever the role of Christianity may have been, it is certainly true that we need to abandon the military-aggressive attitude to nature, with its triumphs and its break-throughs, and must learn to be more humble. 'I am old enough to remember tales that strengthen my belief in a deep semi-religious influence that was formerly at work among our people,' wrote Sherwood Anderson to his friend Waldo Frank, many years ago. ' . . . I can remember old fellows in my home town speaking feelingly of an evening spent on the big empty plains. It had taken the shrillness out of them. They had learned the trick of quiet.' Says Stewart Udall, quoting these words, 'A half-century later we have un-learned, and all but lost, the trick of quiet.'

Policies of conservation rest primarily on our willingness to change our exploitative policies for policies of co-existence. The great ecologist Charles Elton has declared that there are three motives for conservation: first, that natural systems are interesting, beautiful and a source of pleasure in themselves; second, that it is important to protect them, from a practical viewpoint; and thirdly—though he puts it first—the religious reason, that they have a right to exist and we have no right to persecute or destroy them.

Albert Schweitzer once said that the great fault of all ethics hitherto has been that they believed themselves to have to deal only with the relation of man to man. He should, however, have limited the arraignment to western ethics, for some oriental religions (e.g. the Jains) insist strongly on the rights of animals, even insects, to existence. The point is still untaken in many quarters.

Conservation, Elton holds, consists in 'finding a wise princi-ple of coexistence between man and nature, even if it has to be a modified kind of man and a modified kind of nature.' The task is one 'of reducing direct power over nature, not increasing it; of letting nature do some of the jobs that engineers and chemists and applied biologists are frantically attempting to do.' We all too easily assume, for instance, that we have to choose between having a prosperous agriculture and an aesthetically satisfying landscape. There are qualified people who say this is not so.

If society were determined to do so, their proposals could be explored and tested. At present there is small sign of any such tendency, and scientists write to defend 'the rights of man' against the rights of the rest of nature. But the fact is, the issue is not so much a practical as a moral one.

TRIPLE CRISIS

The crisis at which man finds himself is, in sum, a threefold one. First, it is a crisis of values. What is at issue is two diametrically opposed views of how man *ought* to live. Up to now it has seemed that the materialist view—supported equally by parties of the right and the left—must triumph. Suddenly it begins to appear that it cannot triumph. The choice then becomes whether to make an intelligent selection from the gifts of technology and use them to enrich an humane existence, or whether to commit suicide. It is the fact that all parties in western countries are equally committed to materialism that causes the sense of despair and impotence which assails many people today.

Like the lemmings, man is heading for the far bank of the river. Suicide is not his intention. Has he the intelligence to turn back? The lesson of history is that he never avoids catastrophes; he just spends his time recovering from them. No doubt history will repeat itself.

Secondly, we are in a crisis of disconnectedness. As a British observer has said: 'One feels like asking, in the end, how crazy can the world get? . . . no rational men would actually set up conditions in which their very food and water were constantly polluted, their children killed and injured, and their whole environment rendered fouler all the time to ear, eye and nose—not through their failures, but through their very efforts and so-called advances. Imagine you kept knocking your own children down because you always ran to the bottom of the garden to get started on the weekend digging. You'd walk. Imagine you found you were fertilizing your cabbage patch so heavily you were polluting your own water supply. You wouldn't set up a research programme to see how to cancel out the danger; you'd fertilize less, have fewer cabbages and put your feet up more.'

There is the nub; society is too large, hence too impersonal and disconnected. Hence also, impossible to regulate efficiently. As Alfred Korzybski has spent his life showing, when you double the administrative span of an individual, you multiply his administrative problems by many times more. The number of possible relationships between five people and a supervisor is one hundred; in the case of ten people it is 5,210.

Finally, it is a crisis of responsibility.

Man has reached a turning point in his history. Up to now he has lived in a self-optimizing environment. Natural processes have kept him supplied with oxygen and water, with fertile soil, space to move, and even aesthetic pleasures, without the necessity of intervention or forethought on his part. Now he has reached the point where these autonomous natural processes can no longer cope with his demands. So it is not a question of whether he wants to assume control; he is obliged to. In future, man will have to decide how hot or cold he wants the climate to be, how clean he wants the water and air to be, how fertile the soil, how high his disease and mortality rates. And much else besides.

It is a grave responsibility. It is far from clear that man has either the knowledge or the political good sense to exercise this power suitably—that is, so as to ensure for people a life at least as satisfactory as they had under the old arrangement. Indeed, it is quite on the cards that he may mismanage his powers so badly that he causes, in some degree, a disaster.

Only those with a very naïve trust in human nature will prefer to depend on man's good sense rather than on the long-tested self-optimizing processes which made the evolution of life possible.

However, if he does make a mess of it, at least there will be no one around to say: 'I told you so.'

It is the future of the human race that we have been talking about.

Some Organizations concerned to protect the Environment

Readers may feel inspired to give their support to one or more organizations concerned with the issues discussed in this book. There are many bodies, from anglers to landowners, who have an interest in preserving some aspect of the environment. Following is a list of bodies whose primary object is to improve conservation and population policies on a national, or world, basis.

Conservation Foundation: 1717 Massachusetts Ave., NW, Washington, D.C. 20036

Environmental Defense Fund, Inc.: P.O. Box 740, Stony Brook, New York 11790

Friends of the Earth: 451 Pacific, San Francisco, California 94133

Environmental Action Inc.: 2000 P Street, NW, Washington, D.C. 20036

National Wildlife Federation: 1412 Sixteenth Street, NW, Washington, D.C. 20036

Populaiton Reference Bureau, Inc.: 1755 Massachusetts Ave., NW, Washington, D.C. 20036

Rachel Carson Trust for the Living Environment: 8940 Jones Mill Road, Washington, D.C. 20015

Sierra Club: Mills Tower, San Francisco, California 94104

Zero Population Growth: 367 State Street, Los Altos, California 94022

PERIODICALS
There is an increasing number of technical journals and

popular newsletters. Strongly recommended for the ordinary reader are:

CF Newsletter (monthly; 1 yr: $6; 2 yrs: $11; 3 yrs: $15 in U.S. All other countries: $8, $15, $21.) Conservation Foundation, 1717 Massachusetts Ave., NW, Washington, D.C. 20036

Environmental Action (24 issues a year; students $3; ordinary $4; business $10; contributing $50; supporting $100.)

Environment (10 issues a year; 1 yr: $8.50; 2 yrs: $14, plus $1.50 additional postage on foreign subscriptions.) Committee for Environmental Information, 438 N. Skinker Blvd., St. Louis, Missouri 63130

References

These notes are intended more as a general guide to detailed information than as a formal list of sources. Thus when a paper is cited several times in the same section it is only listed once, while one or two important papers not cited are included. Some of these have appeared since the manuscript was completed. Of course, I have not attempted to include *all* the relevant papers; this would have produced a bibliography as long as the book itself.

1 MAN THE MICROBE

page

15 David Price . . . 'Is Man becoming Obsolete?' *Pub. Health Reports* (1959) *74*:693-9.

Fosberg . . . *Proc. Ninth Pacific Conf.* (1957).

Fraser Darling at the Intergovernmental Conference of Experts on the Scientific Basis for Rational Use and Conservation of the Resources of the Biosphere, September 1968 (UNESCO, 1969).

16 Rockefeller Foundation . . . J. G. Harrar in *Rockefeller Quarterly* (1968).

LaMont Cole . . . *BioScience* (1968) *18* (7):679.

Löfroth . . . *New Sci.* (1968) *40*:567, 'Pesticides and Catastrophe'.

Commoner . . . *Science and Survival* (Viking Press, 1967), p. 122.

18 damage to nursery gardens . . . In Low, 'Smog over the Fields', *New Sci.* (1968) *40*:494, where many more instances are given.

Japan . . . *Newsweek* (3 Nov. 1969). On the sea route Tokyo Bay-Uraga visibility is nil on fifty days a year.

19 lakes of Europe . . . see *Information Bulletin* No. 14 (May 1967), 'Protection of Lakes', for a very thorough survey (Föderation Europäischer Gewasserschutz FEB, Zürich).

Baikal . . . P. P. Micklin, 'The Baykal Controversy', *Nat. Resources J.* (1967) No. 4, p. 17; also *Sci. Jnl.* (1968) *4* (4):5.

22 lead . . . cadmium . . . See Ch. 7 for full details.

23 radio-activity . . . See Ch. 8 for full details.

Rajputana Desert . . . Reid Bryson and David Bareis, 'Possibilities of Major Climatic Modification and their Implications: Northwest India, a case for study', *Bull. Amer. Meteorol. Soc.* (March 1967) *48*(3): 136-42.

2 THE PLANETARY ENGINEERS

27 Singer . . . *Science* (1968) *160*: 1476-78, where also Udall cited.

28 Marangunič . . . *Sci. News* (1969) *96*:330.

Chorley . . . R. J. Chorley and R. J. More (eds.), *Water, Earth and Man* (Methuen, 1969), pp. 163*ff*.

29 evaporation . . . V. K. La Mer (ed.), *The Retardation of Evap-*

page

oration by Monolayers (Academic Press, 1962).

STORMFURY . . . *Sci. News* (1969) *96*:153 and *96*:551.

Malone . . . T. F. Malone, 'New Dimensions of International Co-operation in Weather Analysis and Prediction', *Bull. Amer. Met. Soc.* (1968) *49*(12): 114; 'Tinkering with our Atmospheric Environment', *Technology Review* (1968) *70*(7):41-8.

30 irrigating C. Asia . . . V. A. Kovda, 'Land Use Development in the Arid Regions of the Russian Plain, in the Caucasus and in C. Asia'. V. V. Zvonkov, 'Integrated Water Resources Development in the River Basins of the USSR', *Acad. Sciences USSR*, 1957.

32 dam the Amazon . . . R. B. Panero, *Sci. Jnl.* (1969) *5A*(3): 56-60.

Prof. Torki . . . *Le Désaharation Nucléaire: rétablissement de la mer intérieure au Maghreb Centrale*. Rapport CEA 23 (1968), Tunisian Republic.

34 Lake Eyre . . . Ian B. Kiddle, 'Inland Water', *Scientific Australian* (Oct. 1965), pp. 6-11.

35 S. Indian Lake . . . *New Sci.* (1969) *43*:413. The vast Mekong River project with its many new dams may prove a most serious instance. (See G. F. White, 'The Mekong River Plan', *Sci. Amer.* (1963) *208*:49.)

earthquakes . . . J. P. Rothé: 'Fill a Lake, start an Earthquake', *New Sci.* (1968) *39*:75-8.

37 toxic wastes . . . *The Sciences* (Sept. 1969) *9*:7.

David Evans . . . *Dateline in Science* (16 Aug. 1968).

38 Amchitka test . . . *Environment* (1969) *11*(6):2-13, 'Underground Nuclear Testing'. Am-

page

chitka is, or was, a wildlife refuge.

MacDonald . . . 'The Modification of Planet Earth by Man', *Technology Review* (1969) *72* (1):26-35.

40 PLOWSHARE . . . *Plowshare*, Atomic Energy Commission, 1966.

42 Australian harbour . . . V. Brodine, 'Six Questions for Australians', *Environment* (1969) *11*(3):16-19; and 'Unsnug Harbor', *Environment* (1969) *11* (4):54.

another plan . . . W. A. Scholes, 'Nuclear Perseverance', *Sci. News* (1969) *96*:408-9.

43 sea-level canal . . . E. A. Martell, 'Plowing a Nuclear Furrow', *Environment* (1969) *11* (3):2-10, 12-13, 26-8; J. C. Briggs, 'The Sea-Level Panama Canal: Potential Biological Catastrophe', *Bio-Science* (1969) *19*: 79-84; *News Report* (of Nat. Acad. Sciences) Aug-Sept. 1969.

45 Rubinoff . . . 'Central American Sea-level Canal: Possible Biological Effects', *Science* (1968) *161*: 857-61.

46 Borisov . . . 'Can We Control the Arctic Climate?', *Science and Public Affairs* (Mar. 1969) p. 43.

48 Fletcher . . . *The Polar Oceans and World Climate*, cited by S. F. Singer, *loc. cit.*

49 forests . . . The Russians have done a lot on this, e.g. A. A. Molchanov, *The. Hydrological Role of Forests* (Israel Program for Scientific Translations, 1963); V. V. Rakhmanov, *The Role of Forests in Water Conservation* (ed. A. Gourevich and L. M. Hughes, Isr. Prog. Sci. Transl., 1966).

Arno floods . . . R. M. Klein,

page

'The Florence Floods', *Natural History* (1969) 78:46.

50 forest-felling . . . G. Borgstrom, *Too Many, a study of earth's biological limitations* (Macmillan, 1969), Ch. 1: 'The forest and the field in an ominous confrontation'.

51 vanishing hedges . . . *The Times* (3 Nov. 1969), 'Drive to Conserve Hedgerows', and subsequent correspondence.

52 defoliants . . . F. H. Tschirley, 'Defoliation in Vietnam', *Science* (1969) *163*:779; for birth defects caused by defoliants, see *Sunday Times* (30 Nov. 1969) p. 7. See also E. W. Pfeiffer, 'Ecological Effects of the Vietnam War,' *Sci. Jnl.* (1969) *5* (2):33.

3   ICE AGE OR HEAT DEATH

56 Erling Dorf . . . 'Climatic Changes of the Past and Present'. *Amer. Scientist* (1960) *48*: 341-64.

57 Callender . . . 'The artificial production of carbon dioxide and its influence on temperature', *Qtly. J. Roy. Meteorol. Soc.* (1938) *64*:223.

Plass . . . 'The carbon dioxide theory of climatic change', *Tellus* (1956) *8*(2):140-54; *Sci. Amer.* (1959) *201*:41.

5 billion tons . . . Francis Johnson, 'The Oxygen and Carbon Dioxide Balance in the Earth's Atmosphere', at AAAS meeting, 1968.

Deevey . . . E. S. Deevey, Jr., 'Bogs', *Sci. Amer.* (1958) *199* (4):114.

59 Lamb . . . quoted by K. Frazier, 'Earth's Cooling Climate', *Sci. News* (1969) 96:458-9.

Clark . . . 'Return to Hard

page

Winters', *New Sci.* (1968) *37*: 145.

60 Iceland . . . L. Kristiansson, 'The Ice Drifts Back to Iceland', *New Sci.* (1969) *41*:508

Bryson . . . 'Climatic Effects of Atmospheric Pollution', at AAAS meeting, 1968; 'Possibilities of Major Climatic Modification and their Implications', *Bull. Amer. Meteorol. Soc.* (1967) *48*(3):136-42.

62 turbidity . . . R. U. Ayres and I. J. Zucker, 'A Model for Analyzing the Effects of a Dust Cloud in the Stratosphere on the Heat Balance of the Earth' (Hudson Institute, duplicated, n.d.); R. A. McCormick and J. H. Ludwig, 'Climatic Modification by Atmospheric Aerosols', *Science* (1967) *156*:1358.

red dust . . . *Weather* (April 1969) 24:126.

63 Lovelock . . . (privately communicated).
the temperate zones . . . Ayres and Zucker, *op. cit.*

64 Manabe and Wetherald . . . *J. Atmos. Sciences* (1967) 24:241-59.

La Porte . . . S. A. Changnon, Jr., *Bull. Amer. Meteorol. Soc.* (1968) 49:1, cited in *Sci. News* (1969) 96:83.

65 westerly winds . . . *Geogr. Jnl.* (1966) *132*:2.

jet aircraft . . . Bryson, 'Climatic Effects of Atmospheric Pollution', p. 6; for effects of supersonic aircraft, such as Concorde, see R. E. Newell, 'Water Vapour Pollution in the Stratosphere by the Supersonic Transporter?', *Nature* (1970) 226:71. He points out that the time that water vapour remains in the stratosphere is measured in years, as against a week or two in the troposphere below it.

300   References

page

66 which confirms the fact . . . W. O. Roberts, lecture to Advanced Research Projects Agency, Washington (26 June 1969): 'Weather Forecasting and Climate Modification'.

67 ice-cores . . . W. Dansgaard *et al.*, 'One Thousand Centuries of Climatic Record' etc., *Science* (1969) *166*:377; 'Glacier oxygen-18 content and Pleistocene Ocean Temperatures', *ib.*, p. 499.

68 balance . . . Ayres and Zucker, *op. cit.*

Morner . . . *Sveriges Geologiska Undersökning* (1969) *63*:1.

70 Schaefer . . . 'New Field Evidence of Inadvertent Modification of the Atmosphere', *Proc. First Nat. Conf. Weather Modific.*, pp. 163-72 (1968). Dr F. E. Volz, of the Cambridge Air Force Research Laboratories, comments that the explosive eruption of Mount Agung in Bali in March 1963 'may have initiated a breakdown of natural conditions of the chemistry of stratospheric aerosols,' and joins with this the question, 'One may ask whether the contamination of the *upper* atmosphere by man-made aerosols and especially gas traces from the surface and by high-altitude aircraft has not already become significant' (emphasis added). See F. E. Volz, 'On Atmospheric Turbidity after the Agung Eruption of 1963, and Size Distribution of the Volcanic Aerosol', *J. Geophys. Research* (to be published).

Wexler . . . 'Volcanoes and World Climate', *Sci. Amer.* (1952) *186*(4): 74.

Mitchell . . . quoted by Frazier, 'Earth's Cooling Climate', *Sci. News* (1969) *96*:458. See also J. M. Mitchell, Jr., 'Is Man's Industry Upsetting the Weath-

page

er?' *The Futurist* (1969) *3*(2): 34.

Roberts . . . *loc cit.* He, too, thought increasing turbidity would lead to more cloud cover and rainfall.

72 solar constant . . . H. H. Landsberg, 'Trends in Climatology', in J. Bresler (ed.), *Human Ecology* (Addison-Wesley, 1966).

albedo . . . R. A. Bryson, 'All Other Factors being Constant . . .', *Weatherwise* (April 1968) *21*(2): 56-62. *Restoring the Quality of our Environment*, Appendix Y 4.

72 Budyko . . . M. I. Budyko *et al.*, 'Influence of Economic Activity on Climate', in *Contemporary Problems in Climatology* (Leningrad, 1966), cited Gordon MacDonald, *op. cit.*

74 MacDonald . . . Gordon J. F. MacDonald, 'The Modification of Planet Earth by Man', at AAAS meeting, 1968.

Landsberg . . . *Op. cit.*

75 Barrett . . . *U.S. Dept. of Commerce News*, 4 Mar. 1970.

4 NATURE HITS BACK

78 mosquitoes . . . C. Elton, *The Ecology of Invasions by Animals and Plants* (Methuen, 1966).

80 African snail . . . H. van der Schalie, 'Man meddles with Nature — Hawaiian Style', *The Biologist* (1969) *51*(4):136-46.

81 Conway . . . 'A Consequence of Insecticides', in *The Unforeseen Ecological Boomerang*. Supplement to *Natural History*, based on Conference on the Ecological Aspects of International Development Programs at Warrenton, Va., December 1968.

Israel . . . E. Rivnay, 'The Overhead Sprinklers of Israel', *ibid.*

page

85 vanishing animals . . . V. Zis-wiler, *Extinct and Vanishing Animals* (Longmans, 1968); R. Fitter, *Vanishing Wild Animals of the World* (Kaye and Ward, 1968).

86 Hawaii . . . In general, see F. R. Fosberg, *Man's Place in the Island Ecosystem* (The Bishop Museum Press, 1963).

Philip Island . . . Elton, *loc. cit.*

87 sardine industry . . . C. J. George, 'The Role of the Aswan High Dam in Changing the Fisheries of the SE. Mediterranean', EAIDP Conference, 1968.

Nasser Dam . . . 'The Aswan High Dam, a balance sheet', *New Sci.* (1964) 22:406.

88 schistosomiasis . . . H. van der Schalie, 'Egypt's New High Dam —Asset or Liability?', *The Biologist* (1960) 42(3-4):63-70.

89 Wright . . . 'Medical Parasitology in a Changing World', *J. Parasit.* (1951) 37:1-2.

Kariba . . . P. R. Hira, 'Transmission of Schistosomiasis in Lake Kariba', *Nature* (1969) 224:670-2; T. Scudder, 'The Ecological Hazards of Making a Lake', in *The Unforeseen Ecological Boomerang* (see p. 82 above).

91 oxygen . . . LaMont Cole, 'The Ecosphere', *Sci. Amer.* (1958) 198(4):83.

93 LaMont Cole . . . 'Protect the Friendly Bacteria', *Sat. Rev.* (1966) May.

95 nitrates . . . B. Commoner, 'Threats to the Integrity of the Nitrogen Cycle', AAAS meeting, 1968; 'Poisoning the Wells', *Environment* (1969) 11(1):2.

97 Great Ouse . . . *Sci. Jnl.* (1968) 4(5):9, 'Sweetening the land sours the lakes'.

98 tinplate . . . J. H. Jonson, 'Internal Can Corrosion due to High Nitrate Content of Canned Vegetables', *Prot. Flor. Hort. Soc.* (1966) 79:239.

nitrogen oxides . . . E. S. Starkman, 'Chemical Pollution from Transportation Vehicles', at AAAS meeting, 1967.

diminish the capacity of the blood . . . by an average of 20 per cent and up to a maximum of 38 per cent in animal experiments by Prof. Albert A. Bush of UCLA: *Sci. News* (1969) 96:140.

nitroso-compounds . . . S. S. Epstein and W. Lijinsky, 'Nitrosamines as Environmental Carcinogens', *Nature* (1970) 225: 21-3. They point out that nitrites react with secondary amines to produce nitrosamines which are highly carcinogenic in the body.

5 THE LAST GASP

101 Crown of Thorns . . . R. H. Chesher, 'Destruction of Pacific Corals by the Sea-star *A. planci*', *Science* (1969) 165:281-3.

102 team of specialists . . . L. Bickel, 'The Battle for the Reef', *Sci. News* (1969) 96:218-20.

103 red tides . . . S. H. Hutner and J. A. McLaughlin, 'Poisonous Tides', *Sci. Amer.* (1958) 199 (2):92; W. Marx, *The Frail Ocean* (Coward-McCann, 1967), Ch. 2.

104 stinking fish . . . Cyrus Adler (letter) in *Sci. News* (1969) 96: 294.

106 Eco-catastrophe . . . *Ramparts* (September 1969) pp. 24-8.

thousands of products . . . E. D. Goldberg, 'The Chemical Invasion of the Oceans by Man', at AAAS meeting, 1968.

lead . . . C. C. Patterson in D. Hood (ed.) *Impingement of*

page

Man on the Oceans (Wiley, 1970). See also Ch. 7.

107 mercury . . . G. Löfroth, *Report on Methyl Mercury*, duplicated report to WHO (Stockholm, 1968). See also Ch. 7.

shallower parts . . . Edward Wenk, Jr., 'The Physical Resources of the Oceans', *Sci. Amer.* (1969) 221(3):166-76.

the FAO points out . . . Prospectus of Technical Conference on Marine Pollution and its Effects, to be convened December 1970, p. 1.

radio-active wastes . . . E. D. Goldberg, *op cit.* Edward Wenk, Jr., *op. cit.* See also Ch. 8.

108 mixing of the deeper water . . . R. W. Stewart, 'The Atmosphere and the Ocean', *Sci. Amer.* (1969) 221(3):76-86.

109 steel drums . . . Marx, *loc. cit.*

V. T. Bowen . . . 'Strontium-90: Concentrations in Surface Waters of the Atlantic Ocean', *Science* (1969) 165: 825-7.

Revelle . . . cited by R. Furon. *The Problem of Water* (Faber, 1963), See also J. C. Collins, *Radioactive Wastes* (Spon, 1960).

110 kelp forests . . . Marx, *op. cit.*, Ch. 5.

Polykarpov . . . *The Radioecology of Aquatic Organisms* (Reinhold, 1966).

spillage of oil . . . half the world's ocean cargo weight is oil; 700m. tons in 1967. S. Fred Singer, 'The Lesson of Santa Barbara' (duplicated, 1969).

111 *Torrey Canyon* . . . J. E. Smith (ed.) *The Torrey Canyon* (Cambridge U.P., 1968).

anaesthesia . . . R. J. Goldacre, 'Effects of Detergents and Oils on the Cell Membrane'. Field Study Council.

page

Max Blumer . . . 'Oil Pollution of the Ocean'. Material presented at Symposium 'Man's Chemical Invasion of the Ocean', La Jolla, Feb. 1969 (duplicated).

112 Nelson Smith . . . 'Biological Consequences of Oil Pollution and Shore Cleansing', in *The Biological Effects of Oil Pollution on Littoral Communities* (suppl. to *Field Studies* Vol. 2), July 1968. Field Studies Council. This also contains his 'Classified Bibliography of Oil Pollution'.

113 Boyle . . . *Biol. Conservation* (1969) 1(4):319-27.
Pearce, Holt . . . J. Chamblin, 'Rumblings from the Deep', *Sci. News* (1969) 96:213.

114 Lloyd Berkner . . . 'Man versus Technology', *Pop. Bull.* (1966) 22(4):(no pagin.). See also LaMont Cole, 'Can the World Be Saved?', *BioScience* (1968) 18 (7):679.

115 Wurster . . . *Science* (1968) 159:1474.

116 Lovelock . . . J. E. Lovelock and C. E. Giffin, 'Planetary Atmospheres', in Tiffany (ed.), *Advanced Space Experiments* (AAAS, 1969).

6 THE NEW LOOK IN POLLUTANTS

119 asbestos . . . Paul Brodeur did an admirable summary, 'The Magic Mineral', in *New Yorker* (12 Oct. 1968), available as a reprint. Dr. I. J. Selikoff also summarizes, with numerous references: 'Asbestos', in *Environment* (1969) 11(2):2-7. For some technical aspects, see V. Timbrell and S. Holmes, "Suggestions for Criteria for Sampling Asbestos Dust", (Johannesburg Conference on Pneumoconiosis, 1969).

page

124 DDT . . . The literature is, of course, immense. Useful summaries of recent developments are: Justin Frost, 'Earth, Air and Water', *Environment* (1969) *11*(6):14-33 on world-wide distribution; Tony J. Peterle, 'Pyramiding Damage', *ibid.*, pp. 34-40, on biological concentration; Gordon Conway *et al.*, 'DDT On Balance', *Environment* (1969) *11*(7):2-5; and Kevin P. Shea, 'Unwanted Harvest', *ibid.*, pp. 12-17 and 28-31 for effects on animals and man.

Arctic seals . . . There appears to be at least 2,300 tons of DDT in Antarctic snow. T. J. Peterle.

124 'DDT in Antarctic Snow', *Nature* (1969) *224*:620.

in the air . . . K. R. Tarrant and J. O'G. Tatton, *Nature* (1968) *219*:725.

125 fiddler crabs . . . W. E. Odum, G. E. Woodwell, and C. F. Wurster, 'DDT Residues' etc., *Science* (1969) *164*:576.

forests are sprayed . . . *Nature* (1969) *221*:487.

126 Lucille Stickel . . . R. D. Porter and S. N. Wiemayer, 'Dieldrin and DDT: Effects on Sparrowhawk Eggshells and Reproduction', *Science* (1969) *165*:199.

quail . . . F. J. S. Jones and D. B. Summers, *Nature* (1968) *217*:1162.

127 trout . . . J. M. Anderson and M. Peterson, *Science* (1969) *164*:440.

hassle . . . C. F. Wurster, 'DDT Goes to Trial in Madison', *BioScience* (1969) *19*(9):809-13.

128 badgers . . . D. J. Jefferies, *J. Zool.* (1969) *157*:429, cited *New Sci.* (1969) *42*:341.

laboratory worker . . . *Brit. Med. J.* (1947) i.507.

page

129 obese patient . . . *N. Z. Med. Jnl.* (1959) *58*:393, cited Ruth Carson, *Silent Spring* (Hamish Hamilton, 1963), p. 155.

130 drive you mad . . . R. Carson, *Silent Spring*, p. 162.

liver enzymes . . . a long story, well summarized by O'Shea, *loc. cit.* See also R. Kuntzman, 'Drugs and Enzyme Induction', *Ann. Rev. Pharm.* (1969) *9*: 21-36.

Welch . . . R. M. Welch *et al.*, *Science* (1968) *160*:541-2.

131 carcinogen . . . *Congressional Record-Senate*, 1 May 1969 S4412-17: National Cancer Institute Studies of Pesticides.

Hungarian scientists . . . T. Kemeny and R. Tajan, *Experientia* (1966) *22*:748.

Miami University . . . J. L. Radomski *et al.*, 'Pesticide Concentrations in the Liver, Brain and Adipose Tissues of Terminal Hospital Patients', *Food and Cosmetic Technology* (1968) 6:209-220.

Löfroth . . . 'Pesticides and Catastrophe', *New Sci.* (1968) *40*: 567.

132 Swedish soil . . . cited from S. Odén *et al.* of Uppsala by Löfroth, *op. cit.*

133 eagles . . . 'DDT Residues in Pacific Sea Birds', *Nature* (1967) *216*:589. The full story is in J. J. Hickey (ed.), *Peregrine Falcon Populations: their Biology and Decline* (Univ. of Wisconsin Press, (1969).

lard . . . *New Sci.* (1969) *41*: 555.

Dilantin . . . *Sci. News* (1969) *96*:115.

van den Bosch . . . *Science* (1969) *164*:497.

page

135 third-generation pesticides . . . Carroll M. Williams, 'Third-Generation Pesticides', *Sci. Amer.* (1967) *217*(1):13.

136 Jensen . . . *New Sci.* (1966) *32*: 612.

seals and porpoises . . . A. V. Holden and K. Marsden, *Nature* (1967) *216*:1274.

137 two months before . . . D. C. Holmes *et al.*, *Nature* (1967) *216*:227.

137 Peakall . . . 'Pesticide-Induced Breakdown of Steroids in Birds', *Nature* (1967) *216*:505.

Risebrough . . . R. W. Risebrough *et al.*, 'Polychlorinated Biphenyls in the Global Ecosystem', *Nature* (1968) *220*:1098.

139 fertility . . . see also J. C. Street *et al.*, 'Comparative Effects of Polychlorinated Biphenyls and Organochlorine Pesticides in Induction of Hepatic Microsomal Enzymes', paper presented at Amer. Chem. Soc. 158th meeting, New York, 1969. Since I wrote this chapter an excellent summary has appeared: R. W. Risebrough with V. Brodine, 'More Letters in the Wind', *Environment* (1970) *12*(1):16-27.

140 trout . . . J. M. Anderson and M. Peterson, *Science* (1969) *164*:440.

7 BREATHE ONLY OUT!

143 mercury . . . E. Browning, *Toxicity of Industrial Metals* (Butterworth, 1969).

Mad Hatter . . . N. Grant, 'Legacy of the Mad Hatter', *Environment* (1969) *11*(4):18-23 and 43-4; S. Novick, 'A New Pollution Problem', *Environment* (1969) *11*(4):2-9; G. Löfroth and M. E. Duffy, 'Birds Give Warning', *Environment* (1969) *11*(4):10-17.

page

144 Minamata . . . G. Löfroth, *Report on Methyl Mercury*, report to WHO (duplicated), Stockholm, 1968; W. Marx, *The Frail Ocean* (Coward-McCann, 1967).

145 Swedish fish . . . H. Palmstierna, 'Is it a Throwaway World?', *Sweden Now* (1969) *3*:23 and 46.

146 effect on humans . . . *Science News* (1969) *96*:115 Polish scientists S. Kosmider and T. Wocka-Markowa showed functional damage in exposed humans, and a toxic effect on the bulbo-spinal system due to inhibition of enzymes facilitating electron transport in sacrificed animals.

148 lead . . . H. L. Hardy, 'What is the Status of Knowledge of the Toxic Effect of Lead on Identifiable Groups in the Population?', *Clin. Pharmacol. & Therap.* (1966) *7*(6):713-22.

birds . . . W. H. Stickel, 'Lead Shot Poisoning of American Birds', in *Metals and Ecology* (Ecol. Res. Cttee. Bull, No. 5), Swedish Nat. Sci. Research Ccl., Stockholm, 1969. Stickel estimates that 2 to 3 per cent of the American waterfowl population is lost to lead poisoning annually.

in the Pacific . . . *Environmental Science and Technology* (1969) *3*:737, cited *New Sci.* (1969) *44*:112.

Patterson . . . 'Contaminated and natural lead environments of man', *Arch. Env. Health* (1965) *11*:344.

149 symptoms . . . Browning, *loc. cit.*

150 level of lead . . . C. C. Patterson, 'Lead', in D. Hood (ed.), *Impingement of Man on the Oceans.* (Wiley, 1970).

blood-level . . . *BMJ* (1968) *i*.618.

page

150 lettuce . . . *Lancet* (1968) i.1252.

drinking water . . . *Lancet* (1967) ii.1087.

151 Schroeder . . . Numerous papers, especially: 'Effects of Chromium, Cadmium and other Trace Metals on the Growth and Survival of Mice', *J. Nutr.* (1963) *80*:39; 'Effect of Chromium, Cadmium and Lead on the Growth and Survival of Rats', *J. Nutr.* (1963) *80*:48; 'Chromium, Lead, Cadmium, Nickel and Titanium in Mice: Effect on Mortality, Tumors and Tissue Levels', *J. Nutr.* (1964) *83*:239.

152 Goldsmith . . . 'Respiratory Exposure to Lead', *Science* (1967) *158*:132.

Thomas . . . *Arch. Environ. Health* (1967) *15*:695.

153 tetra-ethyl lead . . . E. Browning, *op. cit.*, Ch. 20. L. Danielson, *Gasoline Containing Lead* (Ecol. Res. Cttee. Bull. No. 7), Swedish Nat. Sci. Research Ccl., 1970 (bibl. of 145 items).

chelating agents . . . *ibid.*

154 Patterson . . . *Arch. Environ. Health* (1965) *11*:344.

Mueller . . . *Arch. Environ. Health* (1967) *14*:373.

children . . . *Arch. Environ. Health* (1966) *13*:262; Moncrieff, *Arch. Dis. Childr.* (1964) *39*:1; B. Fristedt, 'Metal Toxicity', in *Metals and Ecology* (Ecol. Research Cttee. Bull. No. 5), Swedish Nat. Sci. Research Ccl., 1969.

155 British food . . . Patterson, *op. cit.*

156 a research vessel . . . T. J. Chow *et al.*, *Environ. Sci. & Technol.*

156 (1969) *3*:737, cited *New Sci.* (1969) *44*:112.

Greenland . . . M. Murozumi and T. J. Chow, 'Chemical con-

centrations of pollutant lead aerosols, terrestrial dusts and sea salts in Greenland and Antarctic snow strata', *Geochim. et Cosmochim. Acta* (1969) *33*:1247-94.

157 cadmium . . . E. Browning, *op. cit.*; R. Nilsson, *Aspects of the Toxicity of Cadmium and its Compounds* (Ecol. Res. Cttee. Bull. No. 7), Swedish Nat. Sci. Research Ccl., 1970.

158 hypertension . . . H. Mitchell Perry, Jr., 'Trace Elements related to Specific Chronic Diseases: Cardiovascular Disease', at AAAS Meeting, 1968; Schroeder, 'Cadmium as a Factor in Hypertension', *J. Chron. Dis.* (1965) *18*:647; some authorities, e.g. Dr G. Kazantzis (Middlesex Hospital) still deny, but see Nilsson, *op. cit.*, for a review.

159 Schroeder . . . see references above, under p. 155.

round the world . . . H. M. Perry *et al.*, 'Variation in the Concentration of Cadmium in the Human Kidney as a Function of Age and Geographic Origin', *J. Chron. Dis.* (1961). *14*:259.

nineteen locations . . . J. Kubota *et al.*, 'Copper, Zinc, Cadmium and Lead in Nineteen Locations', *Arch. Environ. Health* (1968) *16*:788.

birth malformations . . . V. H. Fern and S. J. Carpenter, 'Teratogenic Effect of Cadmium and its Inhibition by Zinc', *Nature* (1967) *216*:1123.

160 beryllium . . . H. Hardy *et al.*, 'United States Beryllium Case Registry (1952-66)', *J. of Occup. Med.* (1967) *9*(6):271-6; E. Browning, *op. cit.*

161 selenium . . . E. Browning, *op. cit.*

thallium . . . E. Browning, *op. cit.*

page

ote. Metal poisoning is a complex subject and in the space available I have had to omit complexities. Technically trained people are recommended to consult the literature, especially the excellent summaries issued by the Swedish Natural Science Research Council (Redaksjonstjänsten, Box 23 136, S-104 32 Stockholm, Sweden), Kr. 10, $2, or £1 each.

8 THE FIFTH FACTOR

165 nuclear power industry . . . *Civilian Nuclear Power* (1967 supplement to Report to President, 1962), U.S. Atomic Energy Commn., 1967.

166 radio-active wastes . . . duplicated summary. The reduced estimates are in J. A. Lieberman and W. G. Belter, 'Waste Management and Nuclear Power', *Environ. Sci. & Technol.* (1967) *1*(6):466-75.

167 Eisenbud . . . *Environmental Radioactivity* (McGraw-Hill, 1963).

containment and disposal . . . W. G. Belter, 'U.S. Operational Experience in Radioactive Waste Management (1958-63)' in *Third Internat. Conference on Peaceful Uses of Atomic Energy*, Geneva, 1964. 28/P/869 Rev 1 (duplicated).

167 55 million gallons . . . Milton Shaw, Director, Division of Reactor Technology, U.S. Atomic Energy Commission: Hearing on AEC Authorizing Legislation, Fiscal Year 1970, testimony before Joint Cttee on Atomic Energy, 24-25 April 1969. Pt. 2, p. 1023.

risk of earthquakes . . . S. Novick, 'Earthquake at Giza', *Environment* (1970) *12*(1):2. See also J. A. Snow, 'Radioactive Waste from Reactors', *Science and the Citizen* (1967).

169 atmospheric krypton . . . *New Sci.* (1963) *20*:488: 'Another Radiation Hazard', citing *Pugwash Newsletter* (1963) *1*:27. By 1967, the estimate had been raised to 1,160 MC of accumulated krypton. Lieberman and Belter, *op. cit.*

tritium . . . D. G. Jacobs, *Sources of Tritium and its behaviour upon Release to the Environment* (U.S. Atomic Energy Commission, 1968).

170 Kenny . . . 'Disposal of Radioactive Wastes', Proceedings of Symposium, May 1966 (Internat. Atomic Energy Agency, 1966).

171 K. E. Cowser . . . K. E. Cowser *et al.*, 'Sec. 4: Engineering, Economic and Safety Evaluations' in Annual Progress Report, to 31 July 1968, of Health Physics Divn., Radioactive Waste Disposal Sectn., Oak Ridge National Laboratory (ORNL-4316).

172 unacceptable exposure . . . K. E. Cowser *et al.*, 'Sec. 5: Engineering, Economic and Safety Evaluations', in Annual Progress Report, to 31 July 1967, of Health Physics Divn., Radioactive Waste Disposal Sectn., Oak Ridge National Laboratory (ORNL-4168).

175 biological concentration . . . in general, see *Radioecological Concentration Processes: Proceedings of an Internat. Symposium, Stockholm, 1966* (1967). C. A. B. Aberg and F. P. Hungate, *Radiological Concentration Processes* (Pergamon Press, 1961).

White Oak Lake . . . S. Novick, *The Careless Atom* (Houghton Mifflin, 1969).

176 New York state . . . J. T. Gentry, 'An Epidemiological Study

page

of Congenital Malformation in N.Y. State', in J. Bresler (ed.), *Human Ecology* (Addison-Wesley, 1966), pp. 223-47.

178 acceptable dose . . . J. C. Collins (ed.), *Radioactive Wastes: their treatment and disposal* (Spon, 1960).

180 Windscale . . . Windscale has announced that it will increase its release of wastes to the Irish Sea by 4½ times—to the dismay of local environmentalists, who are to make measurements during the summer of 1970.

Gofman and Tamplin . . . 'Low Dose Radiation, Chromosomes and Cancer', IEEE Nuclear Science Symposium, San Francisco, 1969 (duplic.); 'A Proposal for at Least a 10-Fold Reduction in the FRC Guidelines for Radiation Exposure to the Population at Large: Supportive Evidence', testimony presented at hearings of the Joint Cttee on Atomic Energy, U.S. Congress, 28 January 1970 (duplic.); 'Studies of Radiation-Exposed Humans', supplement to testimony presented to Sub-Cttee on Air and Water Pollution, Cttee on Public Works, U.S. Senate, 18 Nov. 1969 (duplic.); and other papers.

182 Holcomb . . . 'Radiation Risk: a Scientific Problem?', *Science* (1970) *167*:853-5.

183 near Denver . . . 'Aftermath of a Fire', *Sci. News* (1969) *96*:496. The AEC was very evasive as to whether radioactivity had been released and about the damage done; nor would it say what the normal releases at this plant were.

184 Bodega Bay . . . S. Novick, *The Careless Atom* (Houghton Mifflin, 1969).

'tailings' . . . *ibid.*

page

187 Pendleton . . . Press release by Univ. of Utah, 9 Sept. 1969.

188 Commoner . . . 'Attitudes towards the Environment: a nearly Fatal Illusion', AAAS meeting, 1968. Estimates vary from a 50 per cent increase in the thyroid cancer rate to 1,000 per cent.

Science and Survival . . . Viking Press, 1967.

189 Polykarpov . . . *Radioecology of Aquatic Organisms* (Reinhold, 1966).

9 THE POPULATION LIMIT

193 Fremlin . . . 'How Many People Could the World Support?', *New Sci.*, (1964) 24:285.

194 Clark . . . *Population Growth and Land Use* (Macmillan, 1967).

195 fish-concentrates . . . L. V. Shannon and R. D. Cherry, 'Polonium-210 in Marine Plankton', *Nature* (1967) 216:352-3; T. M. Beasley *et al.*, 'Natural and Artificial Radionuclides in Seafoods and Marine Protein Concentrates', *Nature* (1969) 221: 1207-9.

Solway Firth . . . See also *Morecambe Bay and Solway Barrages: report on Desk Studies*, Water Resources Board (HMSO, 1966) and several similar studies and annual reports.

196 3 billion acres . . . L. Anderson, 'The Mushroom Crowd: social and political aspects of population pressure', *Canad. Med. Assn. J.* (1964) 91:1213-22; R. Calder *et al.*, *World of Opportunity*, UN Conference on application of science and technology for the benefit of the less developed areas (1963) *1*:20; and see F. Osborn, *The Limits*

page

of the Earth (Faber & Faber, 1954), Ch. 3; G. Borgstrom, *Too Many* (Macmillan, N.Y., 1969); R. R. Doane, *World Balance Sheet* (Harper, 1957).

Ozbekhan . . . in R. Jungk and J. Galtung (eds.), *Mankind 2000* (Allen & Unwin, 1969).

197 jungles are lush . . . H. Teuscher *et al.*, *The Soil and its Fertility* (Reinhold, NY; Chapman & Hall, London, 1960). H. Addison remarks, in *Land, Water and Food* (Chapman & Hall, 1961), 'Raising rain crops on semi-arid subtropical land is one of the most precarious and unrewarding types of agriculture.'

Osborn . . . (ed.) *Our Crowded Planet* (Doubleday, 1962).

water . . . R. Furon, *The Problem of Water* (Faber & Faber, 1963); M. Overman, *Water: solutions to a problem of supply and demand* (Aldus Books, 1968).

desalination . . . M. Clawson *et al.*, 'Desalted Water for Agriculture: is it economic?', *Science* (1969) *164*:1141 for a sceptical assessment.

198 fertilizer . . . for an analysis, see R. Dumont and B. Rosier, *The Hungry Future* (Deutsch, 1969; orig. *Nous allons à la famine*). For an optimistic view see H. Osvald, *The Earth Can Feed Us* (Allen & Unwin, 1966). On the whole problem, I particularly recommend C. S. Christian, 'The Use and Abuse of Land and Water', in S. Mudd (ed.), *The Population Crisis and the Use of World Resources* (Indiana University Press, 1966), which also contains many other excellent contributions.

199 energy debit . . . LaMont Cole, 'The Ecosphere', *Sci. Amer.* (1958) *198*(4):83.

201 supplies of uranium . . . *Uran-*

page

tum: production and long-term demand, OECD Report, cited in *Nature* (1969) *221*:1183.

202 phosphorus . . . Cole, *op. cit.* Harrison Brown . . . *The Sciences*.

204 Freeman . . . *World Without Hunger* (Praeger, 1968).

Peru . . . A. J. Coutu and R. A. King, 'Agricultural Development in Peru: a Bench Mark Study' (synopsis). Ford Foundation internal document (duplicated—to be published).

nuclear energy . . . Perry R. Stout, 'Potential Agricultural Production for Nuclear-Powered Agro-Industrial Complexes', Oak Ridge National Lab. (ORNL 4292) 1968. There are countless studies of population trends. A basic summary is 'World Population Projections 1965-2000', *Pop. Bull.* (1965) *21*:73-99; for implications see Paul Ehrlich, *The Population Bomb* (Ballantine, 1968).

207 Mass Observation . . . *Britain and her Birth Rate* (Murray, 1945). Knibbs . . . *The Shadow of the World's Future* (Benn, 1938).

208 family size . . . Judith Blake, 'Ideal Family Size among White Americans', Pop. Studies series, *Demography* (1966) *3*(1):154-73. "Are Babies Consumer Durables?' *Pop. Studies* (1968) *22*(1):5.

210 illiteracy . . . H. Houghton, 'The Effect of the Population Explosion on Education', *Advancement of Science* (1967) *115*:443; UNESCO Survey of Illiteracy, cited *Dateline in Science* (1969) *4*:6.

211 protein shock . . . in a large literature, basic is W. H. Pawley, *Possibilities of Increasing World Food Production* (Food and Agriculture Organization, 1963);

page

see also H. A. B. Parpia, 'Novel Routes to Plant Protein', *Sci. Jnl.* (1968) 4:66-71. This issue (May 1968) was devoted to the theme 'Feeding the World'.

213 kwashiorkor . . . H. C. Trowell, 'Kwashiorkor', *Sci. Amer.* (1954) *191*(6):46.

amino acids . . . F. D. Wharton, 'Worldwide Production of Synthetic Amino-acids', at AAAS meeting, 1969.

214 Sukhatme . . . 'A Statistical Appraisal of the Protein Problem' (duplic.), Food and Agriculture Organization, n.d.

215 erosion . . . R. C. Haw, *The Conservation of Natural Resources* (Faber & Faber, 1959); 'Soil Erosion by Water', FAO Agricultural Dev. Paper No. 81; 'Soil Erosion by Wind', FAO Agricultural Dev. Paper No. 71; R. Furon, *The Problem of Water* (Faber & Faber, 1963).

carried down to the sea . . . S. Judson, 'Erosion', *Amer. Scientist* (1968) 56:356.

217 South America . . . H. F. Robinson, 'Prospects for Food Production' (Symposium on Science, Technology and Latin American Development), AAAS meeting, 1968.

corruption . . . W. & P. Paddock, *Famine-1975!* (Weidenfeld & Nicolson, 1968).

217 intensively farmed . . . W. A. Dill and T. V. R. Pillay, 'Non-Oceanic Living Aquatic Resources': paper to Int. Union Conservation of Nature, Sept. 1968 (duplic.)

American prisoners . . . S. A. Goldblith, 'The World Food Crisis', *Technology Rev.* (1969) 70(8):21.

Robinson . . . *op. cit.* See also Prof. Bunting, 'Improving Traditional Agriculture', *Sci. Jnl.* (1968) 5:61-5.

Note. On the food position generally, the following is little-known and important: R. U. Ayres, 'Technology and the Prospects

for World Food Production', Hudson Institute Discussion Paper, 1966.

10 POPULATION CRASH: WHEN?

219 Sika deer . . . See S. Hall, *The Hidden Dimension* (Doubleday, 1966) for this investigation and an excellent account of the whole issue of crowding.

Christian . . . *J. Mammalogy* (1950):31(3):247-59.

220 snowshoe hares . . . Edward S. Deevey, Jr., 'The Hare and the Haruspex', in J. Bresler (ed.), *Human Ecology* (Addison-Wesley, 1966).

American prisoners . . . *ibid.*

221 mice kept in cages . . . *ibid.*

Hoagland . . . 'Cybernetics of Population Control', *Bull. of the Atomic Scientists* (Feb. 1964) 20(2):2-6, for another good outline, including the flour beetles

223 Kingsley Davis . . . 'The Urbanization of the Human Population', *Sci. Amer.* (1965) 213 (3):40, and many other articles. São Paulo . . . H. Maksoud, "São Paulo in the Year 2000", *Futures* (1969) *1*(3):198.

Russia . . . *Soviet Life* (July 1969), p. 21.

224 Turkey . . . L. Anderson, 'People, Food and Cities in the Years Ahead', presented at AID symposium on Agriculture, Ankara, March 1969 (supplemented by private communication).

310   References

225 Calcutta . . . N. K. Bose, 'Calcutta: a premature Metropolis', *Sci. Amer.* (1965) *213*(3):90.

shanty-town . . . *Urbanization: development policies and planning* (Internat. Soc. Devel. Review No. 1, United Nations, 1968), p. 107.

conditions in cities . . . W. P. Lowry, 'Conditions in Cities', *Sci. Amer.* (1967) *217*(2):15.

incidence of diseases . . . F. S. L. Williamson, 'Population Pollution', *BioScience* (1969).

Faris and Dunham . . . R. E. L. Faris and H. W. Dunham, *Mental Disorders in Urban Areas* (Phoenix Books, U. of Chicago Press, 1967); H. W. Dunham, 'The Ecology of the Functional Psychoses in Chicago', in G. A. Theodorson, *Studies in Human Ecology* (Harper and Row, 1961).

226 Hell's half-acre . . . A. W. Lind, "Some Ecological Patterns of Community Disorganization in Honolulu', in G. A. Theodorson, *op. cit.*, p. 430.

227 Buckley . . . 'Cardiovascular and Biochemical Effects of Chronic Intermittent Neurogenic Stimulation', at AAAS meeting, 1969.

Lockett . . . M. F. Lockett, 'Effect of Sound on Endocrine Function and Electrolyte Excretion', at AAAS meeting, 1969.

Sontag . . . 'Effects of Noise during Pregnancy upon Foetal and subsequent Adult Behavior', at AAAS meeting, 1969.

228 psychiatric work . . . W. R. Bion, *Experiences in Groups* (Tavistock Press, 1961).

230 Calhoun . . . 'Population Density and Social Pathology', *Sci. Amer.* (1962) *206*(2):139; 'Space and the Strategy of Life', at AAAS meeting, 1969. The latter describes Kessler's work.

231 Leyhausen . . . see below.

232 Mental hospitals . . . D. E. Davis, at AAAS meeting, 1968.

Spitz . . . *A Genetic Field Theory of Ego Formation* (International University Press, New York, 1959).

Leyhausen . . . *Discovery* (1965) *26*(8):27 (condensation of a paper given to the Zoological Society, London, 1963: 'The Communal Organization of Solitary Mammals', *Symp. Zool. Soc. of London* (1965) *14*:249-63), 'The Sane Community'; 'Dominance and Territoriality as complements in mammalian social structure, at AAAS Meeting, 1968.

236 ever greater pressure . . . 'Outdoor Recreation threatened by excess Procreation', *Pop. Bull.* (1964) *20*(4):89-105; 'California: after 19 Million—What?', *Pop. Bull.* (1966) *22*(2):29-57.

Norris . . . *BioScience* (May 1968) pp. 14-17.

North Shore Oil . . . 'North Slope: Oil Rush', *Science* (1969) *166*:85; Edward Gross, 'Getting set for a Black Gold Rush', *Sci. News* (1970) *97*:177-9.

237 Churchill Falls . . . P. Kallio, 'A Task for Ecologists around Waterfalls in Labrador-Ungava', *Science* (1969) *166*:1598.

Pacific . . . see for example D. R. Stoddart, 'Catastrophic

238 Human Interference with Coral Atoll Ecosystems', *Geography* (1968) *53*.i. 25-40.

phosphate mining . . . F. R. Fosberg (ed.), *Man's Place in the Island Ecosystem* (The Bishop Museum Press, 1963).

Stegman . . . *Open Horizons* (Knopf, 1969).

240 Calder . . . . *The Environment Game* (Secker & Warburg, 1967).

Hoyle . . . in 'A Contradiction in the Argument of Malthus', St. John's College Lecture, University of Hull, 17 May 1963.

optimum populations . . S. F. Singer: 'Is there an Optimum Level of Population?' (preparatory paper for Symposium, AAAS meeting, 1969). 'Optimum Population for Britain', Symposium, London, September 1969.

241 Fuchs . . . 'Some Notes on the Optimum Size of Population with special Reference to Health', at AAAS meeting, 1969.

242 National Research Council . . . *New York Times* (30 Dec. 1969).

243 Fremlin . . . 'An Optimum Population for Great Britain', *New Sci.* (1967) *36*:717.

Hutchinson . . . 'Land and Human Populations', *New Sci.* (1966) *31*:465-69; also in *The Advancement of Science.* Vol. 23.

Southwood . . . contrib. to Conference, 'The Optimum Population for Britain', London, September 1969; 'The Abundance of Animals', Imperial College, Inaugural Lecture October 1968, *8*:1-16, 1968.

243 Spilhaus . . . 'Technology, Living Cities and Human Environment', at AAAS meeting, 1968.

11   HURT NOT THE EARTH

245 Japan's example . . . unfortunately, Japan now aims to increase its population: see 'Japan: a Crowded Nation wants to Boost its Birth Rate', *Science* (1970) *167*:690

249 Corps of Engineers . . . E. B. Drew, 'Dam Outrage: the story of the Army Engineers', *Atlantic* (1970) *225*(4):51.

Sakharov . . . reprinted in *Technol. Rev.* (1969) *71*(8):18, with comments by I. Rabi, H. Salisbury and D. Bell.

251 Derelict Land Unit . . . 'Mr Price Takes a Derelict Valley', *Sun. Times*, 4 Jan. 1970.

university students . . . for a conspectus of student activities see *Conservation Foundation Newsletter*, Jan. 1970: 'Students Rally to Halt Pollution'.

Japan . . . *Asahi Evening News*, 9 June 1969.

252 Public Prevention Ordinance . . . *The Times* (of Japan), 8 June 1969.

Golovin's Law . . . *New Sci.* (1968) *40*:478.

253 Kiyoura process . . . B. H. Billince *et al.*, 'Reduction of Emission of Carbon and Sulphur Dioxide', Central Electricity Research Labs. (duplic.).

253 Lockheed . . . *Technol. Review* (1969) *71*(9):75.

invisible $80 . . . US Public Health Service estimate cited by Barry Commoner, 'Attitudes towards the Environment', AAAS, 1968.

255 Fred Singer . . . 'Environmental Quality—when does Growth become too Expensive?', at AAAS meeting, 1969.

$275 billion . . . F. F. Gorschboth, 'Controlling Air Pollution', *The Nation's Cities* (1969) *7*(3): 13.

257 Consolidated Edison . . . A. N. Heller, 'A Scientific Approach to Managing our Air Resources', at AAAS meeting, 1968.

public pressure . . . see *Conservation Foundation Newsletter*, Nov. 1969, for these and other instances.

fish in the Thames . . . . A. Wheeler, 'The Fish that Came

page

Back', *Your Environment* (1970) *1*(2):62. He reports a few chub and dace at Vauxhall, but mostly gobies, shrimps, etc.

258 Clean Air Act . . . J. F. Garner and R. K. Crow, *Clean Air—Law and Practice* (Shaw, 1964).

local authorities . . . *1969/70 Clean Air Handbook* (Nat. Soc. for Clean Air).

Peter Gregory . . . *Polluted Homes*. Occasional Papers in Social Administration. No. 15 (Bell, 1965).

260 Seneca Indians . . . Alvin M. Josephy, Jr., 'Cornplanter, Can You Swim?', *Seattle Post-Intelligencer*, 27 Apr. 1969 (reprinted from *American Heritage*).

261 Crosland . . . *Sun. Times*, 25 Jan. 1970: 'Mr Environment'.

National Environment Research Council . . . *New Sci.* (1969) *44*:108. For Select Cttee criticisms of NERC see H. of C. Paper 400. The total grant to the Nature Conservancy is considerably less than is given to the Antarctic Survey.

263 *Economist* . . . The *Economist*, 15 Nov. 1969.

carbon monoxide . . . J. R. Goldsmith and S. A. Landaw, 'Carbon Monoxide and Human Health', *Science* (1968) *162*: 1352-9; for a summary see *Sci. News* (1969) *96*:480: 'The Elusive Polluter'.

264 Great Lakes . . . P. Scrag, 'Life on a Dying Lake', *Sat. Rev.*, 20 Sept. 1969, p. 19.

thermal pollution . . . W. L. Picton, *Water Use in the US, 1960-80* (US Dept. of Commerce, 1960).

Chesapeake Bay . . . J. A. Mihursky, *Patuxent Thermal Studies*. NRI Special Report No. 1 (University of Maryland, 1969).

page

265 noise . . . W. Scheisheimer, 'Noise: Another Pollutant', *Astme VECTORS* (1969) *4*(4):12.

K. E. Farr . . . *New York Times*, 23 June 1967.

Mark Abrams . . . *The Next Fifteen Years* (duplic., n.d.).

266 effects of air pollution . . . see summary of Ninth Air Pollution Medical Research Conference in *Science* (1969) *163*:706-9.

sulphur dioxide . . . T. K. Sherwood, 'Must We Breathe Sulphur Oxides?', *Technol. Rev.* (1970) *72*(3):24.

ozone . . . R. Bryson, *The Climate of Cities* (discussion following the paper; duplic., n.d.). *Note*. The most useful source on the economics of pollution control is Marshal J. Goldman (ed.), *Controlling Pollution* (Prentice-Hall, 1967).

12 THE TECHNOLOGICAL NIGHTMARE

269 electric power . . . P. Sporn, 'Energy for Man and Environmental Protection', *Science* (1969) *166*:555.

270 solid wastes . . . See, for instance, D. G. Wilson, 'Rethinking the Solid Waste Problem', *Sci. Jnl.* (1969) *5A*(3):68.

271 'fusion torch' . . . D. E. Thomsen, 'Fusion Power against Garbage', *Sci. News* (1970) *97*:249.

Lake Trummen . . . D. Jenkins, 'In Search of a Clear Solution', *Sweden Now* (1969) *3*(3):24.

thermal pollution . . . J. R. Clark, 'Thermal Pollution and Aquatic Life', *Sci. Amer.* (1969) *220*(3):19; about half the US freshwater flow will be needed for cooling, except in wettest months, by 2000.

page

272 Brower . . . *Technol. Rev.* (1968) *70*(7):21, 'DNA> GNP'.

rehabilitated . . . for instances of what can be done, see G. T. Goodman, 'The Revegetation of derelict land contaminated with toxic heavy metals', in *Metals and Ecology*: Ecol. Res. Cttee. Bull. No. 5 (Swedish Nat. Sci. Res. Ccl., 1969); also 'Mr. Price Takes a Derelict Valley' etc., *Sun. Times* (4 Jan. 1970).

274 Hardin . . . 'The Tragedy of the Commons', *Science* (1968) *162*: 1243.

275 Crowe . . . 'The Tragedy of the Commons Revisited', *Science* (1969) *166*:1103.

Berry . . . 'Consumers of the River', *The Nation* (17 Oct. 1966), p. 381.

278 Krutilla . . . 'Conservation Reconsidered', *Resources for the Future* (Reprint No. 67), 1967.

279 *Wall Street Journal* . . . *Here Comes Tomorrow: living and working in the year 2000* (Dow Jones, Princeton, 1966).

Foreign Policy Association . . . *Towards the Year 2018* (Cowles Educ. Corp., 1968).

281 Preston Cloud . . . 'Resources, Population and Quality of Life', at AAAS meeting, 1968.

283 *Conditions of Happiness* . . . Bodley Head, 1949; Houghton Mifflin, 1950.

Wilensky . . . 'Work, Careers and Leisure Styles', summarized in *5th Ann. Report of Harvard Program on Science and Technology*, 1969, p. 7.

Hemmende Strukturen . . . Duttweiler Foundation, Zürich, 1969.

page

283 enhanced motivation . . . R. Cooper, 'The Psychology of Boredom', *Sci. Jnl.* (1968) *4*(2): 38.

285 Gell-Mann . . . at symposium of John Muir Inst. for Environmental Studies. *Science* (1969) *166*:723.

287 Medawar . . . 'On the Effecting of all Things Possible', Presidential Address to British Association, 1969. *Technol. Rev.* (1969) *72*(2):30.

288 Stanley . . . 'Technology and its Critics', summarized in *5th Ann. Report of Harvard Program on Science and Technology*, 1969.

292 Lynn White . . . 'The Historic Roots of our Ecological Crisis', *Science* (1967) *155*:1203.

Udall . . . *1976: Agenda for Tomorrow* (Harcourt Brace and World, 1968).

Elton . . . *The Ecology of Invasions by Plants and Animals* (Methuen, 1966).

293 British observer . . . John Holloway (Chairman, Faculty Board of English, Cambridge Univ.), 'The Land of More and More', *The Listener* (20 Mar. 1969), p. 373.

294 future of the human race . . . while passing these pages for press, I read *The Question Mark* by Canon (now Bishop) Hugh Montefiore. In his first chapter, which reads almost like a summary of a large part of this book, he regrets that there is not a fuller study of the subject. Quite coincidentally, and unknown to each other, we seem to have been thinking along the same lines.

Index